the G ATES
to
RECOVERY

the Gates to RECOVERY

Cathy Sweat

Ambassador International
GREENVILLE, SOUTH CAROLINA & BELFAST, NORTHERN IRELAND

www.ambassador-international.com

The Gates to Recovery

ISBN: 978-1-62020-813-7

eISBN: 978-1-62020-814-4

Cover Design & Typesetting by Hannah Nichols
Ebook Conversion by Anna Riebe Raats

AMBASSADOR INTERNATIONAL
Emerald House
411 University Ridge, Suite B14
Greenville, SC 29601, USA
www.ambassador-international.com

AMBASSADOR BOOKS
The Mount
2 Woodstock Link
Belfast, BT6 8DD, Northern Ireland, UK
www.ambassadormedia.co.uk

The colophon is a trademark of Ambassador, a Christian publishing company.

The Gates to Recovery is dedicated to the men and women who are searching for recovery from life's toughest issues. I believe recovery is universal. I pray that, with the help of Jesus, you will be able to use this information to start a new life and to maintain it.

❧ CONTENTS ❧

❧ ACKNOWLEDGMENTS ❧

Twenty years of living with women suffering from addiction has led to this work; yet before I worked with them, I also began recovery. There are so many folks to thank and acknowledge for the work on this project. Janice Brewton has worked very hard over the years to help me develop this program of recovery.

We have used so much printed material over the years to help in the healing of women. I will always be grateful for the work that was done by the RAPHA program. The materials I used early on came from books developed from that program. These books were given to me by Dr. Eileen Essberg.

Though I never met the developers of RAPHA or John or Paula Sandford of Elijah House Ministries, I have gleaned much wisdom from the study of their materials.

I would also like to acknowledge the women themselves who allowed me to speak into their lives and to learn from the situations we were in. I am grateful to each client of Bethesda House of Mercy and Bethesda Recovery.

❧ FOREWORD ❧

THIS MATERIAL WAS DEVELOPED IN an in-house residential program for women in recovery. Bethesda Recovery has used the findings of this book to lead hundreds of women to God and to a life of fullness and healing. I believe Jesus has revealed Himself to the broken and has offered healing to us by using the book of Nehemiah as the basis for this restoration.

This workbook will give you tools to help you see who God is, how He works in your life, and how He wants a relationship with you.

This book is written to help set strong boundaries in a new life. Boundaries are referred to as "gates" in this work. I have studied the gates of Nehemiah, using them as the standard for rebuilding these boundaries.

Boundaries are the limits in our lives that we set for others, as well as for ourselves. The gates are the structures in our lives which allow the good in and the bad out. Using gates as an analogy helps us picture the ability to open and close the twelve essential areas of life. Those twelve areas, as we have discovered, are reality, authority, truth, self, trust, empowerment, freedom, future, relationships, a new harvest, belonging, and joy.

The gates transfer responsibility to the individual—responsibility which has so often been lost through years of addiction.

Sobriety refers to living a life without the substance, relationship, or illness which has destroyed the ability to make right choices in a person's life. Biblically speaking, sobriety means a sound mind.

Addiction is defined in this work as "any activity that cannot be stopped by simply trying." Addiction can be referred to as chemical, emotional, spiritual, or relational.

It is my desire, as the principal writer of this material, that you find new information (or old information presented in a new way) that is helpful in your journey from addiction to change.

PART ONE

INTRODUCTION TO RECOVERY

❧ CHAPTER ONE ❧
THE RECOVERY JOURNEY BEGINS

THE WHOLE RECOVERY JOURNEY STARTED for me with Nehemiah, an Old Testament book of the Bible, so that is where we will begin your journey.

Nehemiah was, according to Scriptures, a cupbearer to the king. He was in a comfortable job—as long as no one was trying to assassinate the king. He was at his side for every meal, every snack, and every drink of water, for nothing touched the lips of the king without Nehemiah tasting it first. In the context of our society today, Nehemiah had a good job, nice house, well-behaved children, and a place of significance and position. He was at ease, surrounded by elegance and sophistication, yet Nehemiah was haunted by the conditions of his people. This favored Jew in exile had family in Jerusalem who were trying to rebuild a city that had been destroyed.

One day, his curiosity got the best of him, and he asked a messenger from Jerusalem how things were going. Nehemiah was surprised to hear that things were not going so well. The messenger told Nehemiah that the workers were discouraged because the progress was slow. It seemed that each time the workers rebuilt parts of the city, enemies would run through the walls, taking everything and leaving the workers to constantly build and rebuild. **"They said to me, 'Those who survived the exile and are back in the province are in great trouble and disgrace. The wall of Jerusalem is broken down, and its gates have been burned with fire'"** (Neh. 1:3).

The temple was not finished due to the discouragement of the workers and the belief they held that they had to protect their families by fortifying their own homes. In verse five of chapter one, Nehemiah appeals to God for help, based on God's great mercy and covenant-keeping promises. Nehemiah confessed his sin and the sin of those in trouble in Jerusalem. He admitted that he and the others had dealt treacherously with God. In verse nine, Nehemiah reminds God that if the people returned to Him, He would redeem them and return them to their homeland. Nehemiah reminded God of His promise to restore. These people were the very ones God had redeemed, and now they needed His help. Nehemiah not only asked God for help for the people but also asked for favor with the king in order for him to go to Jerusalem to help in the restoration.

While in prayer, Nehemiah was given a plan by the Lord. Feeling the urgency to do something, Nehemiah was overtaken with feelings of responsibility, as well as fear, for what the king might do to him if he would take a leave of absence. The Bible says that Nehemiah's countenance was heavy, and the king asked him to explain his mood. Nehemiah at once told the king about his desire to help the people of Jerusalem, and the rest is history. Nehemiah left with money and provisions from the king to begin the work of restoring the walls.

Throughout the book of Nehemiah, we can see that this man of God was not ashamed to ask for help. More than once, Nehemiah did so. From day one, Nehemiah sought God to direct his journey to restoration and recovery.

While Nehemiah found favor with the king, he was not without opposition. As soon as those who had opposed the people in Jerusalem heard that Nehemiah was coming to help, they began at once to cause him trouble. Two of the leaders in Jerusalem, Sanballat and Tobiah, represent the opposition that exists to any recovery plan. You can call this the devil, addiction, co-dependency, or any number of other names; but, nevertheless, it is opposition to recovery. This opposition will be present from the first moment the plan for recovery is set in place and represented by those people who say, "You can't change," and "There is no way you can ever get sober and stay sober."

So often, the difficulties in the life of recovery come from people you would never expect. They are family members, close friends, and co-workers. They never believed they would stop you from recovery. Such was the way of Sanballat and Tobiah. They were greatly "grieved" because Nehemiah showed up to improve the conditions of the children of Israel. But Nehemiah prepared himself for the opposition.

Sanballat and Tobiah were in leadership in the provinces around Jerusalem. They hated the Jews. They did not want the Israelites to succeed. In the recovery process—or let us call it "the change process"—there will be people who do not want you to succeed. They may not want to make changes themselves, or they may just want you to continue to support what they are doing. Your success will not be important to them.

Take notice of what Nehemiah did as he arrived in Jerusalem. First, he didn't tell many what God had put in his heart. So often, people get too excited and too puffed up, and they start making claims and promises before they even know what the job of restoration will take. It wasn't that Nehemiah doubted God, but he did not want to give the enemies any ammunition.

Quietly, Nehemiah surveyed the problem. This indicates that he had sound judgment about making a plan. He counted the cost. He took a look at just how bad the problem was before he made any suggestions as to how to get the job done. From the beginning, Nehemiah had shown restraint in his character, and he had shown strength as he waited on God to show him exactly what should be done.

"As you start your recovery process, you, too, must start at the lowest part of your life."

Next, Nehemiah went and assessed the Valley Gate and the Dung Gate. The Valley Gate was on the west side of the city and opened to the Hinnom Valley. The Israelites were notorious for idol worship. It was at the valley of Hinnom that history reveals the sacrifice of the children of Israel to the god Molech. Molech was said to be idolized as a brazen statue of a "man/beast" that held his arms out to receive the sacrifices. Priests of the brazen "altar" heated the statue to unbelievably high temperatures, and the children were "roasted" in the arms of the god. Hinnom was also known as the Valley of Gehenna, which Jesus referred to in the New Testament as the "eternal fire" or "hell." **If your hand causes you to stumble, cut it off. It is better for you to enter life maimed than with two hands to go into hell, where the fire never goes out" (Mk. 9:43).** It is no wonder God called for the destruction of Jerusalem. Nehemiah saw the destruction and the devastation of the city by examining the worst part of the destruction first.

As you start your recovery process, you, too, must start at the lowest part of your life. You will never begin recovery on the "top." Recovery or change will come only after all the other possibilities are exhausted, and you are at your lowest place for recovery. Restoration begins with looking at where you are and where you want to be.

The gates of each city were specific entrances for different parts of city life. The name of the gate related to the activities that occurred at that gate. The people who helped to rebuild each section and gate directly benefited from the restoration. Likewise, as you rebuild your life, there are specific areas where ideas, people, and dreams can enter. You will rebuild boundaries with the help of people who are involved in your life at the gate.

Next, Nehemiah put together a team of rebuilders to start the restoration. Your recovery will consist of putting together a team of people who are headed in the same direction you are and who will not tear you down or cause you to stumble—those who will hold you accountable as you make your way to a new lifestyle.

Nehemiah began his inspection of the city of Jerusalem at the Valley Gate. On horseback, Nehemiah saw the great devastation of the gate at the lowest portion of the city. As he looked, he knew the work would be consuming. He knew that this could not be accomplished in his power alone, but that the people who lived in despair must garner enough strength to restore their own lives. He would lead them and work beside them, but they must work as well.

You will learn to say, "I need help" at the Valley Gate. You will learn to admit the problem. You will learn to assess what the reality of the problem is. Also, at the Valley Gate, you will begin to choose forgiveness. Forgiveness is a process, but it is also a command of Jesus. He says in Matthew that unless you forgive your brother, God will not forgive you. **"For if you forgive other people when they sin against you, your heavenly Father will also forgive you. But if you do not forgive others their sins, your Father will not forgive your sins"** (Matt. 6:14-15).

At the East Gate, you will learn that God will help, but *you* must commit. You will also learn to choose love. And it is here that authority is restored. Authority, on every level, is destroyed by addiction and other life issues. You give up your own authority; you refuse authority; and you reject authority. It is at the East Gate that authority is the strongest. The Bible speaks of Jesus returning and coming in the East. When Jesus returns, His authority will be completely restored, and He will be the victor over all evil. When authority is restored in your life, you are able to respect God's ability to restore sanity in your life. You also learn to respect the authority that God has given to others over you.

At the Old Gate, you will learn to believe in the truths of God's Word, to submit to those truths, and to choose the truth of the Word of God as it pertains to everyday life.

The Inspection Gate is the gateway to restoring self. At this gate, you will learn that you can look at yourself, take responsibility, and choose self-control. So much of the time, we fail to look at ourselves in a realistic way.

At the Fountain Gate, trust is restored. Trust is so often destroyed by addiction. You cannot trust others or yourself. At this gate, you will learn that you can tell your story to another. You will learn to remember your life as it really was and choose to be vulnerable. It will take additional courage to choose vulnerability, but, as the other gates are restored, the choice will be a little easier.

It is at the Horse Gate that empowerment is restored. As empowerment is restored, you will find that you can change; you can choose; and you can do the right thing. Empowerment implies strength of character, trust, and resources. At this gate, you will begin to recognize the forming of faithfulness and steadfastness in your character.

The Prison Gate is the gateway to restoring freedom. Here you will learn to walk away a free person. You will learn to move forward, declaring that you are free. It is when you have been imprisoned that you can truly know what freedom is. But with freedom comes work. Freedom is a new way of life. It is walking away from the things that have bound us and enslaved us. In freedom, you must learn new skills and concentrate on new things.

The Dung Gate is the gateway to restoring your future. Here you learn that you can dig up, let go, and rebuild. It was at the Dung Gate that Nehemiah realized the devastation of the city, but it was also at the Dung Gate that he decided that there could be a future for Jerusalem.

The Fish Gate is the place to restore relationships. There you will learn to give, to love, and to live. You must set new boundaries in your relationships by giving of yourself and by learning about what real love is meant to be.

The Harvest Gate is where a new harvest is restored. After sowing seeds of evil and destruction and reaping much of that harvest through addiction, you must learn to sow good seeds. It is here you will learn to do good deeds, to build a good work ethic, and to give to the things of God.

The Sheep Gate is the gate where you restore belonging in your life. Addiction and life issues steal your sense of belonging. "I have no place," you may often say. It is here you will learn that you are in the body of Christ and in a new family. In this family, you will learn to serve and know that you belong.

Finally, at the Water Gate, your joy will be restored. When joy is restored to your life, you can speak of that joy; you can share of that joy; and you can celebrate the new life in Christ.

Soul recovery is designed to help those suffering from the agonies of life. Addiction creates such a stigmatized life and covers a wide array of life problems. The definition of addiction covers any habitual problem that can be stopped by an individual. At Bethesda Recovery, we have discovered many habitual problems, which people need help to overcome.

These gates are not designed to be worked through alone. Although the workbook lends itself to self-evaluation, we believe that it is through small groups that the best results are achieved. It is though accountability and reliability that change is accomplished. Accountability to others is like a rubber band; it stretches to allow freedom but holds to require change. Reliability is the idea that trust is earned through faithfulness. With reliability, we learn the character traits of faithfulness and truthfulness, working in conjunction with mercy and grace.

HOW NEHEMIAH RESTORED MORE THAN
JUST THE WALLS OF JERUSALEM

In the Nehemiah study, the pattern for recovery can be used for more than just the walls of the city. Nehemiah rebuilt the twelve "life gates," as well as the city gates, for the people of Jerusalem. The twelve life issues we will look at rebuilding are reality, authority, a belief system based on truth, self-esteem based on biblical morals, trust, empowerment, freedom, a future, relationships, a new harvest, a sense of belonging, and joy. Nehemiah brought reality to the people of Jerusalem by explaining the need for good walls and gates. He restored authority to them by soliciting their help in the process. He helped them recover their belief in God and the goodness of God, as well as the protection and security of God. Nehemiah helped to restore their self-esteem by encouraging them to work and not be afraid. He restored their trust in themselves, in God, and in His authority. He empowered the people of Jerusalem by holding them accountable. He restored their freedom with gates and boundaries. He restored a future by staying on the wall and working until the gates were restored. He restored relationships with the people in the city and with those who came to help them rebuild. A new harvest was exacted because the pillage was stopped. The Israelites had a new sense of belonging, and their joy was restored at the completion of the gates and walls.

Nehemiah restored reality by confronting the situation as it existed. **"Then I said to them, 'You see the trouble we are in: Jerusalem lies in ruins, and its gates have been burned with fire. Come, let us rebuild the wall of Jerusalem, and we will no longer be in disgrace.' I also told them about the gracious hand of my God on me and what the king had said to me" (Neh. 2:17-18).**

In the second part of verse eighteen of chapter two, Nehemiah heard the answer. The people told him that they would rise up and build. **"So, they began this good work."** The reality of any situation often brings a positive response to "get to work" and make the changes needed.

Restored authority comes almost immediately behind the initial start for Nehemiah. At once, his authority and the power of God for restoration are challenged by the evil Sanballat and Tobiah. They laughed at the people of Jerusalem and made jokes about their work. But Nehemiah showed the people the godly authority on his life by responding to the enemy: **"The God of heaven will give us success. We his servants will start rebuilding, but as for you, you have no share in Jerusalem or any claim or historic right to it" (Neh. 2:20).** Throughout the book, Nehemiah was challenged; but, because of his authority as a servant of God, he was able to stand and complete the tasks he was given.

We see the belief system of the Israelites restored in chapter eight as Ezra and all the people gathered together and read the law. **"Ezra praised the LORD, the great God; and all the people lifted their hands and responded, 'Amen! Amen!' Then they bowed down and worshiped the LORD with their faces to the ground" (Neh. 8:6).** What a sign of restoration of their belief system.

Nehemiah restored self-esteem in chapter four as Nehemiah helped the people overcome the opposition of ridicule and discouragement. Nehemiah prayed to God to turn their reproach on the heads of those who ridiculed the Israelites. When the attack continued, Nehemiah continued to pray for help. As they became discouraged, Nehemiah spoke words of encouragement to the people. Their self-esteem was restored through prayer and encouragement.

Trust returned as, day by day, the workers saw that Nehemiah would not leave them. He worked side by side with them. They began to trust him with their lives. As that happened, they began to trust in themselves.

Nehemiah empowered the people through prayer, working with them, helping them accomplish goals, and not giving up. We are told that Nehemiah prayed and talked to the people, but, more than that, he worked with them. **"Neither I nor my brothers nor my men nor the guards with me took off our clothes" (Neh. 4:23a).** How much that must have empowered the people to stay with him and complete the work.

Little by little, the people regained freedom from the terror of their enemies. The people walked in less fear, though they carried weapons of war. They were prepared to live in more freedom from day to day by working for restoration of their city. As the walls were completed, their future was restored. No longer would they have to redo the work they had done the day before because intruders had destroyed everything. No longer would these people have to look to the past for hope because now their families were safe, and they could accomplish much.

As the walls were rebuilt and the gates restored, they were also able to restore their relationships. Neighboring peoples helped the Israelites. In verse five of chapter three, it says that the Tekoites repaired the walls: **"The next section was repaired by the men of Tekoa, but their nobles would not put their shoulders to the work under their supervisors."** Tekoa was a town in Judah which was thought to have belonged to the tribe of Asher. The nobles of Tekoa would not help the people of Jerusalem, yet some of the townspeople came and helped in rebuilding at least two sections of the wall. This is only one way that relationships were restored.

A new harvest came when Nehemiah cleansed the defilement out of Jerusalem and asked God to remember him with the first fruits of the new harvest (Neh. 13).

When the provisions for the Levites were restored, placing the priesthood in the proper position to set the "church" or the worship back in its rightful place, their sense of belonging to God was regained.

Finally, joy was restored to the city as they celebrated the dedication of the wall. **"At the dedication of the wall of Jerusalem, the Levites were sought out from where they lived and were brought to Jerusalem to celebrate joyfully the dedication with songs of thanksgiving and with the music of cymbals, harps and lyres"** (Neh. 12:27).

The walls were built, the gates restored, and the people were joyous because their lives were filled with hope and a future. **"'For I know the plans I have for you,' declares the Lord, 'plans to prosper you and not to harm you, plans to give you hope and a future'"** (Jer. 29:11).

As we study restoration and recovery, we will look at four specific areas. The first one we will look at is the restoration of a relationship with God. Secondly, we will study the need for restoration with self. This includes becoming aware of self from a biblical perspective. We are to walk humbly before God. **"He has shown you, O mortal, what is good. And what does the LORD require of you? To act justly and to love mercy and to walk humbly with your God"** (Mic. 6:8). Many life issues cause—what some call—"losing self." As you find self, you discover empowerment to move to your complete life.

Thirdly, we will study restoration to others. Being restored to others is a sometimes-difficult path to follow, but as you go along rebuilding your boundaries, you will discover that this difficult path leads to serenity. Fourthly, we will study the restoration to community. Often, reputations are destroyed, and the community in which you live is reluctant to accept you.

Of course, no recovery program is without problems. You will discover life is worth living, regardless of the difficulties that must be overcome. The slippery, downhill slide of addiction is never the uphill fight that recovery must be. In recovery, you are building; in addiction, you are tearing down and destroying. Different "muscle groups" are required in recovery. In fact, no positive "muscle groups" are needed to slide downhill. All you need to do is give in to gravity. But with recovery, you are climbing up, one step at a time, one day at a time. The uphill climb is not without commitment. It is one day at a time with a lifetime commitment.

> "The uphill climb is not without commitment. It is one day at a time with a lifetime commitment."

At the Valley Gate, the East Gate, and the Old Gate, your relationship with God is restored. As you rebuild the boundaries and the gates that hold this relationship with God, you will move on to the Inspection Gate, the Fountain Gate, the Horse Gate, and the Prison Gate to restore self to self. That is, you will restore the new self; or, in the words of Paul in **Colossians 3:9-10, "Do not lie to each other, since you have taken off your old self with its practices and have put on the new self, which is being renewed in knowledge in the image of its Creator."** As you put on the new man, you will then begin the restoration with others through rebuilding the Dung Gate, the Fish Gate, and the Harvest Gate. Finally, at the Sheep Gate and the Water Gate, you will be restored to community.

THE WHOLE ARMOR OF GOD

Finally, be strong in the Lord and in his mighty power. Put on the full armor of God, so that you can take your stand against the devil's schemes. For our struggle is not against flesh and blood, but against the rulers, against the authorities, against the powers of this dark world and against the spiritual forces of evil in the heavenly realms. Therefore put on the full armor of God, so that when the day of evil comes, you may be able to stand your ground, and after you have done everything, to stand. Stand firm then, with the belt of truth buckled around your waist, with the breastplate of righteousness in place, and with your feet fitted with the readiness that comes from the gospel of peace. In addition to all this, take up the shield of faith, with which you can extinguish all the flaming arrows of the evil one. Take the helmet of salvation and the sword of the Spirit, which is the word of God" (Eph. 6:10-17).

The following is a declaration of faith, rewritten from Ephesians six and other Scriptures to help those in recovery retrain the brain to think in a positive way. Each section will be briefly explained in this chapter.

"By faith, I put on the helmet of salvation to protect my mind from the fiery darts of the enemy."

The helmet is a protective device used to cover the head. The head houses the brain. The number one trick of the devil is to cause us to think negative thoughts. These thoughts are transmitted throughout the atmosphere all the time by the enemy. You have only to tune in to them, and the fiery darts begin. With the helmet of salvation on, our minds are protected from any enemy transmission.

"I put on the breastplate of righteousness—not my righteousness, but the righteousness of Christ."

The breastplate covers the area of the heart. It was the heart that was considered the center of man's being. The heart needs to be right with God and man. The breastplate of righteousness cannot be made of man's goodness because man can always fail. Jesus is the perfect Goodness. With His righteousness covering your heart, you can meet life head-on, knowing that you will be doing the next right thing.

"I put on the girdle of truth; I will tell the truth, and I will believe the truth."

The girdle holds the armor together. Truth is what holds our lives together. You must tell the truth and believe the truth. We have all experienced some negative thought reaching our minds, and, even though it was false, we accepted that thought as truth. It is so important in recovery to know the truth and believe the truth.

"I put on the shoes of the Gospel of peace; and everywhere my feet take me, I will take the Gospel of peace."

The *Gospel* means the "Good News." In the past, your feet have taken you to places where you were part of the bad news. Now, you will put on the shoes of the Good News of peace. These shoes deal with anger and resentment, fighting, and outbursts. These shoes deal with peace. The good news is that through Jesus Christ you can have peace. Peace is a lost commodity in the world of addiction. To get peace and keep it is worth the trouble of recovery.

"I take up the Sword of the Spirit, which is the Word of God, and it 'is a lamp unto my feet, and a light unto my path.'[1] Its Word will I hide in my heart that I might not sin against God.'"[2]

The sword is the only defensive weapon of the armor of God. The defense we have is the Word of God, the Bible. If you know the Word, then you have a light for your journey. The Word gives instruction and produces wisdom to live the new, sober life. If you hide the Word in your heart, you will not sin against God because it produces a desire to serve a great and powerful God.

"I take up the shield of faith—not my faith, but Your faithfulness."

The shield is the final protection while moving forward. To every person is given the measure of faith, but that faith will often wane at certain times of our life. You cannot count on your faith to get you through, but Jesus is always faithful. He is true, and His faithfulness never wanes.

"And over all that, I put on the garment of praise, and I will be thankful."

The garment of praise covers our backside. It is gratitude that keeps the past in the past. It is gratitude that separates us from the pain of yesterday. The garment of praise completes the armor that protects us from our former life.

---

1   Psalm 119:105 KJV
2   Psalm 119:11 KJV

"Left Foot: I am dead to the demands of my flesh," and **"Right Foot: I am alive unto Christ."**

I was once told by my mentor, Dr. Eileen Essberg, that if I spent ninety days telling myself that I was dead to the demands of my flesh and alive unto Christ, my life would be changed forever. She said that when I put on my shoes each morning, to say with every step that I was dead to the flesh and alive unto Christ.

The flesh demands what it wants when it wants it. The flesh can never be satisfied. We are to die daily to the wants of our flesh and remind ourselves that we are alive or resurrected in the power of Jesus Christ. That same power that raised Him from the dead is resident in our lives. We must recognize that power and use it for overcoming the enemy.

DEUTERONOMY TWENTY-EIGHT: BLESS YOURSELF

Until now, your life has been part of one curse after another. You must learn to speak blessings over your life. The power of Jesus' blood has broken all the curses, but in order for you to be an overcomer, you must convince yourself of His love.

Deuteronomy twenty-eight speaks of the blessings that will overtake us if we obey God. The following declaration is taken from this passage. Every blessing is spoken out loud and repeated daily for announcing to the devil and to yourself that you are blessed and not cursed by God. You also agree to obey God. You ask for forgiveness of the things where you have failed.

> Lord, today I choose life, and I choose to obey Your voice and heed Your commandments. Forgive me where I have failed You. I desire to have all that You have promised in Your Word. Therefore, I declare to myself that I am what Your Word says I am.

> I am blessed in the city; I am blessed in the country. My children are blessed in the city and the country. My ground is blessed; my animals are blessed; my basket is blessed and filled. My kneading dough is enough to supply all my bread. I am blessed when I come in, and I am blessed when I go out. When my enemies rise up against me, You will cause them to flee seven different ways. My storehouse

is blessed; every job I undertake is blessed. My future is blessed; my destination in life is blessed. Wherever I am is blessed.

Everybody will know that I belong to You, Lord, and they will respect me. I shall have a surplus—more than enough money and more than enough everything, so I can lend and never have to borrow. My children are prosperous. The work of my hand is blessed. I am a lender and not a borrower. I am the head and not the tail; I am above and not beneath. I am the beloved of the Lord, and I will live and multiply.

The blessing speaks of prosperity in a way that brings self-esteem and reassurance. Recovery is rocky, at best, in the first stage, so continual reassurance is necessary for all of us to continue. David said in one passage of Scripture that he encouraged himself (1 Sam. 30:6). Sometimes, there is no one to help you when you are down in the dumps. You must learn to bless and not curse in these times of despair.

THE IMPORTANCE OF ACTION STEPS

Recovery is often called a spiritual journey. I personally think that most people believe it is a spiritual journey because there is nothing tangible about it. They just sit around and think recovery is going to fall out of the sky for them. This is not so.

As with the armor of God, putting on the armor is action. The soldier must do something himself. The warfare may be spiritual, but there are tangible action steps that must be taken.

Each of us must take personal responsibility for recovery. Nothing is going to happen if someone else is taking responsibility for our recovery. The action steps given here are necessary. Recovery is elusive. It is like the blue butterfly. It does exist, and we know the region where it lives; but finding it is one thing, and capturing it is something else altogether. The legend of the blue butterfly is that if the butterfly is spotted and captured, it will bring great success or failure. Recovery may be the same. Once a person has captured recovery, success may come for life, or one may fail at the process. Either way, the person has seen the butterfly and knows that it really exists. With recovery, once you have sincerely tasted sobriety, you may fail, but you will forever be searching for it and trying to attain it because you know it really does exist.

CHAPTER TWO
INTRODUCTION: RECOVERY EXPLAINED

THE STORY OF REDEMPTION IS really a story about recovery. Jesus was sent to earth on a mission from His Father to recover what had been lost in the Garden of Eden. Sin entered the world and began an avalanche of destruction, which drove mankind deeper and deeper into sin that he could not get out of by himself.

An early story of recovery in the Bible is the story of Lot and Abraham. Lot was kidnapped by sinful kings, and Abraham went after him to recover his belongings and his life. He was on a mission of recovery and restoration. Likewise, Moses was sent to recover and restore the Israelites to God, to themselves, to others, and to a community. It is simple to see that the Israelites needed to be restored back to God, back to what they were originally intended to be, back to each other, and, finally, back to a thriving community.

The basis of recovery of human lives from the effects of sin—whether it is drugs, alcohol, pornography, depression, lifestyle issues, or life-threatening illness—is in the Bible. The pattern for recovery and restoration is simple to learn but complicated to follow. In this course, you will discover how the pattern works through the deliverance in Exodus and the restoration of the gates of Jerusalem in Nehemiah. The basic pattern for restoration and recovery of any of life's issues, including addiction, is restoring self to God, restoring self to self, restoring self to others, and restoring self to the community.

"Restoring the soul to God, to self, to others, to community."

According to *Strong's Concordance*, the Hebrew word for recovery is *natsal*. This word is translated as "recover" and means "to snatch away, deliver, rescue, save, strip, or plunder."[3] It is used in 1 Samuel 30:8 when David prayed and asked God if he should pursue a group of renegades, who had stolen his wives and looted his camp. The Lord answered him by telling David to pursue the renegades and to recover all that had been stolen from him. When a loved one has been ravaged by addiction or other life circumstance, recovery is necessary. Sometimes the recovery process will seem like a snatching away, sometimes like deliverance, sometimes like rescue, and sometimes like being plundered. Nevertheless, God speaks to us today to take the recovery process from a secular world and bring it back into the church, where it has always belonged.

Another Hebrew word for recover is *chayah*. This means to "live, to have life, remain alive, sustain life, live prosperously, live forever, and be quickened, be alive or be restored to life or health."[4] We see that to recover means both to rescue what was lost and to sustain life.

Since Jesus came to give us life, He means for us to recover from life's issues by having life, by sustaining life, and by prospering in this life. Is there something to recover from? Ahaziah, according to **2 Kings 1:2,** fell down in his chambers and was sick. **"Now Ahaziah had fallen through the lattice of his upper room in Samaria and injured himself. So he sent messengers, saying to them, 'Go and consult Baal-Zebub, the god of Ekron, to see if I will recover from this injury.'"** He inquired from a source other than Jehovah as to whether he would recover from his disease. This is exactly what is happening to the myriad of people who are "sick" and looking for answers other than from God. They are seeking recovery from sources other than from the One Who can give them full recovery.

Two other Hebrew words relate to recovery. **Michyah** means "to restrain, halt, and stop or to retain."[5] **Shuwb** means "to turn back to God or repent; to

---

3   *Strong's Concordance*, s.v. "natsal," accessed October 9, 2017, http://www.eliyah.com/cgi-bin/strongs.cgi?file=hebrewlexicon&isindex=natsal.

4   *Strong's Concordance*, s.v. "chayah," accessed October 9, 2017, http://lexiconcordance.com/hebrew/2421.html.

5   *Strong's Concordance*, s.v. "michyah," accessed October 9, 2017, http://lexiconcordance.som/hebrew/4241.html.

turn back from evil."[6] From these Hebrew words, we can get a picture of what it means to fully recover today.

"Restoring the soul one gateway at a time."

In the New Testament Greek, Paul tells Timothy **"that they will come to their senses and escape from the trap of the devil, who has taken them captive to do his will" (2 Tim. 2:26).**

The Message says it this way:

> **Run away from infantile indulgence. Run after mature righteousness—faith, love, peace—joining those who are in honest and serious prayer before God. Refuse to get involved in inane discussions; they always end up in fights. God's servant must not be argumentative, but a gentle listener and a teacher who keeps cool, working firmly but patiently with those who refuse to obey.** *You never know how or when God might sober them up with a change of heart and a turning to the truth, enabling them to escape the Devil's trap, where they are caught and held captive, forced to run his errands"* (italics mine).

This last sentence explains in a nutshell what happens when a person gets free from addiction. Addiction is a trap of the devil. You are caught and held captive and forced to do things that are evil. As we study the addiction process, we will see exactly how the devil has been able to manipulate people into this deceptive lifestyle.

Who needs recovery? In some form or another, everybody needs recovery. Everybody has lost something—whether it is a material loss or the loss of a loved one. Everybody has, at one time or another, had to stop doing something. Everybody has been sick or has known somebody who was sick. Everybody needs recovery.

How does recovery happen? It happens through restoration to God, restoration to self, restoration to others, and restoration to community.

---

6   *Strong's Concordance, s.v.* "shuwb," accessed October 9, 2017, http://lexiconcordance. som/hebrew/7225.html.

RESTORATION TO GOD

In the recovery process, the first area of restoration is that of self to God. This is a three-part plan: admit your need for God; commit your failures to God; and submit your life to God.

Human beings have built into their DNA a desire to direct their own lives. They are taught from a young age to be self-sufficient. Babies are nurtured to be independent. Toddlers learn "me" before any other word, except *mama*. They learn *mama* first because, somehow, they know that she will help them with their "me." Even those of us who are brought up in the church still have a hard time understanding that we need God. Many of us think we will need God at death or in a crisis but never on a day-to-day, moment-to moment basis. When the pain of life shows up, and only after everything else has been tried first, some of us will turn to God for help.

This is why we might hear someone say, "They haven't hit bottom yet." It is believed that when you hit bottom, you have nowhere else to go but up, and that sometimes means turning to God.

It doesn't matter how you get to the understanding that you need God; it only matters that you get there. Without that understanding, recovery will never begin. You may stop drinking or doing some other unacceptable behavior for a while, but without God, relapse is inevitable.

When you admit the need for God, then you can come to the revelation that all of your failures must be committed to Him. The failures of life are sometimes the most cherished things we possess. That statement may seem unusual, but failures cushion addiction. What I mean by that is that the failures of life can form a bed of excuses. A person who wants to stay in addiction will use their failures as an excuse to blame someone else. If it's someone else's fault, then it will be another's responsibility. Your failures form a comfortable place in which to stay addicted. If you commit your failures to God, then God can take your failures and use them as a foundation for learning and change. Committing failures to God holds you accountable for past mistakes and requires you to learn from those mistakes.

Finally, you must submit your life to God. This submission may also come in stages. Since God is a triune God—Father, Son, and Holy Spirit—the submission has to be to the total personage of God. God must be submitted to as the Father that He really is. Because many of us have not been exposed to godly fathers, the thought of submitting to God as Father may be extremely difficult. You will have to learn that God is a loving Authority, a faithful Provider, and a dependable Father. If you have no experience with an earthly father who is loving, faithful, and dependable, you may resist submitting your life to God the Father.

Submitting to God as Jesus the Son may also cause some difficulties. Jesus is Savior, Redeemer, and Lord and must be seen as all three for you to submit and to give over your life completely. Since many have been betrayed by mankind, this can cause some issues in surrender.

Submitting to God as the Holy Spirit may seem spooky to us. Many people have a misconception of the Holy Spirit. They may not believe in the Holy Spirit at all, so submitting to God as a Spirit to be their Friend, Counselor, and Helper may take some time. Surrendering to the Holy Spirit comes through an intimate knowledge of God.

All of this surrender will include repentance.

> **"The Lord is not slow in keeping his promise, as some understand slowness. Instead he is patient with you, not wanting anyone to perish, but everyone to come to repentance" (2 Pet. 3:9).**

> **"Repent, then, and turn to God, so that your sins may be wiped out, that times of refreshing may come from the Lord" (Acts 3:19).**

> **"Repent of this wickedness and pray to the Lord in the hope that he may forgive you for having such a thought in your heart" (Acts 8:22).**

> **"From that time on Jesus began to preach, 'Repent, for the kingdom of heaven has come near'" (Matthew 4:17).**

> **"I tell you that in the same way there will be more rejoicing in heaven over one sinner who repents than over ninety-nine righteous persons who do not need to repent" (Lk. 15:7).**

> **"In the same way, I tell you, there is rejoicing in the presence of the angels of God over one sinner who repents" (Lk. 15:10).**

"Whoever conceals their sins does not prosper, but the one who confesses and renounces them finds mercy" (Prov. 28:13).

"God is a loving Authority."

"When the people heard this, they were cut to the heart and said to Peter and the other apostles, 'Brothers, what shall we do?'" (Acts 2:37).

"Grieve, mourn and wail. Change your laughter to mourning and your joy to gloom. Humble yourselves before the Lord, and he will lift you up" (Jas. 4:9-10).

Over and over again in the Word of God, man is told to repent. *Repent* in the simplest terms means to turn from evil and turn toward God. To repent is to humble yourself. To repent is to stop doing the evil things you have been doing and begin doing good.

RESTORATION TO SELF

The second stage of recovery comes with restoration to one's self, which has been lost in addiction. The self that must be restored is the one God intended a person to be from birth. No one's life ambition is to become addicted and out of control.

What does it look like to be restored to self? I see it like this: a person must be able to trust himself again. Even in the worst addiction I have ever known, there are still some boundaries that are set and will not be crossed. For example, one person won't steal from family but will steal from strangers. One person will not harm an older person, while another will not harm a child. However, in most other areas of this life, there are no boundaries. In order to trust one's self again, you must restore the boundaries of your life. These boundaries can be restored through forgiveness. First, you must receive forgiveness from God and then humble yourself to take the gift of forgiveness through Jesus Christ. Forgiveness is never earned. It is a gift from God. The word is for/give/ness. Right in the middle is the word *give*. Forgiveness empowers a person to change. It softens hard hearts and changes minds. After you receive God's forgiveness, then you can give forgiveness to yourself. A person needs to understand what has happened in the past is not going to change. You cannot go back to yesterday and redo it. Past failures, once committed to God, must be forgiven by you. It is a gift you give yourself.

No person ever intends to lose his soul to addiction."

Finally, in restoring self to self, a person must make restitution to self. The only way to make this restitution is to change the behavior which caused the problem. This step cannot be left out. You must be able to trust yourself. But you will not be able to trust yourself if you continue to do the same sinful, addictive behaviors.

"When he came to his senses, he said, 'How many of my father's hired servants have food to spare, and here I am starving to death! I will set out and go back to my father and say to him: Father, I have sinned against heaven and against you. I am no longer worthy to be called your son; make me like one of your hired servants'" (Lk. 15:17-19).

"Yet now I am happy, not because you were made sorry, but because your sorrow led you to repentance. For you became sorrowful as God intended and so were not harmed in any way by us. Godly sorrow brings repentance that leads to salvation and leaves no regret, but worldly sorrow brings death" (2 Cor. 7:9-10).

"He refreshes my soul. He guides me along the right paths for his name's sake" (Ps. 23:3).

RESTORATION TO OTHERS

Restoring self to others is the third area of recovery. Specialists say that the first stage of recovery usually lasts one month for every year in addiction. Therefore, restoration from life's other issues will take about the same amount of time. They also say that a person stops maturing emotionally on the first day the first drink is taken. I have concluded that emotional growth often stops at the first emotional trauma. With this compounded with addiction, a person may be stunted in emotional growth for a long time.

If you stop growing emotionally on the first day of the first drink or the first cigarette, it can take years to be restored to full recovery. I use the term premature to relate to brain maturity, even after a person has reached adulthood.

Premature refers to the stage the brain is in before complete maturity. It is speculated that the cognitive brain is not fully developed or mature until age twenty-four, meaning that any drugs or alcohol or addictive behavior done before that age stunts the maturity of the individual. This premature state could mean that an adult who is forty acts like a thirteen-year-old. Imagine the havoc a thirteen-year-old child could wreak in a forty-year-old body.

> "To restore self to others, the premature, emotional brain must gain some maturity."

Relationships with parents, children, spouse, co-workers, friends, and neighbors can all be in complete chaos in the life of a person who is seriously premature.

A person may be right with God and may even have trust in self, but restoring self to others can take years. In this stage, the process of confession, honesty, repentance, and complete forgiveness has to be embraced. You also must come to terms with personal responsibility for restoration to others to be effective.

To restore self to others, the premature must gain some maturity. One area of maturity is understanding the damage that has been done to some or all relationships. Damage to the relationships must be repaired by both parties. You have no control over whether the relationship will be restored to a previous state, but you do have control over how you will behave toward that relationship.

The recovering person should make the first effort to forgive the other person. They must then seek forgiveness for what they have done. This may come in the form of an apology—either in person, by phone, or through written communication. No matter how the apology is given, sincerity is the key. Humility and sincerity will go a long way to restore a broken relationship. They may not always bring a restored relationship, however. Sometimes the pain that has occurred cannot be overcome without much work. You must be willing to give the injured party time to heal.

Making restitution is yet another way to restore relationships. The injured party will have little excuse not to forgive the injuring party if he or she is making every effort to "pay back the offense." One of the best ways to make restitution is to keep promises through faithfulness and commitment. Restoration must be made first to the family, then to friends, and, finally, to acquaintances. This restoration must reach to the co-worker, the neighbor, and even the stranger.

The New Living Translation uses the word family 123 times in seventy-six verses. God believes in family and relationships. He wants families restored and relationships healthy.

> **"God decided in advance to adopt us into his own family by bringing us to himself through Jesus Christ. This is what he wanted to do, and it gave him great pleasure" (Eph. 1:5).**

> **"Now this is what the Lord says to the family of Israel: 'Come back to me and live!'" (Amos 5:4).**

Psalm 38:11 sums all of this up: **"My loved ones and friends stay away, fearing my disease. Even my own family stands at a distance."** Loved ones and friends stay away from us, fearing what our problems will do to them.

RESTORATION TO COMMUNITY

The last area of restoration and recovery comes to the community. The community where you have lived is affected by your life. People love to think that nobody knows. You convince yourself that nobody talks about you because you are anonymous. The truth is that most communities know the troubles of the addicted. The community knows about the person with the "problem." People may not know what is wrong, but they know something is wrong. The work place is affected; the church family is infected; and the neighborhood is involved.

"Serving the church is yet another way to be restored to community."

The community restoration begins with a job. This job requires steady and faithful service. The job must be honorable. There can be no absenteeism, no employee theft.

The restoration continues in the community when you begin to volunteer in the church or elsewhere. You can rebuild your reputation by giving back. Serving the church is yet another way to be restored to community. There you continue to be held accountable and continue to mature emotionally and spiritually.

WHAT HAPPENS WHEN THE CHURCH IGNORES RECOVERY?

The following is a true story of a pastor's wife who had been separated from God, self, others, and community.

"Sundays are rough around my house," the pastor said to me.

"What do you mean by that?" I asked. "Well, if she is going to have an episode, it's going to be on Sunday morning." Tears were dripping from eyes that were weary of looking for a solution to a major problem in his life and in his wife's life.

The man sitting across from me was a well-known, retired minister. He was well-acquainted with Jesus and the Word of God. Sitting next to him was his wife of many years who was well-acquainted with drugs.

The weary family took turns expressing the pain of what had happened to their loved one. She, however, sat quietly with a far-off look in her eye. In the middle of the serious discussion about how to help this "first lady," she urinated on the sofa.

Her husband told of time after time on Sunday morning when she would lock herself in the bathroom and begin screaming obscenities at him. Pill bottles left empty by her bed or on the floor were the telltale sign of a major, devastating addiction.

The pastor's wife had what I call 'a little help from her friends.'"

The minister admitted that he had known about the problem for years, but, "in his position" in the church, he was ashamed that he could not get her "delivered."

It all had started about twenty years prior when a nurse in his church offered his wife a Valium®. His wife was under a lot of stress, trying to meet the needs of the women in the church and maintain the perfect appearance of an up-and-coming minister's wife. The pills were a "lifesaver." At first, he encouraged her to use the drug because it made her seem more at ease with the congregation. The nurse kept her supplied, and, for a season, all was well.

What the family did not know is that this is a highly addictive drug. Once a person is addicted, the chemistry in the brain begins to change. The natural, God-given chemicals stop producing, and, when the person doesn't get the drug of choice or the chemicals it has become familiar with, withdrawal symptoms begin. As a result of the "unknown factor," this Christian pastor's wife began to experience some withdrawal signs.

It is important to know that when you take another person's prescription, especially a scheduled drug (one that the government tracks as addictive), you have broken the law. When she began experiencing "symptoms" like a nervous breakdown, she told her doctor the symptoms, but she left out the important part of the story, which was the addiction.

With all addiction, the process is progressive. At first, one pill at night is enough. It makes you sleepy and does its job to calm the nervous system. But the tolerance level grows; withdrawal symptoms continue; and you must have more relief.

Just a sidebar here to tell you that central nervous system drugs work in the brain. In the mid-brain, it is speculated that most of the "God activity" occurs. If this is true, the drug does its magic in the brain, and the person using the drug loses all spiritual feeling. In a sense, they are "dead" to the things of God because their feelings are so numbed.

This pastor's wife had what I call, "a little help from her friends." She continued to take Valium, then added pain pills, then added any pill available. This is the quick progression of tolerance to drugs in your system. She did not go to the streets to buy drugs; she went to her doctor. As the addiction progressed, her mind was more and more numbed; her feelings completely changed; and the love she once had was destroyed and replaced with the idol of central nervous system drugs.

On the day she arrived, she was not really interested in change. The drugs had changed her thinking. Her rational brain was so affected, she could not begin to understand the consequences of her behavior. By this point, she would take any kind of pill she could get her hands on. On this particular day, she had gotten some over-the-counter medicines for allergies and taken so many that her bodily functions were out of her control.

She "dried out," going through hallucinations, evil visions, and radical homosexual behavior, plus scaring the socks off the rest of the women in the ministry. The once-beautiful pastor's wife, who led hundreds of women, was reduced to a "servant of Satan" (in her own words).

Once the drugs were gone, the woman began to crave the feeling of being on more drugs. That insane behavior drove her from our ministry into the streets, where her family rescued her. This was extremely difficult because they did not want to rescue her. But what else could they do? They sent her again to another treatment facility, but she ran away from there. Keep in mind that this is a woman in her sixties. What a sad story! This story haunts me as I continue to work with addicts. Here's what I have ascertained from her:

First, secrets kill us. Pride stops us from asking for help. The church has a façade of perfection. When a less-than-perfect person finds her way into the church, rather than marring the façade, she keeps her secrets. The secret, of course, is not only hers, but her family's as well. Her husband can't expose the issue because of what they might think in the ministerial association.

Next, the church has failed with people who need recovery. In the case of this woman, she had been taught all her life that her sin was forgiven. In an altered brain, where rational thoughts are destroyed, that one truth becomes perverted. You believe that no matter what you do, Jesus will forgive you. But instead of understanding the power of forgiveness to change, you use it as an avenue to continue to sin. Paul addresses this attitude in Romans six. But with an altered mind, there is no explaining that grace is not a license to continue in sin.

Finally, you need help. The church needs help to understand the issues of addiction. Sometimes, I believe that Christianity has reduced itself to a form of paganism by using drugs to expand the mind and "go deeper in the spiritual world." This is a personal opinion. I say this because so many in ministry smoke or drink a little. As you will learn later, cigarettes are called the "perfect drug." They hit on every major brain receptor and alter the flow of chemicals in the brain. If you are nervous, smoke. If you are hungry, smoke. If you need to relax or need a "pick-me-up," smoke.

Alcohol is a system depressant, but one drink begins the chemical change in the brain. This is one reason alcohol helps people who drink to unwind, be social, and go to sleep. The chemicals alter the brain immediately. There is also the matter of the millions of pain pills—which are narcotics—which are given to church folks every day. Of course, then there's caffeine, and don't forget sugar and carbohydrates. So, if you think about it, is there anybody who has not altered their brain?

America is an altered society. The church is an altered church. As for addicts, well, let's just say that some of us are still living with secrets. Here's the real problem: the church has become a hiding place for addicts to continue using or a place of ignorance about drug treatment. Jesus said, **"The truth will set you free" (Jn. 8:32b).** The church needs to know the truth about addiction, and then addicts will be set free. However, there is a point of no return for some.

❧ CHAPTER THREE ❧
SIN/DISEASE CONCEPT EXPLORED

PATHOLOGICAL BEHAVIOR IS HABITUAL, MALADAPTIVE, and compulsive. Negative, addictive behavior is habitual, maladaptive, and compulsive. Sin/ disease is missing the mark of a productive plan for life by participating in behavior that is habitual, maladaptive, and compulsive. What starts out as a slight veering off-course for a productive life ends up as a progressive development of negative, behavior-seeking vulnerability to relapse to that behavior and a slowed ability to respond to positive, rewarding activities.

The Diagnostic and Statistical Manual of Mental Disorders (DSM-IV) defines drug addiction as a pathological condition. The disorder of addiction involves the progression of acute drug use to the development of drug-seeking behavior, the vulnerability to relapse, and the decreased, slowed ability to respond to naturally rewarding stimuli.[7]

"Virtually all drugs which cause addiction increase the Dopamine release in the brain."

According to the *DSM-IV*, there are three distinct stages of addiction: the first stage is preoccupation/anticipation, followed by binge/intoxication, and concluding with withdrawal/negative effect. These stages are characterized by constant cravings and preoccupation with obtaining the substance; using more of the substance than necessary to experience the intoxicating effects; and experiencing tolerance, withdrawal symptoms, and decreased motivation

---

7   American Psychiatric Association. 1994. *The Diagnostic and Statistical Manual of Mental Disorders (DSM-IV-TR)*. New York: American Psychiatric Association.

for normal life activities.[8] According to the American Society of Addiction Medicine, drug addiction differs from drug dependence and drug tolerance.[9]

If there is mental illness involved, the church can be completely lost as to how to handle the day-to-day actions of the individual. As an ordained minister, I can attest to the fact that there was nothing in my ministerial training that told me how to know when a person is on drugs or alcohol or how to tell if someone is addicted to gambling or pornography. At the same time, in all the churches that I am affiliated with, there are hundreds of individuals still engaging in these negative behaviors.

Virtually all drugs which cause addiction increase the dopamine release in the brain in addition to the specific effects caused by particular drugs. For example, in cocaine use, the brain is stimulated and gets excited, but, at the same time, the dopamine, which makes us feel rewarded and happy, is increased. The brain is flooded with a release of dopamine, which eventually turns off the natural pumps that cause users to feel happy and satisfied. At this stage of addiction, only chemically induced dopamine will cause an addict to feel "good." This is the reason so many are miserable when not using drugs. The simple pleasures do not cause the natural dopamine release because the brain has stopped making it naturally. This one chemical change is enough to cause relapse. Misery must be relieved. Since holding a baby won't release the natural dopamine, the mother of a precious baby will leave the child to find her drug of choice to feel normal again. The feelings of happiness, which occur for most when attending church, do not occur if you are using. Only the chemical release of dopamine can cause those feelings. You may see someone in early stage recovery leave church, seeking a more "exciting" event. What does the Bible say about all of this?

Who has woe? Who has sorrow? Who has strife? Who has complaints? Who has needless bruises? Who has bloodshot eyes? Those who linger over wine, who go to sample bowls of mixed wine. Do not gaze at wine when it is red, when it sparkles in the cup, when it goes down smoothly! In the end it bites like a snake

---

8   Ibid.
9   American Society of Addiction Medicine. "Definition of Addiction." ASAM.org. http://www.asam.org/for-the-public/definition-of-addiction (accessed November 13, 2017).

and poisons like a viper. Your eyes will see strange sights, and your mind will imagine confusing things. You will be like one sleeping on the high seas, lying on top of the rigging. 'They hit me,' you will say, 'but I'm not hurt! They beat me, but I don't feel it! When will I wake up so I can find another drink?'" (Prov. 23:29-35).

"Wine is a mocker and beer a brawler; whoever is led astray by them is not wise" (Prov. 20:1).

"You ate no bread and drank no wine or other fermented drink. I did this so that you might know that I am the LORD your God" (Deut. 29:6).

"'I have the right to do anything,' you say—but not everything is beneficial. 'I have the right to do anything'—but I will not be mastered by anything" (1 Cor. 6:12)

"Do not get drunk on wine, which leads to debauchery. Instead, be filled with the Spirit" (Eph. 5:18).

"The acts of the flesh are obvious: sexual immorality, impurity and debauchery; idolatry and witchcraft; hatred, discord, jealousy, fits of rage, selfish ambition, dissensions, factions and envy; drunkenness, orgies, and the like. I warn you, as I did before, that those who live like this will not inherit the kingdom of God" (Gal. 5:19-21).

"Nor did they repent of their murders, their magic arts, their sexual immorality or their thefts" (Rev. 9:21).

"They promise them freedom, while they themselves are slaves of depravity—for 'people are slaves to whatever has mastered them'" (2 Pet. 2:19).

Some additional problems caused by the disease of addiction are explained by Dr. Alan Leshner, director of the National Institute of Drug Abuse (NIDA).

The most immediate, extensive, and long-lasting problems caused by drug abuse, both for individuals and for society, are often medical in nature. For example, known drug-abuse-related health problems and resulting lost productivity alone cost our society more than $33 billion each year.

Illicit drugs directly cause many medical problems. Stimulants such as cocaine and methamphetamine increase the heart rate while constricting the blood vessels. In susceptible individuals, these two actions together set the stage for cardiac arrhythmias and strokes. The club drug methylenedioxymethamphetamine (MDMA, also called ecstasy), which many users mistakenly believe to be safe, has caused malignant hyperthermia, permanent kidney damage, and death. MDMA also damages serotonin nerve fibers in the brain. Heroin can cause a life-threatening kidney condition called focal glomerulosclerosis. The list continues. NIDA research has shown that almost every drug of abuse harms some tissue or organ.

Marijuana, while being the least harmful of all of the illicit drugs, is still potentially lethal. Marijuana enthusiasts take comfort in the fact that, unlike most other illicit drugs, it is seemingly impossible to fatally overdose on "weed" by means of normal consumption (i.e. smoking it). But this does nothing to diminish the potentially fatal risks of lung cancer, emphysema, and other forms of chronic obstructive pulmonary disease (COPD) caused by marijuana smoke. While marijuana can be ingested without smoking it, thereby eliminating these risks, there are negative physiological and psychological consequences including damage to the reproductive system, the immune system, and cognitive ability.[10]

THE DISEASE PART

The Bible says in **Psalm 139:14** that we are **"fearfully and wonderfully made,"** indicating that God's design of man is awesome and mysterious. God has allowed science to peek into His design to learn about some of the specifics

---

10   Dr. Alan I. Leshner. "Addressing the Medical Consequences of Drug Abuse," NIDA Notes, 15 (2000): 1, accessed November 10, 2017, http://www.nida.nih.gov/NIDA_notes/ NNVol15N1/DirRepVol15N1.html.

of how the brain works. For example, science explains that virtually all drugs causing drug addiction increase the dopamine release in the mesolimbic pathway (dopamine pathways) in addition to their specific effects.

Serotonin is also affected by alcohol and other substances in the brain. Serotonin helps control moods, impulses, cognition, and sleep. All of these areas of the brain are changed as alcohol consumption increases. The brain naturally produces dopamine. We need dopamine to experience pleasure, so, naturally, the more dopamine, the more pleasure.

Addictions affect the physical organs of a person. Addiction is sometimes called a brain disease or disorder because it changes the physical chemistry of the brain and changes the pathways of those chemicals. Addictions are not limited to the emotional part of mankind in that they change the way a person feels, what he thinks, and what he chooses. Addiction is said to be a mental illness and is listed in the *DSM-IV* as such. Addiction is not limited to the spiritual aspects of man in that it separates us from God and from others. Addiction is sometimes called a curse or spiritual problem. Those in the church have a limited understanding of addiction and think it can be easily overcome solely by prayer. Using the sin/disease concept, an addict can be treated as a spiritual being, a physical being, and an emotional being at one time.

Physical brain disease treatment can begin simply by taking a daily vitamin, which helps the chemicals in the brain find the needed nutrients for rebuilding. Exercise, especially walking for forty-five minutes each day, helps the brain to rebuild pathways and changes the chemical structure to a new normal. A balanced diet rich in protein, low in fat, and moderate in carbohydrates also helps the physical body be restored. Adequate sleep also restores the brain.

Soul treatment requires work in the area of changing the mind. The mind must be changed from a negative mindset to a positive mindset for recovery to last. When the mind changes, choices improve. With improved choices or decisions, the emotions eventually come in line with the truth of recovery. Meditation, studying the Word of God, and memorizing Scripture or other positive declarations speed the healing of the soul from the effects of addiction.

"The mind must be changed from a negative mindset to a positive mindset for recovery to last."

Recovery for the spiritual aspect of the person wounded by addiction calls for prayer, counseling, church or meeting attendance, fellowship with like-minded people, and accountability.

As you begin to get sober and stay sober, the spirit, soul, and body become more at peace. It takes work in all areas to have a sober life. This is also a balanced life. Since obsession is such a large part of addiction, it is important to work in a balanced way in all three areas.

Changes come through persistence and through determination to not be distracted by anything. Everything must be reevaluated in light of staying sober. This is a lifestyle change. Even church events have to be evaluated. So many church members are casual drinkers. You must be careful not to be pulled in by someone saying, "One drink won't hurt you." Jobs have to be evaluated in light of staying sober. If a bar has the only job available, don't take it. If the substance abuse history does not involve alcohol, remember it is a gateway drug. One drink for a pill taker or cocaine user could open the door for using the drug of choice.

PART TWO
12 GATES RECOVERY

CHAPTER FOUR

VALLEY GATE: GATEWAY TO RESTORING REALITY

"By night I went out through the Valley Gate toward the Jackal Well and the Dung Gate, examining the walls of Jerusalem, which had been broken down, and its gates, which had been destroyed by fire. So I went up the valley by night, examining the wall. Finally, I turned back and reentered through the Valley Gate" (Neh. 2:13, 15).

"The Valley Gate was repaired by Hanun and the residents of Zanoah. They rebuilt it and put its doors with their bolts and bars in place. They also repaired a thousand cubits of the wall as far as the Dung Gate" (Neh. 3:13).

"Look on my affliction and my distress and take away all my sins" (Ps. 25:18).

DAY ONE—REALITY

DO YOU WANT TO BE RESTORED?

"Hey, Cathy, wanna hear what I found in the Bible?" asked the woman, who, like so many others had, stood before me in my kitchen. "Sure," I said as I turned from the sink to dry my hands. "I always want to know what you find in the Bible."

Quite attractive, the woman looked older than her years because of her "mileage." She was staying with me in the mission, attempting yet again (of who-knows-how-many times) to get sober and stay sober. She had some experience staying in a mission. She had lived in an orphanage as a child. Her life had been filled with thirty-eight years of mostly pain—pain deadened by excessive abuse of alcohol. This woman had come to Bethesda, with a friend, quite "messed up," as they say on the streets. She had lost her job and, in an alcoholic stupor, had ended up at a truck stop, fleeing from her hometown and her life. Anything to get away. Anything to stop the memories.

What memories? Memories of being a child left by parents who were too concerned about their own addictions to care for her. Memories of being told not to tell the secret because "it's just between us" (the classic statement of sexual abuse). Memories of losing a brother in a terrible automobile accident. Memories of having her mother snatched away from her as a little girl and being left with strangers. Memories. Anything to get away from those memories. And there were the recent memories of failed jobs and relationships. Thirty-eight years of them clouded her judgments and caused her to be at Bethesda.

"Hey, Cathy, did you know Bethesda is in the Bible?"

"Yes, I did," I said.

"Hey, Cathy, that man in the Bible was thirty-eight years old. I'm thirty-eight years old. He was at Bethesda when Jesus came by."

"That's right."

"Jesus asked that man, 'Do you want to be healed?'"

"What did the man say?"

"He said, 'Nobody will help me.'"

"And what did Jesus say?"

"Take up your bed and walk. Be healed."

"What do you think about that story?"

"I'm thirty-eight years old, and I am at Bethesda, a healing place."

"Do you want to be healed?"

The woman dropped her head and said something to me I will never forget: "I don't know. I don't know what it would be like to be healed."

"But," I said, "This is your opportunity to be completely healed. Take up your bed and walk, my friend."

"I'll think about it," she said.

What would cause a person to stand on the threshold of change and turn back? *Stuck* is what. Stranded in the noise of the past, it is hard to hear the whisper of change. You need a life song of hope, a whisper from God through a Nehemiah.

KEY FOR THE VALLEY GATE

I Need Help

This week, you will learn to ask for help. This is the key to reality. Denial is broken with asking for help. Others see truths that you cannot see in early recovery.

ACTION STEPS TO TAKE IN WEEK ONE

- Schedule your time for getting up, and set the alarm. Have a back-up plan for being up at the same time each day.
- Schedule your bedtime.
- Get at least one hour a day of sunlight.
- Eat three meals a day, always adding a little protein.
- Take a vitamin, and get exercise.
- Write in your journal, and begin a personal, daily devotional time. As you begin your journal this week, choose a picture from a magazine to symbolize the topic. This will help you to visualize the topic and help you retain the information you are learning.

- In your prayer journal, add items that will help you make your prayers real.

- Make a God box. Keep it close to you; and every time you have a problem, recognize a sin, or have a prayer request, put it in the box. This exercise will cause you to think of God as a real Person and help you to develop your relationship with Him.

PRAYER TO ASK FOR FORGIVENESS AND TO FORGIVE OTHERS

(Use this prayer daily as you work through this gate.)

"Whoever would foster love covers over an offense, but whoever repeats the matter separates close friends" (Prov. 17:9).

"Okay, so I admit I am not able to help myself. My addiction has taken over my life. I did not mean for this to happen, but it has. It has become a giant in my life, and I really don't feel like fighting it, but I know I must. I need Your help today. This thing has caused me to be depressed and angry and hopeless. Give me hope today.

"They say I have a lot to do to get better, but I don't know if I can do this or not. Please make me willing to be willing. As much as I can, I surrender myself to You. I am depressed and angry. I don't really want to be here, but I know that I must if I am going to get better. Right now, all I know is that I am in a lot of pain. I have been hurt, and I am angry and sad about a lot of things in my life. In obedience, I want to ask You to help me forgive these people for what they have done to me in my life. I don't know how to forgive them today, but I am asking that You help me. My mother, my father, my siblings, my spouse, my friends, authority figures who have offended me, relatives, my abuser, my accuser, my best friend, and my worst enemy."

(Make a personal list of these people and repeat their names as you read this prayer.)

TODAY'S SCRIPTURE

"Be kind and compassionate to one another, forgiving each other, just as in Christ God forgave you" (Eph. 4:32).

TODAY'S PRAYER

"Lord, help me to be still. Just for today, Lord, help me want to recover. Just for today, help me to ask for help when I need it. Just for today, just for today."

TODAY'S JOURNAL QUESTION

What have I learned about my addiction today?

DAY TWO

HOW CAN I BEGIN?

Rebuilding begins with assessing where you are and where you want to be. This is reality. In the book of Nehemiah, we are told that he put together a team of people to help him rebuild the walls and, especially, the gates of Jerusalem.

> "Rebuilding begins with assessing where you are and where you want to be."

The gates of each city were specific entrances for different parts of city life. The name of the gate related to the activities that occurred there. The people who helped to rebuild that section and gate directly benefited from the restoration. Likewise, as you rebuild your life, there are specific areas where ideas, people, and dreams can enter. You will rebuild boundaries with the help of people who are involved in your life.

Recovery will be putting together a team of people who are headed in the same direction you are and who will not tear you down or cause you to stumble—those who will hold you accountable as you make your way to a new lifestyle.

The first gate you will find destroyed is the Valley Gate. Nehemiah began his inspection of the city of Jerusalem at the Valley Gate. On horseback, Nehemiah saw the great devastation of the gate at the lowest portion of the city. As he looked at the reality of the destruction, he knew the work would be consuming. He knew that this could not be accomplished in his power alone but that the people who lived in such despair must garner enough strength to restore their own lives. He would lead them and work beside them, but they must work as well.

Hanun and inhabitants of the Low Country rebuilt this wall. One of the valleys that the Bible speaks about is the valley of Elah. In 1 Samuel 17:3, the giants stood on one side of the valley and the Israelites on the other. This was a valley of decision and a valley of victory. When you come to the point of discovery that addiction has overtaken your life, this is a low point, a valley. In the valley, emotions are intense. You are scared and intimidated. Things are bleak on one side of the valley, but on the other side is hope because discovery leads to decision. Just as David looked across at the giant and said he would face that giant and take him for the cause of God (1 Sam. 17:32), you, too, can look across the valley of decision and see the victory that awaits.

At the Valley Gate was the Hinnom Valley. In the winter, the valley was filled with torrential waters, but in the summer, the valley was dry. The Hinnom Valley was also known as the Valley of Gehenna or "the Valley of the Shadow of Death." It is the valley of recognition and of pain, yet it is also the valley of hope. It is in this valley that you begin your climb to the new life that you desperately desire.

It is interesting to note that the rebuilders of the Valley Gate were from the marshland about ten miles away from Jerusalem. Hanun, whose name means "graciously given," was a son of Zalaph, which means "wound."[11] In the Bible, names were always given for distinctive meaning. The name would often reflect what the person's life would be or God's intention for the family or nation. It would not be hard to imagine that after a wound, God gives graciously to help in restoration.

At the Valley Gate, or "Reality Gate," you admit you have been wounded by the actions of others and by your own actions. You also admit what you need is gracious help. This is a time of facing the reality of your life. If you want real deliverance and healing, you must face reality.

WORD STUDY

> **"The acts of the flesh are obvious: sexual immorality, impurity and debauchery; idolatry and witchcraft; hatred, discord, jealousy, fits of rage, selfish ambition, dissensions, factions and envy; drunkenness, orgies, and the like. I warn you, as I did before, that those who live like this will not inherit the kingdom of God"** (Gal. 5:19-21).

Witchcraft is translated from the Greek word *pharmekia*. American words such as *pharmacy* come from this word. *Pharmekia* means "the use or the

---

11   *Bible Study Tools, s.v.* "Hanun," accessed November 13, 2017, http://www.biblestudytools. com/dictionary/hanun/.

administering of drugs; or poisoning; sorcery, magical arts often found in connection with idolatry and fostered by it; metaphorically it means the deceptions and seductions of idolatry."[12]

At the Valley Gate, you restore reality to your life. No more denial. No more deception. You must live in today and experience today's good times and today's pain. Coming out of denial seems cruel at first, but denial is costly and painful to you. Witchcraft is a fake or phony solution to life's situations. Facing the truth is the only way to have true recovery.

Drugs and alcohol are in our flesh. It requires personal responsibility to stop doing anything that has found its way into the flesh. The flesh simply means that soulish area of a person, which is the mind, will, and emotions. In other words, addiction has taken up residence in the personality. You think, choose, and feel like the addiction wants you to think, choose, and feel. "In the flesh" may also mean that the addiction has altered your body. It is a proven fact that chemicals like marijuana stay in the cells of the brain for up to one year after a person has stopped smoking marijuana.

"Drugs and alcohol have taken up residence in the personality."

As you rebuild this gate, you will need perseverance. You will get that perseverance from the weekly work you have begun. Answering the questions honestly, writing in your journal, attending meetings, and talking to your life coach and/or sponsor are all critical at this point.

Without the Word, you will not be able to open and close the gates you are rebuilding. Each gate will have structural recovery points, such as a word study and action steps. Other important activities hinge gates to the wall of your will. Journaling and prayer are two such activities. The final structure for your rebuilding is deliverance. The Names of God will assist in your growing in spiritual intimacy with Jesus as they reveal a portion of His character with each Name. Safe people will assist you in your recovery and life-rebuilding. They will hold you accountable and be like the mortar between the bricks of

---

12   *Blue Letter Bible, s.v.* "pharmekia," accessed November 8, 2017, https://www.blueletter-bible.org/lang/lexicon/lexicon.cfm?t=kjv&strongs=g5331.

the new walls you are constructing. You have work to do today to rebuild the gate in your valley. Let's begin by answering these questions:

- Where are you living today?
- What is going on today?
- Who is in your life today?
- When are you most likely to give up?
- What makes you the angriest?
- What are the obstacles you have overcome today?

There is a dimension for God to become real to you and for you to be real to God. For some, the idea of God is so very wrong that they have to pray some very revealing prayers to the God of the Bible before they can accept Him. The God of the Bible is not the manmade God of the sinner's theology. He has dimensions and character the average sinner cannot imagine. He is Love. The sinner has known a love man has introduced him to, but to imagine the love of God is inconceivable at first. They must be vulnerable to let go of the "sinner's ideas," and honest prayer will begin this introduction to the God of the Bible.

TODAY'S SCRIPTURE

"Create in me a pure heart, O God, and renew a steadfast spirit within me. Do not cast me from your presence or take your Holy Spirit from me. Restore to me the joy of your salvation and grant me a willing spirit, to sustain me" (Ps. 51:10-12).

TODAY'S PRAYER

"Lord, I have developed a defense to keep myself from being seen. I have built a hiding place to protect myself from hurt. I know that this protection blocks the love and nurture I long for. I come to You, Lord, because I am helpless to change. I want You to be my defense, Lord. Help me to become vulnerable to risk love. This defense has become a heart of stone. I admit I am unable to love You, others, or myself.

"Lord, I am choosing to let go of my offense—and even hatred of—those people who have wounded me. I have blamed, You, God, for allowing these wounds in my life. I am choosing to let go of my resentment of You, God, so that I can begin to have a trusting relationship with You. This blame and resentment has been my hiding place. I do not know how to trust You, and I do not know how to let go. Help me today to believe You are a loving and kind God, Who has my best interest in mind.

"I am choosing today to let go of my hatred toward myself for the way I have reacted to the painful experiences and for building a heart of stone. Father God, please forgive me for the way I have acted toward the people who have hurt me and the way I have responded to You because I resented them and blamed You. I have chosen to retaliate by doing very wrong and spiteful things and have hurt loved ones by keeping them out of my life. I repent for the destruction in my own life and for wounding You with my sin, Lord."

TODAY'S JOURNAL QUESTION

What have I learned that I need to change today?

DAY THREE

SIN/DISEASE CONCEPT: ADDICTION IS BOTH SIN AND DISEASE

The sin/disease concept of addiction is not a new one. It has been around for years, and more and more Christian counselors are presenting this concept as a viable treatment option for addiction. We are offering it for more than addiction in the traditional sense. We suggest that the sin/disease concept is one that is supported by Scripture. Sin is translated from the Greek word *hamartia*, which means "to miss the mark."[13] It has the concept of a marksman aiming his bow at the perfect score, the bull's eye. As the arrow travels away from the bow, the wind shifts it up or down, and the bull's eye is missed. The arrow has missed its mark, resulting in sin.

This definition of sin "missing the mark" helps us understand the target of our lives should never be addiction of any kind.

Actions and behaviors may also be sin. Sin, in this case, is any action or behavior that violates a standard or code of ethics. For Christians, that code of ethics is the Bible. Even if you do not know what the Bible says, some of your behaviors easily violate your own code of ethics. You find yourself involved in activities you never thought you would be involved in. You have, at the very least, sinned against yourself by your own actions. Your soul is lost in missing the mark. We are, indeed, sinners. We need a Savior, but that is not all we need. The habits of sin cause "brain damage." The habitual structures of doing the sin over and over forms a sort of groove in your brain. I call it a rut. This rut in your brain is similar in design to any other natural rut. To stop the habitual pattern, you will need to develop a new pathway around the "damage." This "brain damage" causes you to be diseased, so now you need a Healer.

A simple definition of disease is "'dis,' or not, at ease." This "dis ease" has altered our bodies. It has caused medical and mental disorders that are now clinical. This habitual sin, or addiction, has altered our thinking and caused some chemical dysfunction in our brains. Some of these dysfunctions will

---

13 *Strong's Concordance*, s.v. "Hamartia," accessed October 9, 2017, http://biblehub.com/greek/266.htm.

not go away. Some of them may be reversed. Using the sin/disease concept, you learn that you are responsible for your actions, which led to the disease; but, once the disease is in place, you have to learn that your responsibility is to keep the disease in remission. This is very similar to any other chronic and critical disease. Habitual sin or addiction is both chronic in that it is not going away and critical in that it is deadly.

> The habitual structures of doing sin over and over forms a sort of groove in your brain. I call it a rut. This brain damage causes you to be diseased. Now, you need a Healer.

The brain is changed as the sin becomes rooted. The chemicals in the brain are changed for life, and the only way the brain can recover is to reroute the receptor pathways. This takes time and work. The damage done in the receptor pathways is why most people can't just quit without help. The disease concept also relates to the emotional and spiritual aspect of the person. "Dis ease" causes a person to become emotionally unstable, paranoid, or depressed. Spiritual "dis ease" causes us to turn away from God because of guilt and shame.

RELAPSE

Relapsing into habitual sin is a matter of grave consequence. It is not inevitable. It does not have to mean you must be lost to your addiction. Relapse can be prevented if you understand what leads to it and how to take steps to avoid it. A slip is different than a full-fledged relapse. A slip is a onetime, unintentional act. A slip is a onetime occurrence; relapse is prolonged usage. The cycle can be stopped with no permanent damage being done.

One of the first things many people in recovery learn is **HALT**. Never get too **H**ungry, too **A**ngry, too **L**onely, or too **T**ired. It is important to maintain good physical health in order to maintain good mental health. You cannot afford to let things go—physically or emotionally; it is too dangerous to recovery.

> "The target of your life should never be full-blown addiction."

Emotional health can be charted in many areas, so that we will not be caught totally by surprise. We have learned, through our work at Bethesda, that understanding cycles is very important to the recovery process. You have emotional and physical cycles that affect your behavior. You can realize that these waves of emotion are actually quite predictable. These waves come in cycles of three, seven, twenty-one, and twenty-eight days. These are critical times for you. You must be able to recognize them. You need to understand to be on guard during these times. These are not the only times that relapse can occur. However, an awareness of cycles can be an invaluable tool in preventing relapse. It often occurs first in the mind. I have listed a few signals to watch for:

EXHAUSTION: You cannot afford to become overly tired. Proper rest is critical. Attempt to schedule eight hours of sleep per day and one hour of sunlight each day. The sunlight produces melatonin, and the darkness releases it to promote sleep and rest.

DISHONESTY: Total and complete honesty is a must for us. Honesty is usually a foreign concept for those beginning recovery. White lies are lies. Lying is like all other aspects of the disease in that it is progressive. This includes lying to yourself as well as others.

IMPATIENCE: You are used to expecting instant gratification, and now you find it difficult when things do not seem to be happening fast enough or when other people do not seem to be doing what you think they should. You must learn that the world does not revolve around you. Getting impatient leads to anger, which will lead you backwards.

ARGUMENTATIVENESS: Finding fault in every little thing, no matter how minor, and always arguing about ridiculous things are sure danger signs. It is time to stop and reevaluate. What you may be doing is looking for an excuse to give up.

FRUSTRATION: This emotion is closely related to impatience. Frustration comes when it is not possible to achieve a goal or when things do not go according to our will.

SELF-PITY: "Why me? Why can't I have just one? It is just not fair!" And the list goes on. Instead of dwelling on how bad and unfair things seem, take an honest look at how much better things are now and will be later.

COCKINESS: You can get into real trouble when you begin to think that you have your disease licked and that now you know all the answers. Many have relapsed after several years simply because they get a little too sure of themselves.

COMPLACENCY: Complacency is a feeling of quiet security, often while being unaware of unpleasant possibilities. Most relapses occur when things are going well. Awareness, not obsession, is the key.

EXPECTING TOO MUCH FROM OTHERS: You cannot expect others to give more that they are able to give or are ready to give.

"Self-Pity: 'Why me?' Instead of dwelling on how bad and unfair things seem, take an honest look at how much better things are now and will be."

LETTING UP ON DISCIPLINES: Whatever you are doing to stay sober now and to stay away from negative activities, you will have to continue until the pattern of sobriety is entrenched in your lifestyle.

USE OF ANY MOOD-ALTERING CHEMICALS: Anything that can cause drowsiness or increase alertness is only a stepping stone back to our drug of choice. No drug is completely safe, even if a doctor has prescribed it.

FORGETTING GRATITUDE: You need to be grateful for each breath. You don't need to concentrate on what is wrong in life, but you need to be grateful for all that is right.

THINKING IT CAN'T HAPPEN TO ME: Never forget that you are only one sin, one drink, or one drug away from all the insanity that you have fought so hard to escape. Nobody is immune. The sin/disease is progressive. If you return, things will get worse than ever in a short amount of time.

TODAY'S SCRIPTURE

"Wash away all my iniquity and cleanse me from my sin" (Ps. 51:2).

TODAY'S PRAYER

"Lord, forgive me for not wanting to be here today. I wish I could be anywhere else but here. Here reminds me that I can't have what

I want, can't do what I want. I really don't like anybody telling me what to do. I am angry. I don't really know if I can do this sobriety thing. My nerves are shot. I want to run. Help me not to run. Help me to want to be willing to stay. Help me. Will You hear me? Will You answer me? I need to know Who You are and what You can do for me. I am screaming inside.

"Wash me thoroughly [and repeatedly] from my iniquity and guilt, and cleanse me and make me wholly pure from my sin. Lord, feelings keep waking up. I don't want to feel; I want to be numb. Is there any way I can get sober without feeling or remembering? I guess not. That is the definition of being high or drunk . . . numb, not feeling. There are too many new things to deal with at once. Help me."

TODAY'S JOURNAL QUESTION

What have I learned about others today?

DAY FOUR

DELIVERANCE

It is said a little bit of knowledge is a dangerous thing, especially concerning addiction. Knowing the problem does not guarantee positive results or healing. It has been the experience of many that the only true relief from addiction comes through Divine deliverance. To many people, the word *deliverance* conjures thoughts of screaming demons, people foaming at the mouth while rolling about the floor, and other misconceptions delivered by Hollywood via *The Exorcist* and other movies of this type. Biblically, the exorcism of demons was accomplished by the simple words of Christ or His followers. A manifestation of the demon might be audible or physical, but it was ended by the admonition to go and walk in the deliverance and healing the individual received. It was an orderly procedure—careful, calculated, and complete. You can read about one such deliverance in Luke 8:26-36.

In studying deliverance, let's look at the most famous deliverance in all of biblical history. The deliverance of the children of Israel from their bondage in Egypt to their arrival in the Promised Land parallels true deliverance from the bondage of addiction.

In the study of Exodus, we notice there are many aspects to the story. Notice in chapters one through three that Moses' story is told. It seems he was almost destroyed before being saved himself, exiled from his homeland, and then restored to his birth heritage at eighty years of age. Moses was chosen by God to deliver the people of Israel. He did not live as a slave himself; he was reared in the palace of the pharaoh. He had to learn what it was like to be held captive. The time Moses spent in the wilderness helped him to learn the lessons needed for freeing his people. Some say that only those who have been where you have been and done what you have done know what it will take to help. As with Moses, God can train the person to lead the deliverance. We don't go to the doctor because he has the flu; we go to the doctor because he has the cure for the flu.

"We don't go to the doctor because he has the flu; we go
to the doctor because he has the cure for the flu."

When the children of Israel finally began their journey, it wasn't as easy as you might think. The plight of the Israelites seemed hopeless. Many became resigned to their fate and continued in their forced labor, never believing that anything would ever change. Others cried out, desperate for relief, yet there was no escape. Perhaps some, in their desperation, attempted to free themselves, but there was no freedom to be found. Every attempt at flight was foiled by the cruel hands of those in power.

Today, you are in the same situation—unable to free yourself, even through desperation. You may become resigned to a life of addiction, even unto death. Some cry out and attempt to escape under their own power, but they are hunted down and ensnared again. It is the sin/disease itself that renders you powerless.

Part of the Exodus story includes the trip of the twelve spies into the Promised Land. Of these twelve spies, only two were ever able to enter the Promised Land. The Israelites were empowered to receive their deliverance, but they refused to see the tools God had given them.

These tools included their own names. Children were often named in a prophetic way.

Joshua was the son of Nun. He was born in Egypt. When Moses rescued the people, Joshua quickly became a follower. His name means "Jehovah is salvation."[14]

He was with Moses at the exodus, with him as he went up the mountain to see God, and with him in the tabernacle. In fact, Joshua stayed in the tabernacle after Moses left just to be near God. He knew in his heart God was his salvation. Joshua was one of the two spies who trusted God to occupy the Promised Land.

Joshua and Caleb were the only two Israelites who survived the wilderness trip and crossed the Jordan into Canaan. He had been a slave, but, somehow, he was different. His name was different—"Jehovah is salvation"—"God is the rescuer." Joshua changed his lifestyle. In deliverance, everything about a person is changed.

---

14   *Bible Hub, s.v.* "Joshua," accessed October 24, 2017, http://biblehub.com/hebrew/3091.htm.

A complete change may not appeal to you at first. You may want to keep some of the old, familiar personality traits. You may even balk at the changes that must be made in order to overcome. You must think this change completely through. Meditate on the meaning of changing a whole lifestyle.

- What will a new lifestyle look like for me?
- What do I want to keep that may not be good for me?
- What do I need to change?
- Who will help me change?

Look up the word *change* in the dictionary, and write down the meaning. Look up the word *change* in a concordance, and write down what it means according to the Bible.

Can you find biblical references related to change?

TODAY'S SCRIPTURE

"If we confess our sins, he is faithful and just and will forgive us our sins and purify us from all unrighteousness" (1 Jn. 1:9).

TODAY'S PRAYER

"Lord, I confess that I have sinned. I have missed the mark in my life. I have pursued my own way. I have not chosen the right path. I have gone the wrong way. Please forgive me. Show me the right path to follow and the right choices to make."

TODAY'S JOURNAL QUESTION

What have I learned about God today?

DAY FIVE

NAMES OF GOD

In the Old Testament, the names of God reveal certain aspects of His character. He was revealing His omnipotence, His omnipresence, and His omniscience by showing Himself and by giving a name to remember Him by. For example, He revealed Himself to Abraham as *Jehovah Jirah*. *Jehovah* means "lord or ruler or master," and *Jirah* means "provider."[15] As Abraham had to trust God for preserving Isaac's life or resurrecting his son, God showed Himself as able to provide whatever was needed.

We could almost think of the names of God as we think of nicknames today. We usually give a nickname to someone because of what they do. This is a simple way to relate to the names of God. We also become more intimate with someone when we know all their names. For example, when someone calls me Cathy, I know that they know me as a friend or acquaintance. If someone knows my last name and calls me by it, that also lets me know how well they know me. But if someone knows all of my names, they know me best. As we learn the names of God, we become more acquainted with Him.

"Therefore, say to the Israelites: 'I am the LORD, and I will bring you out from under the yoke of the Egyptians. I will free you from being slaves to them, and I will redeem you with an outstretched arm and with mighty acts of judgment'" (Exod. 6:6).

The Bible speaks of *Haggo'el*, the redeemer.[16] The redeemer pays the ransom for those he is redeeming. Our Redeemer, Jesus Christ, has paid the price for us so that we may be put in right standing with God, with ourselves, and with others. He has seen the situations in our lives and has agreed to pay the price for us to be changed and delivered from the wreck of our present situations.

The Lord told Moses that He saw the distress of the lives of His people and would free them from their slavery. He sent a deliverer in Moses to the people of Israel, and He has sent a Deliverer in Jesus Christ to free us from the slavery

---

15   *Wikipedia, s.v.* "Jehovah-jireh," accessed October 24, 2017, https://en.wikipedia.org/wiki/Jehovah-jireh.

16   John J. Parsons. "Hebrew Names of God." Hebrew4Christians.net. http://www.hebrew-4christians.com/Names_of_G-d/Redeemer/redeemer.html (accessed October 24, 2017).

of addiction and sin. It is when we are at our lowest that we need a Redeemer. We need the Lord, our Redeemer.

We can understand redemption by thinking about manufacturer's coupons. A manufacturer wants to introduce a new product to society. The manufacturer prints a coupon for the product, which in and of itself is worthless. The coupon isn't worth the paper it is printed on, but the manufacturer of the product says the coupon is worth something.

"What do we get when we get redemption? We get forgiveness."

When you receive the coupon, you think, "I will take this worthless thing to the store and redeem it for something of value." The coupon is worthless, but the item you receive from taking the coupon to somebody who does know the value is of worth to you. That is what we do when we take our worthless, broken-down lives to Jesus and give them to Him. In return, He gives us His pure and powerful life to use as we see fit. You can take this wonderful gift and store it in a closet, or you can use it every day for your benefit. We need redemption.

What do you get when you get redemption? You get forgiveness. At this stage of restoration, you receive forgiveness for your mistakes, failures, sins, disappointments, and pain. You must receive forgiveness for yourself individually. Forgiveness is a gift. It cannot be earned. Trust and forgiveness are not the same. Trust must be earned. You will have to prove trustworthiness, but forgiveness must be given. This is in the word, *for given*. Forgiveness is a gift for us to receive and then give away. To receive redemption, you must choose. You choose to open your heart to the gift God is giving you through faith in Jesus Christ. You exchange your life with the life of Jesus working in and through you.

TODAY'S SCRIPTURE

"Look on my affliction and my distress and take away all my sins" (Ps. 25:18).

TODAY'S PRAYER

"Help me with this stinkin' thinkin', Lord. My mind keeps going back to the 'good, ol' days.' I know I shouldn't, but it is there. Help me to change my mind. I choose now to learn new ways to think. I choose to take back my mind from the addiction. I choose to think and to talk about positive things. Help me with these choices today."

TODAY'S JOURNAL QUESTION

What have I learned about stinkin' thinkin' today?

DAY SIX

COMMITMENT

Admit. Commit. Submit. These three words say a lot for the beginning of change. They are simple to say but hard to do. *To admit* implies the reality of our lives at this present moment, with no excuses. Admitting the problem is ours is of utmost importance at this stage. It is very easy to blame circumstances and the actions of others for what is going on with us now, but that will not get us to recovery.

To commit declares change. It is for more than a moment. *To commit* means "to go without stopping until it is complete." Commitment means time.

To submit is to yield, to give over, and, ultimately to give up. You must be willing to submit.

Today is day six of the week of reality. Reality will force you to examine the past five days to determine if you want to be in reality. It is a choice.

Admit . . . hmm . . . Does this mean more than to speak out? I think it does. I think admitting you have a problem is very deep. It goes to the depth of our souls; it searches our minds; it tingles our feelings; it questions our choices. There is nothing easy about admitting you have a problem. It is the kind of knowing that makes you put up or shut up. Admit you have a problem, and it thunders through your being so loudly, you have to make a decision.

Commitment has lost its meaning in America. *Commit*, to most of us, means "stay until the first sign of trouble." But change requires commitment of the lasting kind. The kind of commitment it takes to recover is the kind that won't give up, regardless of the circumstance. It is a determination, a drive, to hold on and finish what has been started. Persistence, bulldog tenacity, and a death grip all embody the type of commitment needed for you to recover. We often say, "One day at a time with a lifetime commitment." You will change one day at a time, but without a commitment, the change will not last.

Submit is almost a dirty word now. Americans hate to submit to anything or anyone. We have to change the word for people to submit. We say things like, "discipline," "just do it," or "teamwork" in order to have a group of people submit to the workplace authority. The Bible says we should **"submit to one another" (Eph. 5:21)**; but in today's world, you will be in deep trouble trying to suggest submission to the average person. We live in a domination society. We equate submission to being a doormat. However, the truth is that submission to a new life is one of the keys to recovery. "Submitting to one another" implies respect and love for others. It drives a stake into the heart of the self-centered and pours the oil of forgiveness and acceptance into that heart.

New life submission deals with agreeing with a brand-new way of dealing with life, people, and problems. You have to learn to give in to a discipline of learning. You have to give up your wills and choices to God and to others who have gone a little farther in recovery than you have. Submission is another form of surrender. But it is not dying; it is living. Surrender gives over, and submission gives in.

All three—admit, commit, and submit—speak to the volition of man. You must make a choice to admit, commit, and submit. These choices are voluntary. That, in itself, is part of the submission.

TODAY'S SCRIPTURE

"Bear with each other and forgive one another if any of you has a grievance against someone. Forgive as the Lord forgave you. And over all these virtues put on love, which binds them all together in perfect unity" (Col. 3:13-14).

TODAY'S PRAYER

"Lord, help me be kind today. Help me to learn the lesson of quick forgiveness in the little things of life. Help me to turn the other cheek and to say nice things to others, instead of being such a smart aleck."

TODAY'S JOURNAL QUESTION

What have I learned about my feelings today?

DAY SEVEN

PREPARE YOUR HEART FOR WORSHIP AND FELLOWSHIP AT CHURCH TODAY

In this day and age, we get the impression that everything can be handled via the internet. We have Facebook for friends and texting to communicate; but for us to grow as Christians, we need human support and contact. *Fellowship* is a biblical word. Fellowship involves sharing food, sharing testimonies, and sharing life. It is hard to share yourself in reality with internet friends. The reality of worship in a church community brings healing in all areas of the spirit and soul.

From the beginning of the Old Testament, corporate worship established a pattern of how man meets God and how God meets man. In Leviticus, worship was important for the stability of man's understanding of the monotheistic truth about Jehovah. The pattern promoted holiness, reverence, and respect for God the Father as the one and only God. Jesus encouraged worship and church attendance by attending the synagogue each week. Jesus kept all the rites of Judaism.

Relationship with God is necessary on an intimate level, but aloneness can lead to unhealthy worship. Corporate worship keeps us in reality. Independent theology at the early stages of recovery can be dangerous because you may so often become confused by your own thoughts and ideas.

To prepare for worship, begin by quieting your negative thoughts. Get into a mode of expectancy. Plan to learn something. Plan to worship God from your heart.

One way to help prepare is to set aside a time of private prayer, praise, and worship music. Saturday night is a good time to think about the Sunday service. In ancient days, when the Sabbath began at six p.m. on Friday, the Sabbath morning was the time to bring tithes and offerings to the temple.

Sunday worship is more than prayer, preaching, and praise. It is also a time to give your tithe and offerings. A tithe is ten percent of your earnings for the week. An offering is anything over the amount of your tithe. If you write checks for your tithes and offerings, go ahead and write it before the meeting on Sunday morning. Some churches have the option of paying by debit card. Learn the methods of giving that your church offers.

I used attendance at church as a way to get faithful. I prayed that God would make me faithful. He began to show me that my pattern of running away included church attendance. I asked Him to help me start with attending church regularly.

As I requested help from God to make me faithful, I also got immediate help from Satan to make me unfaithful. Every Sunday morning, my family would be in turmoil. We would argue on the way to church and then smile at the people in church. We were two-faced. As I began to complain to the Lord about making my family more agreeable to church attendance, He told me to stop arguing. I learned it takes two to argue, and if one stops, the argument stops. Soon my family was going to church without the drama.

TODAY'S SCRIPTURE

"'Then I acknowledged my sin to you and did not cover up my iniquity.' I said. 'I will confess my transgressions to the LORD.' And you forgave the guilt of my sin" (Ps. 32:5).

TODAY'S PRAYER

"Help me to walk in obedience today. Help me to submit to authority. Help me, Lord, to be teachable today. Help me to know You better and to choose Your ways."

TODAY'S JOURNAL QUESTION

What did I give to God today?

CHAPTER FIVE
EAST GATE: GATEWAY TO RESTORING AUTHORITY

"Next to them, Zadok son of Immer made repairs opposite his house. Next to him, Shemaiah son of Shekaniah, the guard at the East Gate, made repairs. Next to him, Hananiah son of Shelemiah, and Hanun, the sixth son of Zalaph, repaired another section. Next to them, Meshullam son of Berekiah made repairs opposite his living quarters. Next to him, Malkijah, one of the goldsmiths, made repairs as far as the house of the temple servants and the merchants, opposite the Inspection Gate, and as far as the room above the corner" (Neh. 3:29-31).

"But if I were you, I would appeal to God; I would lay my cause before him" (Job 5:8).

DAY ONE

AUTHORITY

Prison Is a Terrible Place

Prison is a terrible place to be, but it is an even more terrible place to be *from*. At least, that is what Rose thought. She really didn't want me to know her past. She wanted her past to be her past, so she walked into the house with her head held high.

"Cathy," she said, "you know my clothes and stuff are in storage. I need an opportunity to go and get them out."

This was a Saturday morning. I wondered if I should ask who had paid the storage fees while she was in prison, but I didn't because I was letting her past be the past. At Bethesda Recovery, I never really know who will return once the door closes behind them; and watching Rose leave that morning, I wasn't sure that she would be back or that she would find the past wasn't so past after all. In other words, she might run into someone on the street, and she could be at a crack house for days. My heart's prayer was that God would take care of her and bring her back. Rose was gone for most of the day. Then a wilted Rose returned. Her wilting wasn't from the heat but from disappointment. I didn't pry but noticed that she carried no bags and no stuff.

The Bethesda House is a one-hundred-year-old house right in the downtown section of Waycross, Georgia—complete with porches and shade trees for afternoon breezes. As a custom, I would sit on the porch and enjoy the afternoon in some quietness. We didn't have rockers at that time, so I sat on the steps. I don't remember what I was thinking, but I was probably wondering how in the world I had gotten myself into such a mess. I had no money and no specialized training. I had only the Lord for my Hope and Guide, which, by the way, is plenty; but to be frank, in the natural, I really needed a manifestation of His promise.

As I sat on the steps, Rose came over and sat down beside me. She was in much worse shape than I. She had only the clothes on her back—no money, no job, and no hope in God. She was wilted for sure. She hesitated as she spoke.

"Cathy, all my clothes are gone; all my stuff is gone. I have nothing."

The time in prison taught her to control the tears, but her voice quivered. In my own desperate plight, what was I to say? There was only one thing that I had that Rose didn't have. I had hope.

"Rose, my preacher once told me that God was not surprised at my circumstances—that He knew right where I was and how I got there. God is not surprised at where you are and what your circumstances are. He knows you have nothing, and He can provide. He has clothes and shoes and stuff for you. Hold on, Rose. God's going to show you something. He'll bring those things right to this doorstep."

I finished my faith message and got up to walk away, hoping there would be no arguing, and there wasn't. Rose just sat there quietly, head in hands.

I went on working and wondering if I should do anything to help God out with Rose's problem. But, quite frankly, I had no way to help God out. I only whispered a prayer, "Help her, God."

Rose was still sitting on the steps when a car pulled up at the front of the house. "Is this house for women?" the driver asked. "I've got some women's clothes if you can use them."

Could she use them? What a question that was! Rose jumped from the steps and went out to get the bags of clothing. She thanked the lady and brought the bags inside. There were shoes and clothes, underwear, and socks—all in Rose's sizes.

I came from out of the back of the house, and Rose began to tell me the story of the woman and the clothes. She was overjoyed. She was happy. God had surely seen her need and fulfilled it in a short time. If you think about it, God had been working on that day for some time. The woman had bought the clothes, changed sizes, and decided to donate them to a shelter. That, my friend, did not take the few minutes that Rose was sitting on the porch. God, Who sees and knows everything, set that miracle in motion a long time before Rose went to prison.

Even though Rose went through a lot of things after that, even returning to prison, she has never forgotten how God touched her life that day. She is now in ministry with her husband. Rose learned an important lesson in authority—God is not out to get you because He is the right kind of authority.

RESTORING A RELATIONSHIP WITH GOD
CONTINUES WITH RECOGNIZING AUTHORITY

The gates were often used as a makeshift court system—not too different from our lower courts of today. At the gates, property could be exchanged, wills probated, credibility given, and politics practiced. In the days of King David, Absalom sat at the city gate and heard minor cases for the people. He also wooed the hearts of the people while planning a takeover from his father. It was at the city gates that Ruth's fate was determined. There, Boaz secured the land from Naomi's closest kin, so he might be in a position to marry Ruth.

Kings and others would often sit at the city gates. In Jerusalem, the East Gate was of most significance. It was where the high priest had to stand on Yom Kippur, then look through the East Gate into the Holy of Holies. On Palm Sunday, Jesus rode into Jerusalem through the East Gate. This gate symbolized the coming of the Messiah, redemption for all mankind. This gate is the gate of true authority. God's authority to save and change man is symbolized here.

In our lives, there are at least three levels of authority to be restored. First and foremost is the authority of God in our lives. Next, there is the authority we possess as children of God. And last is the authority of others who have authority over us.

Since God was not created and since He created all things, His authority is from everlasting to everlasting.

"God created man in his own image." Genesis 1:27

God's authority rests in His Being. He is the Ultimate, the Beginning, and the final Authority on everything. He has all power and authority. Yet, in His omnipotence, He gives certain authority to us as believers and disciples.

"To recognize the power and authority of God requires accepting personal limitations."

The power and authority that God gives you requires accepting personal limitations. Some say, "You have to resign as master of the universe." Rebuilding the gate of authority takes submitting to the ultimate authority that God has.

Realizing God is the ultimate Authority begins to quash our resistance and rebellion. God has the final say, or the last word, in everything. Accepting God as the ultimate Authority will take some work. For many, the authority figures in life are often less-than-appropriate role models. A father or mother may abandon or abuse his or her child emotionally, setting up negative ideas about authority figures in the child's mind. Teachers, police officers, and even pastors may neglect their responsibilities, and a child or young adult will assume that all authority figures are untrustworthy.

God made man in His own image, according to Genesis 1:27, giving mankind a natural love for the Creator. This natural love for man's Creator is a spiritual desire, manifesting itself in a physical and emotional way. For example, a young girl is adopted at birth. The child's natural mother places her for adoption, and she is adopted by a loving and responsible family. But before she knows she is adopted, the child feels there is something missing—a hole in her heart, so to speak. When she learns of her adoption, she wants to know her natural parents. It will not matter too much what kind of parents the natural mother and father would have been. The girl wants to know her "creator." Her natural creators are her natural mother and father. This natural, emotional desire for parents is part of the DNA that God put in all mankind to know their Creator. I know what some of you are saying: "Not everybody wants to find their parents." This may be so, but the hole in the heart is still there to know who created them and why they were born.

This desire to know the Creator is so powerful that man will fill the "God hole" with anything that gives temporary relief. The hole will be filled with lovers, drugs, sex, money, power, children—you name it. But the hole requires filling.

When a person turns to drugs or alcohol or sex or gambling, the hole for the Creator is temporarily filled. Pleasure fills the hole for a season, but it will never fill it completely or effectively forever. As recovery begins, the search may take a turn toward filling the "God hole" with other things such as meetings, people, and good deeds. Fear may even take over the search because God may seem austere and very scary. This is simply because God represents ultimate authority, and all the authority a person in early recovery may have known was abusive, over-reactive, or absent. The Scriptures reveal who God is and what He is capable of in our lives.

> **"For who is God besides the LORD? And who is the Rock except our God? It is God who arms me with strength and keeps my way secure. He makes my feet like the feet of a deer; he causes me to stand on the heights"** (2 Sam. 22:32-34).

> **"If you return to the LORD, then your fellow Israelites and your children will be shown compassion by their captors and will return to this land, for the LORD your God is gracious and compassionate. He will not turn his face from you if you return to him"** (2 Chron. 30:9).

> **"For the LORD God is a sun and shield; the LORD bestows favor and honor; no good thing does he withhold from those whose walk is blameless. LORD Almighty, blessed is the one who trusts in you"** (Ps. 84:11-12).

> **"The LORD is gracious and righteous; our God is full of compassion"** (Ps. 116:5).

All other authority may be questionable, but God's authority is never questionable. The Scriptures prove that God is able to restore you to a sound mind and fill the void in your life. All you have to do is accept His authority. Jesus has also given you the power, or the authority, to be the son or daughter of God.

In Luke, Jesus gave His disciples power and authority to trample on snakes and scorpions to heal the sick and deliver those who were demon-possessed. When you recognize the authority of God in your life and become a child of God, He gives you authority. This is a gift. God empowers you to accomplish feats you never could before. This newfound authority sets you in a position as an overcomer and not as a limp, powerless individual bound by an enemy within. The authority God gives you is to overcome and conquer the enemy.

The word *authority* used by Jesus is the Greek word *exousia*, which means "power of choice or liberty of doing as one pleases."[17] He told His disciples

---

17   *Blue Letter Bible, s.v.* "exousia," accessed October 24, 2017, https://www.blueletterbible. org/lang/lexicon/lexicon.cfm?t=kjv&strongs=g1849. 7.

they had authority over devils and diseases. In the world today, freedom of choice has become entitlement, but that was not the intended purpose of the power to choose.

Because the freedom of choice is such a powerful responsibility, you must learn to exercise that authority in all of your life choices. This authority includes taking responsibility for the result of your choices. Satan knows you have the power of choice and can do as you please, so he begins to persuade you to use your authority in a negative context. Take, for example, addiction. You have learned that addiction subdues your power to make right choices. But if we go one step further with the biblical definition of authority, addiction deceives you by telling you there is no choice.

Let's go even further. Satan knows that you have authority to make your own choices, so he gives you opportunities to be pleased by negative choices. Think about it this way: Because you can choose what you want, you choose cocaine. The power of cocaine or the authority of cocaine is like that of a king; it forces submission. You continue to do as you please, making the authority of cocaine stronger until you do not want to do anything else. As a Christian in addiction, you may feel stuck. The devil has used your authority against you. This is why you must want to get better.

That "want" can only come with an internal desire from God. It is a special grace for the recovery to begin. That special grace is Jesus. The problem is not that you have no authority; it is that you do not use your God-given authority appropriately. At the East Gate, where the King of kings will return, you can garner your faith and take that leap to accept God's authority and believe in your authority.

"The problem is not that you have no authority; it is that you do not use your God-given authority appropriately."

The final restoration at this gate is with the authority of others. Accepting the authority of the law enforcers of our country is a huge step for us. Accepting and restoring the authority of others to choose their own boundaries will set us free from control. This may take some doing on our part because sin is built in rebellion. Rebellion against all authority is just par for the course. All of the aspects of authority can and will be restored as you practice the personal disciplines of prayer, meditation, and submission.

Nehemiah encouraged the people of Jerusalem to rebuild the gates and the walls of the city to provide the needed protection from enemies. Each time the people of Jerusalem made progress in rebuilding their lives, the enemies pillaged their homes, destroying the work and causing great discouragement. It was only after the walls and gates of the city were rebuilt that the Israelites were able to restore their homes and live their lives without constant fear.

It is much the same with your life. You try to get sober and stay sober, but each time, an enemy slips in through a hole in your defense system and robs you of any progress. This robbery causes you to get discouraged and, often, to give up, and then a relapse is on the way. Restoring your boundaries is crucial.

The Levites were in charge of the East Gate. They were the tribe without an inheritance, who served God and the community day and night. All the other tribes were given an allotment from the Lord as their inheritance, but the Levites were expected to trust God for everything. They were the priests and were under the direct authority of God. They also held authority with God for the care of His people. As they rebuilt the East Gate, the authority of God was restored to the city of Jerusalem. They did not have to fear any longer.

Being teachable is one strong pillar of restoration. An attitude of "I know it all" causes rebellion to creep into the framework of our character. To become teachable, you must choose to listen. You must listen with an attentive ear. Teachable people may know what another is speaking about, but they listen to hear something new. The other important pillar of the East Gate is respect. Respect is given. It is often said that respect is earned; but, because of where you have been, no matter what someone has done, you must choose to respect their humanity and the office that they hold.

When you begin to accept responsibility for your life, you gain personal authority. So much of your responsibility and authority have been relinquished. You have given up the authority over your children and even over your personal character. Area after area of responsibility is relinquished, and you have stopped taking authority over the things that you can change. You sometimes think you can't speak or act on your own behalf.

As the gate of authority is restored, legal problems begin to get under control. You become less and less afraid of the authority issues in your life, such as old warrants or probation or parole. Your destiny is also reestablished because your destiny is determined by how you relate to God's authority and the authority of others.

Questions to ask yourself about authority:

- Who is my authority?
- Do I trust God's authority? Why or why not?
- How can I begin to take authority over the problems in my life?
- What is my plan for respecting another person's authority?
- Who do I have to learn to respect as an authority in my life?

KEY TO AUTHORITY

God Can Help

This week you will discover that because you are willing to ask for help, God can help. Use this key to develop your relationship with the Lord.

ACTION STEPS

- Read one chapter of Proverbs each night. There are thirty-one chapters of Proverbs so you can coordinate the readings with the days of the month. Chapter one would be read on day one of the month and so on. Our subconscious is cleansed by the reading of the Word. Doing it at night right before you go to bed will help you become more in tune with the wisdom of God.
- Write in your journal each day.
- Continue to have your daily prayer time.
- Learn to meditate. Christian meditation is not an emptying of the mind but a filling of the spirit. Joshua said to meditate on the Word of God, and that would bring success (Josh. 1:8).
- Pick a Scripture, and write it on a notecard. Think about what that word would mean if it were personally written to you. Personalize it with your name being added where possible.

PRAYER TO FIND GOD

Use this prayer every day in addition to other prayers this week

"Everything else has failed me, so I am looking to You for new direction. I don't even know if You will come to me or not, but I am looking. So, by faith, I am praying this prayer and every prayer until I see You at work in my life.

"Honor and glory be unto You, O Lord, as I look toward the East to Your soon appearing. Your glory and Your representatives come from the East. Wise men came from the East after Your birth, and wise men will still be seeking Your appearing. Today, I pray that Your ministers, prophets, and teachers receive a clear understanding from heaven. Remove all hindrances from their lives that will keep them from doing Your perfect will. Give them new eyes to see and new ears to hear and new hearts to receive Your Word. Make Yourself real to them today as I pray for them.

"Give me eyes to see and ears to hear the voices of authority in my life. Help me recognize my rebellion and then give me courage to change my rebellious behavior.

"Help me to recognize authority and to feel secure with that authority. Help me to trust the authority figures in my life. I choose now to pray for authority figures in my life who failed me. I ask you to bless... (Place names of those people in authority who have failed you here. Pray for these people daily that God will bless them.)"

TODAY'S SCRIPTURE

**"Commit your way to the LORD; trust in him, and he will do this"
(Ps. 37:5).**

TODAY'S PRAYER

"Lord, it is hard to give all of myself to You. After all, I don't know You very well. But just for today, I will commit some time to You to say this prayer. I will ask You to bless me because I need to be blessed. I am still trying to understand. Will You help me?"

TODAY'S JOURNAL QUESTION

What will I do to commit to rebuilding the authority in my life?

DAY TWO

AUTHORITY

Prayer is a direct avenue for restoration. As you talk to God, the greatest Authority, about your life, your heart will become softened to all others. Through prayer, you acknowledge the power Jesus has. His power is greater than your problems. You recognize God has placed others in authority over you. As you pray for these people, your mind will change about how you think about authority. Respecting others will return respect to your own life.

COMMITMENT

This week, we will continue to look at recovery from a standpoint of renewing your relationship with God. We discovered in order to live in reality, you must first admit that you have a problem.

Recovery is sometimes related to steps, but, for me, steps symbolize a climb to the top of something with nowhere else to go. I relate recovery to a circular puzzle, its pieces in place. When the pieces are in the circle, the circle is whole. As you continue to gather all the pieces of recovery, you will have a whole person. Any time a piece goes missing, recovery is in jeopardy. Commitment is a piece of the puzzle, which adds stability to early recovery.

Recovery is not self-contained, however. The puzzle is three-dimensional. The surface of the puzzle is foundational and internal. Then there is a second dimension, moving upward toward God. And finally, the third dimension is outward toward others. These dimensions give you hope. Your new belief system may take years to fully develop. Even though this new belief system is not accomplished in an instant, for some, there may be an instantaneous awareness or breakthrough. Though you are learning to live in the present, you must believe everything will not happen now. It is believing. It is a process of faith.

We teach the most important thing to promote lasting change is the holy God, Jehovah, in whom we come to trust through a personal relationship with Jesus Christ. It is true that some will have misconceptions about Jesus Christ, God, and the Holy Spirit; but we will attempt to clear up some of the misconceptions. This is the God of creation. God spoke, and the world was formed. God breathed His breath in man, and man became a living being. God loved the world so much that He sent His own Son to live in human form and redeem fallen man. This Jesus suffered at the hands of cruel humanity to form a pathway to God, which had long been broken. God knows us by name and cares for us.

Jesus Christ, God the Father, and the Holy Spirit are a trinity. A trinitarian God Who is one God is more than we can understand. This God of creation is bigger than us. He is bigger than our worst nightmare. He is powerful enough to heal a leper, and He is powerful enough to restore our sanity.

Sanity means "soundness of mind." The sanity that you need and the sanity that God gives is the ability to face reality. Truth is reality. No matter how bad the truth may seem, truth is always positive. The Bible says, "Then you will know the truth, and the truth will set you free" (Jn. 8:32). The truth about addiction is that it has impaired the rational brain. The reasoning ability of an addict is greatly reduced. You can easily understand that reasoning ability and mental capabilities are impaired. Long after the using has stopped, the brain is still suffering. Many studies show that the brain of a teenager is stunted in its ability to mature because the chemicals in drugs and alcohol change the brain chemistry of a person. This is especially true the younger a person is when they begin to use. As the disease progresses and using continues, the brain also continues to be changed. Add emotional trauma, an unstable living environment, and a harmful lifestyle, and a person can be robbed of their developmental years.

With believing comes commitment. "One day at a time with a lifetime commitment" speaks of a lifestyle change. Believing without commitment is like dating without marriage. The breakup is inevitable. You can date a person for life and perhaps even love that person, but with the marriage ceremony, the lifestyle is changed.

So, what do you commit to? It is a day-by-day process with a lifelong commitment to change. Of course, you cannot promise that you will be sober for life, but just for today, you can. Commitment requires a heart change. A contract signed by two parties forms a legal commitment. If you got married and thought *I will marry for a day at a time*, the marriage would never work. You can only make a marriage last by living the marriage one day at a time, but the commitment to the marriage is for a lifetime.

This is the way it is with sobriety. You must make a lifetime commitment to sobriety and live that lifestyle commitment one day at a time. You may not be sober for life, but you are committed to the lifestyle of sobriety. Sober living is sane living. Sanity is sobriety. All of this is a process. At first, thinking about living life without a drug or habit seems overwhelming. You may be only able to commit to one day at first. The day by day of sobriety eventually brings us to a deeper commitment.

Ask yourself these questions:

- What do you believe about God?
- Who do you say God is?
- How do you explain Who Jesus is?
- How do you explain the Holy Spirit?

WORD STUDY

Believe

The Greek word for believe is *pisteuo*, which is translated, "To think to be true."[18] Thinking is the initial action to believing God exists; however, thinking must be taken one step further. You will need to direct your thoughts and beliefs toward the God of the Bible.

To believe in faith is far different than simply to believe in something. For instance, the demons believe God exists and fear Him, but they are not saved or changed by that belief. The Scriptures use the terms to "believe in" and "to believe on." *To believe on* connotes trust. *To believe in* simply agrees that something is.

You must be convinced that Jesus has the power to do something about your problems. It may take you twelve weeks to believe, or it may take you years to believe that Jesus can restore you to sanity. This is not an instant fix. Lifestyle changes may start in an instant, but they take a lifetime to complete.

---

18   *Bible Study Tools, s.v.* "pisteuo," accessed October 24, 2017, http://www.biblestudytools. com/lexicons/greek/nas/pisteuo.html.

All of this begins and ends with your thoughts. Thinking that Jesus is able to change you will take some practice. It takes actively participating with the words in the Bible to make faith come to life.

TODAY'S SCRIPTURE

"Trust in the LORD forever, for the LORD, the LORD himself, is the Rock eternal" (Isa. 26:4).

TODAY'S PRAYER

"I have refused authority in my life. I have rebelled against the very things that I know to be right. I have disrespected You, Lord. I have disrespected others. Make me willing to accept authority—especially Your authority—in my life."

TODAY'S JOURNAL QUESTION

Who is in my life that I consider authority?

DAY THREE

SIN/DISEASE CONCEPT: PART TWO

Every person is born with an Adamic nature. This is the nature which passes through our DNA from the first man, Adam. It is the ability to sin against God without reason. Even the smallest baby has the Adamic nature.

Children don't need classes to learn rebellion or selfishness, they already are programmed with this information. This nature cannot be cast out as if it were a demon because this nature is part of our being—that is, the human being. Because of the fall in the Garden of Eden, mankind is cursed with this nature. It is only by and through faith in the death and resurrection of Jesus Christ that this Adamic nature can be truly dealt with. When Jesus Christ was born in the flesh, He took on the war that wages between the Spirit of God and that of man. As man, He became the Second Adam. The First Adam sinned and broke fellowship with God, opening the door for all to sin against God. The Second Adam (Jesus) restored fellowship with God, opening a door for all who walk through it to live in harmony with God.

Jesus, as man, was tempted, yet He did not sin. He was tried, and He succeeded. Jesus suffered and yet did not give in to the suffering. He was all the First Adam was supposed to be. Because He is sinless, He is the perfect Sacrifice for the sin nature. He died to take away our sin. Of course, this is hard to understand because, though we receive the new nature through and by Jesus, we are left to experience the old nature's death, which comes by behavioral changes. If you do not choose to change your behavior, you have no experiential understanding of the power of Jesus Christ to change your sinful nature. Your spirit is in a right relationship with God through Jesus Christ, and your actions come into line with His will as you choose different behaviors. This is the experiential side of the spiritual application.

As the behavioral changes are put into practice, you can know the power of Jesus to help you succeed with the changes. You have a part to do in the change, and He has a part to do in the change. His part is to change your want, and your part is to learn new and better habits. Very simply put, He changes the inside; you change the outside. You change where and how you do things.

He changes the way you feel about things. It is through God's love for you that you can change. Once you accept the love of God, you then experience the love for God. This reciprocal love creates the desire to become less and less sinful. You now become sinless by sinning less.

THE DISEASE PART

The Bible says we are fearfully and wonderfully made, indicating that God's design of man is awesome and mysterious. God has allowed science to peek into His design to learn about some of the specifics of how the brain works. For example, science explains that virtually all drugs causing drug addiction increase the dopamine release in the mesolimbic pathway (dopamine pathways) in addition to their specific effects.[19]

When the dopamine levels begin to drop, the neurotransmitters are, in a way, fumbling around in the brain to try to get the same feeling. This causes the cravings for the drug or the experience. The natural amount of the dopamine will not produce the same feeling of pleasure. Over time, the brain forms a new pathway around the natural pathway. The natural pathway is damaged by the overproduction of dopamine.

When a person stops using drugs or alcohol, the brain's reward center has been changed from what God designed to what the drug demands. Therefore depression, agitation, anger, and other negative emotions are hard to handle because there may be no natural dopamine to signal the reward center that the person is experiencing pleasure. It takes time, exercise, the proper diet, and, sometimes, psychotropic medications to restore a new natural reward pathway. This can take up to five years of sobriety. When we tell someone to just quit, get a job, and get on with their life, we are, in effect, asking a person with cancer to ignore all their symptoms or discontinue treatment.

Another way to look at the disease is to think of it like diabetes. Diabetes, when left untreated, can take a person's life. Ignoring diabetes is deadly. Denial is also deadly. Once you have diabetes, you must do anything and

---

19   National Institute on Drug Abuse. "The Neurology of Drug Abuse: 7: Summary: Addictive Drugs Activate the Reward System Via Increasing Dopamine Neurotransmission." DrugAbuse.gov.   https://www.drugabuse.gov/publications/teaching-packets/neurobiology-drug-addiction/section-iv-action-cocaine/7-summary-addictive-drugs-activate-reward (accessed November 8, 2017).

everything to keep the disease from progressing too quickly. Being in control of diabetes means eating the right foods, getting the right exercise, and taking the medication prescribed by a doctor. Having the disease of addiction under control is similar. You must continue to do the next right thing in order to be sober. Working your program may be the only way you can keep the addiction in remission.

Nehemiah encouraged the people of Jerusalem to rebuild the gates and the walls of the city to provide the needed protection from their enemies. Each time the people of Jerusalem would make progress in rebuilding their lives, the enemies would pillage their homes. This destroyed the work and caused great discouragement. It was only after the walls and gates of the city were rebuilt that the Israelites were able to restore their homes and live their lives without constant fear.

Restoring our boundaries is crucial in recovery.

At the East Gate, you believe that there is a God who can restore sanity to your life. It is here that you look to Him for the answers that you need. It is here that you wait for the winds of change to blow on your life and send direction to you. The East Gate is a spiritual place; it is the building block of awareness of a God who is bigger than your problems. This points out that you need help, and you can't do this alone. Accepting that you need help is the one of the most powerful tools you can have to rebuild your life.

It is at this gate that you learn to pray for others in authority over you in ministry. Prayer is an avenue for restoring authority, because, as you talk to God about His authority in your life, you soften your heart to all authority. Through prayer, you acknowledge there is power in Jesus. You then begin to recognize that God has placed others in authority over you. As you pray for these people, your mind will change to accepting that authority and respecting it in your own life. How has prayer played a part in your life up to now? What will be your commitment to prayer?

TODAY'S SCRIPTURE

"Commit your way to the Lord; trust in him and he will do this" **(Psa. 37: 5).**

TODAY'S PRAYER

"Lord, I've been told that You are committed to me. I've been told to commit to You. The truth is that I am not sure what commitment means in my life. I am not sure who has been committed to me and why they would even want to be committed to me. Show me what that commitment means. I need help."

TODAY'S JOURNAL QUESTION

Who has been committed to me?

DAY FOUR

DEALING WITH THE MISERIES

The "miseries" is a term I use with people in recovery. The "miseries" sum up all the negative feelings about change. It is a period of time dedicated to seeing and feeling and making everything around you miserable.

Nothing looks right, feels right, tastes right; you can't do anything right, and nobody else can either while you are in the "miseries." The "miseries" are just miserable to you and to those around you. You must get relief; you just can't go on indefinitely with them. This condition won't go on too long because you will seek relief from past habits if the change doesn't come quickly from a positive direction.

Will you move from the "miseries" into change or revert back to old patterns because change is too hard for us? In his book *Addiction and Grace*, Dr. Gerald May refers to what I call the "miseries" as a desert place. He describes this desert as a place between what was in the past and what will be in the future. Some have referred to the "miseries" as the dark place or the dark night of the soul. No matter what you call it, this place is uncomfortable.[20]

Change is what recovery is all about. Change is hard. Thousands have studied change, and many have developed elaborate theories of how change occurs. But my theory is simple: change happens because of pain or pleasure. Change that happens in pleasure is fast and furious, like that of taking drugs. A teenager is doing well in school, is socially adept, and is maturing nicely. Suddenly, he makes a change for the worse. He starts dressing differently, hanging around a different crowd, and allowing his grades to drop. This is a sudden change brought on by the pleasure of taking drugs. Smoking pot, drinking alcohol, or doing any drug all produce a euphoric effect, which requires more and more to feel the same pleasure. The pleasure is so intense, he is willing to risk anything to experience it again. Let me repeat this: change brought on by pleasure is fast.

The other way we change, in my opinion, is pain. When something hurts enough, the long, agonizing path to life change begins. One reason pain change

---

20   Dr. Gerald May. *Addiction and Grace*. New York: HarperCollins, 2009.

is so long is the pleasure aspect. For example, drugs cause the same teenager grief with his parents, maybe even with the police. The pain is there—that is for sure—but after a few days, the pain subsides, and the thought of pleasure returns. If the teenager has a chance to do the drugs again and feels the pleasure from doing the drug, he forgets the pain. Pleasure trumps pain in us over and over again until the pain is so significant that we must change or die. It is when change can continue, or it can be deflected to a later time. How you deal with the "miseries" will determine if real change takes place.

Why do the "miseries" come? Negative thoughts over past events can cause you to sink into the "miseries."

> "How you deal with the 'miseries' will determine if real change takes place."

Romans 12:2a tells us, **"Do not conform to the pattern of this world, but be transformed by the renewing of your mind."** What you think about is very important in recovery. You have to make an inventory of past events, confess all sin, and replace those negative events with rich and positive things. Sometimes in this process, you will dwell too long on the mistakes and the negativity of the past, causing yourself to go into a miserable place mentally. At this point, you should seek help to change your mind. If no help comes from a positive source, you will return to the old, normal lifestyle. No matter how negative a lifestyle was, it was your normal life. Normal is not really normal; it is simply routine.

True guilt is guilt over something you have actually done. True guilt is a positive emotion for a person if he or she will confess that guilt to God and receive godly sorrow, which leads to repentance. That godly sorrow acts as a deterrent to committing the act again. However, if you refuse to receive forgiveness, the guilt can lead you to the "miseries."

Time is another cause of the "miseries." When you try to make a forever change in your life, you run into the time factor. It takes a long time to change, and "long" is not a word that fits your lifestyle. Everything is instant gratification in our world, so when things take time, you begin to suffer. You must learn how to suffer, since suffering has never been acceptable. You get miserable thinking about the future. You cannot see the future or even begin to picture the future as being a content place to be based on what your past has looked like.

Pressure from family and friends to "hurry up and change" is another source of frustration that leads to misery. Almost anything can cause the "miseries" in early recovery, but this is not the only place for the "miseries." Anybody can get miserable. But, in order to change, one has to face the "miseries" and allow them to have their way without turning back to the old normal. The Bible says it like this: **"Let perseverance finish its work so that you may be mature and complete, not lacking anything" (Jas. 1:4).**

How does one get out of the "miseries" successfully? First you wait. **"But those who hope in the LORD will renew their strength. They will soar on wings like eagles; they will run and not grow weary; they will walk and not be faint" (Isa. 40:31).** If the "miseries" hit, wait five minutes. If they are still there, wait five more. Repeat this exercise until the "miseries" leave you. This waiting five minutes at a time is a simple mental redirection tactic. It helps us to break down things into smaller units. Five minutes is a short enough span to learn to wait.

Next, change your mind. Remember Romans 12:2. Turn on some praise music; call a friend; walk outside; and look for some visible sign that God exists. Make a list of all the things you are thankful for. If thinking about positive things doesn't lift your "miseries" quickly, then wait. Giving up and leaving or going back will only cause you to have to face the miseries again. The miseries are a certain part of change. They mark the end to the old and the beginning of the new.

When the "miseries" end negatively, it is called "relapse." Relapse always starts in the mind. Some have questioned the difference in a relapse and a slip. I will try to explain what I believe is the difference. A slip is one drink, one pill, one snort, or one behavior, which is interrupted by feelings of guilt and shame over throwing recovery away. The slip is not planned; there is not a plan to continue; and it might be brought on by seeing a doctor who gives medication with a narcotic in it.

I use the term "slipping and sliding" to refer to a time when someone is in denial and says that they only had one drink, but this has happened several times. "Relapse" is abusing the drug or alcohol, using more than enough to cause a high, or having a blackout. One night or one weekend is a relapse if a person gets high or gets drunk. A relapse occurs if law enforcement is involved in any way, no matter if it is the first time in a long time or just one time.

Now, I do teach people to get up quickly. If you have called out for help, that is very positive. Relapse can be a teaching tool. Denial is very strong in addiction. Sometimes, people in recovery still have the idea that they are unique and that the rules of addiction don't apply to them. Relapse doesn't have to happen, but when it does, those in the helping ministry should be prepared to give positive feedback to the person who relapsed.

As I said in the beginning, pain or pleasure initiates change. Relapse can be so painful that the changes required in early recovery are cemented into a foundation for a new life. Relapses that occur over and over in a short amount of time aren't really relapses, but simply lapses of using. A relapse is only a relapse after a person has had a significant amount of time, more than a week or two, of sobriety.

Sobriety is more than abstaining from the behavior. The definition of sobriety is that you are truly sober when you exhibit self-control, have been restored to a sound mind, and are calm and collected in your spirit. Many are abstaining but not sober. Sobriety is a long and drawn out process.

Abstinence means not using the drug, substance, or behavior that is the choice for the individual. You can abstain but not be sober. However, you cannot be sober without abstaining from all mood-altering substances or negative habitual behaviors.

I do believe "miseries" come to everyone. It is up to us individually to seek the right relief from the "miseries," or you will return to the old way of life as a relief.

TODAY'S SCRIPTURE

"Lord Almighty, blessed is the one who trusts in you" (Ps. 84:12).

TODAY'S PRAYER

"Lord, help my rebellious heart to respond to Your discipline instead of running away. Help me to recognize and seek out authority, so I may grow to be more like You and less like me."

TODAY'S JOURNAL QUESTION

Who or what have I committed to in the past?

DAY FIVE

DELIVERANCE

In the biblical book of Exodus, the journey to the Promised Land was interrupted by rebellion. Rebellion, according to 1 Samuel 15:23, is as the sin of witchcraft. The children of Israel had lived in slavery for 400 years. Their fathers and grandfathers had lived in slavery. The customs were infiltrated with paganism, brought on by the exposure to Egyptian culture. When they made the trip across a desert through enemy territory, they fell back to old patterns of behavior. Those old patterns were rebellious to the ways of God. Yes, they wanted to be free. They wanted a new job, which did not include making bricks or hauling straw. They wanted shorter work days; they wanted a new master. But when the trip became difficult, these children wanted to go home. They wanted to find something that was familiar. They wanted to complain, to run, to get some relief. They turned to the gods of Egypt to help them.

When God was parting the Red Sea, they were able to walk across on dry land; they followed God. He seemed to offer them the best deal. But when the excitement of the "new deal" waned, or life became more difficult, the children of Israel complained and looked elsewhere. This is rebellion.

Slavery isn't just a method of work, but a state of mind. In the life of the slave, everything is decided for him. The master chooses everything. Generation after generation is educated to believe that only the taskmaster can think, and individualized thinking is punished. With year after year of no individualized thinking and no creativity, the slave is not only in bondage in the flesh, but also in his mind and in his spirit. Now he thinks like a slave. When given a choice to make, he can't make it. If he does make a decision, he has to consult a "god" who answers quickly and doesn't expect anything from the person except more of the slave mentality.

The trip through the desert was example after example of slaves being reconditioned to the ways of God through one act of rebellion, followed by discipline, and then another act of rebellion, followed by more discipline.

It takes time to recondition the thoughts to the thoughts of God. In our language, that could mean relapse, followed by jail, then relapse, followed by residential treatment, and then relapse, followed by a hospital stay. Of course, all of this is avoided if you make the choices to commit to your recovery early and follow the rules of recovery.

NAMES OF GOD

When the children of Israel moved in the wilderness, they moved under the direction of God as the cloud moved by day. God promised them He would be their leader in the wilderness. He provided the leadership and authority through natural phenomenon, and men surrendered to Him. As the cloud moved, they moved. The cloud led the entire group throughout the wilderness from bondage to freedom.

They were divided into twelve tribes, and each tribe moved according to leadership. They moved under their banner. Each tribe followed the authority that was represented in their tribal banner. God promised to be their Banner. As you submit to God, you will find *Jehovah Nissi*, our Banner and our Authority.[21]

TODAY'S SCRIPTURE

"I do believe; help me overcome my unbelief" (Mk. 9:24b).

TODAY'S PRAYER

"How can I believe when my feelings are in such a state of turmoil? Who are You? Can You really restore my sanity? Can You really help me? What will my life be like if You restore my sanity? I admit that I have been out of control, but that is all I have known. Can I be a different person? I need help. Can You help me?"

TODAY'S JOURNAL QUESTION

Do you believe that God can restore you to sanity?

---

21   *Bible Hub, s.v.* "Yhvh Nissi," accessed October 24, 2017, http://biblehub.com/hebrew/3071. htm.

DAY SIX

If you are emotionally immature and have been using a substance almost all of your life, everything about you has to change. The problem is that this life is the only life you have ever known. There is no point of reference for you. Anything prior to using was your childhood, and everything since childhood is related to use and abuse of substances or behaviors.

What a sober person thinks looks normal does not look normal to a person whose whole life has been under the influence. There are two major factors in this way of thinking for an addict. One is that your emotional age is stunted, and the other is that every activity in life has been seen and done from an altered mindset. The negative lifestyle has given you a false sense of understanding.

For example, you may watch a movie while in the throes of addiction. Then, in recovery, you say, "I've seen that movie. It was so funny. Let's watch it now." When the movie is watched during sobriety, it changes the complete meaning. What was funny drunk or high may or may not be funny in recovery.

Change is very hard. *Change* means everything for an addict. Sometimes in recovery, you will have to get a new job or a new career. New friends are a must, and often where you live will have to be evaluated. The way you drive home, the places you go—you name it. Everything will have to change. Can you begin to understand that sometimes you will get overwhelmed and get the "miseries"?

What can be done to help? Learn to say no appropriately. Those caught in a negative lifestyle will press you for the answer they want to hear. No is the best answer most of the time; only say yes to what will keep them in recovery. Never say yes to anything illegal, immoral, or un-Christian.

Give proper support. By proper support, I mean only those areas that will encourage recovery and long-term sobriety. Financial support must be limited or excluded. By limited, I mean only financially support an addict in recovery. If they are not in recovery, do not give them money. Do not give them anything if they are not in active recovery. Do not feel guilty for not being able to save everyone. Life is all about choices. You must choose to do the next right thing for yourself and others. You must be able to set boundaries and keep boundaries.

One day, many years ago, a volunteer was teaching a class at the recovery house. He was talking about freedoms that he enjoyed, such as drinking a beer at a barbecue. There were several women at the house and in the meeting. One definitively stated there was no such freedom for an addict because one beer could trigger a relapse, and that relapse, for her, could mean death. The volunteer was very passionate about being able to drink. He told the women that he would always be able to drink a beer and that he believed that they could drink one as well. He went on to tell them that God would not hold it against them if they drank. The one woman was very upset about his statements because she had tried on numerous occasions to drink just one.

In that meeting was a very sick alcoholic who was also diabetic. She was very deep in her addiction. She was older and had retired from a very lucrative business. This woman could handle business but not the bottle. She was elated with the news that at the next barbecue (or even sooner), she could drink a beer. She was relieved that somebody had let her off the hook, so to speak, about drinking. After all, she longed to drink. We had a discussion, she and I, about what was said in the class. She was angry because I told her that she could not drink one, that one would be the death of her. Her anger was so intense that she called me "Satan." She then called her son and left the next day. I was so sad to see her go because I knew that she was headed for the nearest liquor store.

It was months before I heard from her again. In the few months since she had left Bethesda, she had already been near death twice. Several times, she had made it to detox, only to leave and get drunk again. She wanted to come back to Bethesda. We had a few details to work out. She used her cats as an excuse and said she would let me know.

The next phone call I got was one from a mutual friend, saying the woman's roommate had found her dead. Complications from diabetes and, of course, drinking were to blame. Her son was not a believer; he was an angry man. A few days after her death, he called to let me know that I had killed his mother because of my rigid doctrine.

It took a few months for me to get over that. I examined myself over the issue. I have often wondered what would have happened if the volunteer had not spoken of his freedom. I have often thought of how things would be different if she had gotten through her "miseries" and stayed. But, sometimes, the desert is a very dry place. Sometimes, the longing for a drink is so strong, you believe you have only one choice, and that is to break out running for that drink. You find the mirage is not an oasis but quicksand.

Death can be imminent for those in addiction. I say there is always another relapse, but there may not be another recovery. The progression of the disease aspect of the addiction is so strong that it often drags a person into a deathtrap.

"I say there is always another relapse, but
there may not be another recovery."

However, there are those who do make it out of the addiction cycle. The picture of addiction that I most relate to is that of a tug-of-war. You are on one side of the mudslide, and addiction is on the other side. The rope that holds the two together is thick and strong. It is a love/hate relationship. At first, addiction pulls you any which way, and you are dragged into the mud bath. In early recovery, you get up and pull yourself up with the help of a few friends. You are always holding onto the rope that binds you to addiction. Back and forth goes the addiction tied to you. The stress of the addiction often feels to you as if it is the only thing holding you up. Friends and family see the problem. The rope is wrapped around your arm. After much struggle, the rope is freed from your arm; but over and over, you pull, and addiction pulls back. Once in a while, you pull the addiction into the mud, but then the addiction drags you back.

Once again, the friends and family see what the problem is. You are clutching the rope that holds you to addiction.

"Release the rope!" the family cries.

"I can't!" you cry back.

"Release the rope!"

"I can't; it has me; I don't have it."

"Look at the rope!" the family cries. "You are holding on to addiction."

Finally, after much tugging, you look at your hands and see that you are holding on to the addiction. It is true that once the addiction had you wrapped up in ropes that bind, but after so much struggling, you now hold onto the addiction as your way of life. You must let it go. Addiction makes one final tug—this one really hard—but you release the rope that holds you to your addiction. You are free. Addiction is down, and the rope that bound you is across the field of mud.

One day, you must let go of the things that bind you to addiction. If the struggle is one tug-of-war after another, you should examine your life to see what the rope is. The rope could be a relationship that is ungodly. It could be a job or an attitude. The rope could look like something that seems okay to somebody else but will not work in your life. The rope that binds could be some disobedient act that you continue to do. I have found that God has told us what we have to do to be completely free. Time and time again, in early recovery, I have heard a woman say, "I need to give up this thing." But year after year, they struggle with their sobriety and finding true recovery because they would not give it up.

Some women describe their addiction as their lover. They sometimes refer to it as their best friend. They say it is the only thing they have been able to depend on. This relationship with drugs and alcohol goes deep; but so does the relationship they have with a negative lifestyle, negative thoughts, and negativity in general. Negativity is complicated, yet predictable. It is complicated because everyone is different. It is predictable in that the principles of addiction work the same way for everybody.

TODAY'S SCRIPTURE

"'But I will restore you to health and heal your wounds,' declares the Lord, 'because you are called an outcast, Zion, for whom no one cares'" (Jer. 30:17).

TODAY'S PRAYER

"I feel that nobody cares about my problems. I feel alone and mis-understood. I feel that people treat me as an outcast. Lord, can You restore my emotions? Can You restore my health and heal my pain?"

TODAY'S JOURNAL QUESTION

How do your feelings affect your belief that God can restore you to sanity?

DAY SEVEN

PREPARE FOR FELLOWSHIP WITH OTHER BELIEVERS AND CORPORATE WORSHIP
The Importance of Gathering with Other Believers

You may recognize the local church is not perfect or mature enough to handle the difficult and complex problems you are experiencing, but it is a place to begin. At church, you learn the boundaries necessary for interdependence. In a local church environment, participants can be active in corporate worship without feeling odd about singing to God or praying to Him. It is a safe place to learn that others are in need of God, and you are not alone.

When you learn about how to attend a church, it is important to recognize that each church has its own special culture. You can find the very formal churches with quiet reverence or the modern enthusiastic church filled with loud music and active worship.

Keep in mind as you begin your journey toward change that authority is important. You will find a new representation of authority in the church setting. The culture of the American church is diverse, so you can find a place where you fit to begin to restructure your life around a biblical authority.

If the first church you visit is not the best place for you, don't give up because the church family is so important in the maturity of your life. The church family holds the representation of a biblical family. You may find the mother you have always wanted or the brothers and sisters you have never had.

Denominations have culture, but inside each denomination, the individual church also has culture. We recommend looking into the denominational doctrines before making a decision about becoming a member. Please do not align yourself with a denomination which does not have doctrines you believe.

If you like the atmosphere of a church, then visit again. It usually takes three or more consecutive meetings to determine what the culture is. Once you like the culture, look at the doctrinal structure. You can do this by talking to the pastor or reading online about the denomination.

TODAY'S SCRIPTURES

"For everyone born of God overcomes the world. This is the victory that has overcome the world, even our faith" (1 Jn. 5:4).

"He replied, 'Because you have so little faith. Truly I tell you, if you have faith as small as a mustard seed, you can say to this mountain, *Move from here to there*, and it will move. Nothing will be impossible for you'" (Matt. 17:20).

TODAY'S PRAYER

"If faith like a grain of mustard seed is all I need, then help me, Lord, to have that grain of faith."

TODAY'S JOURNAL QUESTION

What will you believe God for today?

❦ CHAPTER SIX ❦
OLD GATE: GATEWAY TO RESTORING TRUTH

"The Jeshanah (Old) Gate was repaired by Joiada son of Paseah and Meshullam son of Besodeiah. They laid its beams and put its doors with their bolts and bars in place. Next to them, repairs were made by men from Gibeon and Mizpah—Melatiah of Gibeon and Jadon of Meronoth—places under the authority of the governor of Trans-Euphrates. Uzziel son of Harhaiah, one of the goldsmiths, repaired the next section; and Hananiah, one of the perfume-makers, made repairs next to that. They restored Jerusalem as far as the Broad Wall. Rephaiah son of Hur, ruler of a half-district of Jerusalem, repaired the next section. Adjoining this, Jedaiah son of Harumaph made repairs opposite his house, and Hattush son of Hashabneiah made repairs next to him. Malkijah son of Harim and Hasshub son of Pahath-Moab repaired another section and the Tower of the Ovens. Shallum son of Hallohesh, ruler of a half-district of Jerusalem, repaired the next section with the help of his daughters" (Neh. 3:6-12—parentheses mine).

"Surely God is my salvation; I will trust and not be afraid. The Lord, the Lord himself, is my strength and my defense; he has become my salvation" (Isa. 12:2).

DAY ONE

TRUTH

What Is the Truth?

I answered the phone, and it was an agency with a referral.

"Do you have any beds?"

"Not really," I said, but making room for another woman was my specialty.

"This woman is really in need," came the reply.

"What is the problem?"

"She has missed her bus and doesn't have anywhere to stay for the night. Can you keep her until she can get on her way?"

It turned out she was in her mid-seventies, alone, and very misunderstood. She had a couple of boxes and no real suitcases when she arrived on our porch. She walked like a very old lady, taking about ten steps for every one of a younger person. She was soft-spoken and quiet. We exchanged a few words about her stay, and then she was to settle in with her things in a bed on the first floor. This precious lady would be sharing a room with two others—one a staff member.

In a house full of women, it doesn't take long for the rumors to start flying.

"She is really strange," was the first of such rumors.

"I don't think so. She is just a little old lady with no place to go."

After a good twenty-four hours, she was really the talk of the house. It seemed that our guest was very special. She was African American in origin and, in her own words, a "woman of color." She did have, according to her own testimony, a marking on her forehead, which only other women of color could see. I told her I was a woman of color; it was just light tan, and I did so want to see the markings.

She smiled patiently with me and said, "Miss Cathy, you know what I mean."

I really loved hearing her interesting stories of the star, which shone just for her and appeared in the sky the night she was born. She had something wrong with her leg, too. She told me it had eels in it. They moved around and caused her great pain. But the most interesting thing of all was the package she carried wherever she went. This package was properly covered with brown bags and protected from intruders by massive amounts of duct tape. Granny, as we called her, said you needed duct tape for everything, including wrapping special objects of value. But the package got the best of the women because she would not let them peek in and see what it was.

In my office one afternoon, a woman, who had a few of her own odd mannerisms, told me that Granny had Satan's bible in her package.

"What else could it be, Cathy? She holds it when she prays, and she will not let anyone look at it to see what it is."

"You are overreacting," I told the woman.

"We have got to get her out of this house; she is a Satan worshipper. I'm telling you."

"Don't worry," I said, "she will be leaving in a few days. She is staying only until she finds someplace to go."

By the next day, Granny was sitting in my office, suggesting to me that she leave. She wanted to get an apartment and stay in Waycross. I told her that we just didn't have the money to set her up. She could always stay with us. She politely told me she didn't need our money. She had money of her own and started the plunge, as older women sometimes do, by sticking her hand down her bosom and pulling out another package, secured with duct tape and filled with one-hundred-dollar bills. So, we began the process of helping her get into an apartment, moving in some furniture, and, of course, keeping that precious package with her.

My associate, Janice, and I would stop by to see Granny on occasion; and in the year or so she lived in Waycross, we moved her again. It was after the second move that I was made privy to the package. She, Janice, and I were visiting one afternoon when, out of the blue, Granny said, "I have something I want to show you. You might just want one like it someday." Off she toddled to her bedroom and back she came, holding the package, still wrapped with brown bags and duct tape.

I have to admit that she took me off-guard because I really didn't know what was in that package. It could have been something strange—like a Satan's bible, for all I knew—but whatever it was, she trusted me enough to show it to me.

She sat down in the chair and neatly and slowly loosened the duct tape and unwrapped the precious object of value.

As she handed it to me, she said, "It's a *Nelson's Bible Dictionary*. I like to read about those people in the Bible—mainly Sarah. You ought to get you one, Miss Cathy."

In my entire ministry, I have never felt so honored as that day. I shall never forget it. It was the day that I realized that some differences just don't matter. Granny left Waycross shortly after that, and I have not seen her since. But she is always with me. Maybe one of these days, I'll see that mark that's on her forehead.

THE TRUTH ABOUT GOD ACCORDING TO SCRIPTURE

God is Magnificent

> **"Great is the LORD and most worthy of praise; his greatness no one can fathom. One generation commends your works to another; they tell of your mighty acts" (Ps. 145:3-4).**

God is Righteous

> **"Who will not fear you, Lord, and bring glory to your name? For you alone are holy. All nations will come and worship before you, for your righteous acts have been revealed" (Rev. 15:4).**

God is Just

> **"But the LORD Almighty will be exalted by his justice, and the holy God will be proved holy by his righteous acts" (Isa. 5:16).**

God is Perfect

> **"He is the Rock, his works are perfect, and all his ways are just. A faithful God who does no wrong, upright and just is he" (Deut. 32:4).**

God is the One True God

> **Gather together and come; assemble, you fugitives from the nations. Ignorant are those who carry about idols of wood, who pray to**

gods that cannot save. Declare what is to be, present it—let them take counsel together. Who foretold this long ago, who declared it from the distant past? Was it not I, the LORD? And there is no God apart from me, a righteous God and a Savior; there is none but me. Turn to me and be saved, all you ends of the earth; for I am God, and there is no other" (Isa. 45:20-22).

God is the King of Glory

"Who is the King of glory? The LORD strong and mighty, The LORD mighty in battle" (Ps. 24:8).

God is Salvation

"Then I heard a loud voice in heaven say: 'Now have come the salvation and the power and the kingdom of our God, and the authority of his Messiah. For the accuser of our brothers and sisters, who accuses them before our God day and night, has been hurled down'" (Rev. 12:10).

God is Faithful

"Let us hold unswervingly to the hope we profess, for he who promised is faithful" (Heb. 10:23).

God is the Protector

"But the Lord is faithful, and he will strengthen you and protect you from the evil one" (2 Thess. 3:3).

The Lord is Wise

"By wisdom the LORD laid the earth's foundations, by understanding he set the heavens in place" (Prov. 3:19).

"And said: 'Praise be to the name of God for ever and ever; wisdom and power are his. He changes times and seasons; he deposes kings and raises up others. He gives wisdom to the wise and knowledge to the discerning. He reveals deep and hidden things; he knows what lies in darkness, and light dwells with him'" (Dan. 2:20-22).

God is Love

"Whoever does not love does not know God, because God is love"
(1 Jn. 4:8).

KEY TO TRUTH

You can believe the truth. The truth of God is the basis for your belief system. You can use this key to unlock the truth in your recovery.

ACTION STEPS

- Do a random act of kindness today. The act of kindness should be to someone who cannot repay you in any way.
- You could write a note of encouragement.
- Do an anonymous act of service for someone.
- Write a letter to God. Express your feelings to Him and about Him.
- Memorize Scripture.
- Take a walk today. Make the walk spiritual by looking for evidence of God in the natural surroundings.

PRAYER FOR THE OLD GATE
Daily Prayer for This Week

"Father, much has happened in our cities and towns which have become traditions of men. Many families have taken a place of leadership in our town from ancient days. Today, I pray that Your perfect will be done in the lives of these families. I pray that Your kingdom of peace will reign in their lives, and those who do not know You as their personal Savior will be brought to salvation. I bless these families with the riches of heaven according to Your will. I pray that traditions of men—age-old things that separate men from Your grace—will be broken in the lives of these families. Bring peace and joy to them in Jesus' name.

"Today is the day I choose to turn my will over to You. I have made a mess of my life so far, trying to do my own thing. I am not so sure what this means, but I know I cannot make it like I am. Take my will and make it willing to be made willing.

"I will begin today to praise Your holy Name and to thank You for all those things You have done for me."

TODAY'S SCRIPTURE

"For God so loved the world that he gave his one and only Son, that whoever believes in him shall not perish but have eternal life" **(Jn. 3:16).**

TODAY'S PRAYER

"God, I have questions about You and Who You are, but I am choosing today to believe in You. I do not want to die the way I am today. Help me to receive this eternal life and deliver me from the curse of negativity."

TODAY'S JOURNAL QUESTION

What is your first memory of thinking that there was a God?

DAY TWO

DECISIONS AND BELIEF

Have you ever once thought of what it takes to make a decision? Have you ever considered that you have a choice in the decision-making of your life? Decision-making sounds like personal responsibility. You have to be responsible. Some people want instantaneous deliverance by God when they come to Him for help. What He does, more often than not, is cause us to go through a process to gather tools for the rest of our lives.

Now, choosing God's way doesn't mean He will do everything for you. Instead, He sets up a series of events in your life for you to learn His will. As you begin to be positive, you will have more and more opportunities to choose God's way over your own way. God will not destroy every problem area on your path from home to the next meeting, but He will give you tools to bypass those areas. He will not destroy every person who has hurt you or rewrite your medical charts to tell your doctor that you have an addiction. But He will give you tools to avoid the next big hurt and opportunities to tell your doctor the truth.

The work of this gate is to help you find the best of the old traditions and to build new traditions. It is at this place in your life that your belief systems will require examination. Some of us are so hardheaded, we want to ignore anything good about our upbringing. Surely, there are some who have had little good to salvage from their upbringing, but, nevertheless, even those of us who have had horrible childhoods must take a look at the "old stuff" which made up our beliefs and our "truths."

I am thinking of a family I know whose belief system is very convoluted. This system is not spoken but taught by continual action and reaction. No one sits around a dinner table and says, "This is our belief system. You are a sexual object, and, in order to get ahead in life, you must have sex with people. This is how we roll." The way this system becomes the "truth-lie" is by demonstration. Mama is happy when the man is around. He brings "fun" into the house. The children get things when he is around. He leaves, and Mama is devastated. He comes back, and life is good again.

Several "truth-lies" are in this lifestyle. One is that sex brings happiness. And another is that I am only sexual; without sex, I am nothing. Finally, it teaches that love is conditional. I call these "truth-lies" because it is truth to the person but a lie to God. These "truth-lies" are everywhere. When you have an encounter with God and the "truth-lies" are exposed, you have an identity crisis.

Prejudice is one of those "truths" you need to look at. When I grew up in the Deep South, prejudice was acceptable. There was prejudice against race, culture, economics, heritage—you name it, there was some type of prejudging going on. But as I began to examine my "truths," I discovered that God is not prejudiced. He frowns on prejudice, in fact. I needed to throw my "truth" away and embrace God's truth.

How I felt about myself was another of those "old things" not necessary in my new life. I had to accept the truth about myself from God's perspective. Other beliefs of my life had to be tossed, and I am sure your belief system needs to be challenged by God's Word.

Each new choice about change will need to be cemented into your belief system or your "God" system. You must make that decision to rebuild your life based on the truth of God's Word. Once you determine whether an action or choice is godly, then you will still have a choice to do it God's way or your way. You will have to believe it is the right thing to do. The motto, "Do the next right thing," is imperative for your life. "Doing the next right thing" will be the godly choice, but, of course, you can always do the next wrong thing because God never takes your choices away from you. Sometimes, doing the next right thing will feel like it will kill you, but it won't. This is one of your new God-truths to embrace.

"This is what the LORD says: 'Stand at the crossroads and look; ask for the ancient paths, ask where the good way is, and walk in it, and you will find rest for your souls. But you said, *We will not walk in it*'" (Jer. 6:16).

These ancient paths Jeremiah was talking about were the customs of following God and obeying His Word.

Imagine that your life is a walled city. This city has definite boundaries, an entrance, and exit points. The city has a central point, and that is the temple. It has structures and buildings and wells. The city can maintain itself for a season, but someone must go in and out to gather fresh materials, fresh water, and other supplies. This walled city has been ravaged by enemies, wild animals, and neglect. The city needs restoration because every gateway is destroyed, and all that is ungodly can enter without reservation and wreak havoc with everything inside.

When life strikes you, it can leave you defenseless. It destroys boundaries. Tough issues rob you and then allow other enemies—such as depression, anxiety, and mental illness—to steal everything that is worthwhile from you. You need a plan. You need help.

At the Old Gate, truth is restored. You submit. You make the decision to believe the truth about the past, the present, and the future. You need to decide the way you have been living is not working and give up control to Jesus.

The Bible says that Jesus is **"the way and the truth and the life" (Jn. 14:6)**. You realize that Jesus can restore God in your life. The Holy Spirit brings you into all truth. Truth restored will replace traditions from the past with new traditions for the future.

Let's explore the traditions of the past:

- What did you do as a child on holidays? Are those memories good or bad memories? Why?

- What did you do as a child on vacation?

Now, let's look at the present:

- What traditions do you have with your family now?

- What traditions will you continue with your family?

- What traditions will you discontinue?

Let's explore the truth about your parents:

- What good things did they teach you?

- What are some things that you will not continue in your life that your parents did to you?

Let's examine the truth about yourself:

- List the things that you can do well.
- List the things that you cannot do well.
- What is one thing that you like about yourself?
- What is one thing that you wish to change about yourself?
- What do you believe about yourself?
- What is one thing that would stop your recovery at this point?

Now, let's examine how you view God and the Church:

- What do you know about God?
- Is what you know about God based on the Bible?
- What do you believe about church?
- What do you believe about Jesus?
- Are you ready to give over control of your life to God?

Complete honesty will not be easy. Denial has established a stronghold of dishonesty in your personality. What may seem perfectly honest to you will seem like a total lie to another person.

There are at least three types of denial. First, there is simple denial, in which a person denies the fact of an unpleasant reality altogether. Next, there is minimization, in which a person admits the fact but denies the seriousness of the situation. Finally, there is projection, in which a person admits that there is a problem but refuses to take responsibility for the problem.

You rationalize behaviors, rather than admit the truth about what the behaviors are doing to others and to yourself. The problem may be bad—you may rationalize—but it isn't as bad as some other problem you may have encountered.

Another defense mechanism people use to keep from being God-honest is reversal. When being confronted with issues in your life, you reverse the conversation by pointing out the problems in the confronter's life.

All of these behaviors are defense mechanisms. But what are you defending? Are you defending your right to be broken? Or are you defending the "truth-lies" of your life?

WORD STUDY

Character: one of the attributes or features that make up and distinguish an individual; moral or ethical strength; a description of a person's attributes, traits, or abilities.

Many of the attributes of God are stated in the Bible. He is faithful, true, trustworthy, mighty, and worthy. He never leaves us stranded. He always cares for us. He is eternal. He is able. He knows us by name. He is loving and merciful. He is a wonderful Counselor. God's character is absolutely perfect.

It is very important to know God's character if you plan to give your life and will over to His care. You can study what the great writers of the Bible have said about Jesus, God, and the Holy Spirit before you make the decision to submit to God's will for your life.

You develop a godly character as you interact with the Holy Spirit through belief and choose different actions.

TODAY'S SCRIPTURE

"All your words are true; all your righteous laws are eternal" (Ps. 119:160).

TODAY'S PRAYER

"Lord Jesus, I do not know what Your truth is. I have formed my own truths and believed what I thought was right in my own eyes. I want to learn the truth of Your Word and the righteousness of Your rules. Forgive me because I have believed lies about You and about myself."

TODAY'S JOURNAL QUESTION

In what ways has God shown you that He loves you?

DAY THREE

SPIRIT, MIND, AND BODY

God designed us to be a triune person. Mankind is spirit, soul, and body. The human spirit is where God meets man, where man meets God, and where man meets others. The soul is the mind, will, and emotions of a person. This is where man meets with circumstances. It is where personality lives and where character is built. The body is the flesh and blood of an individual; this includes the organs of the person, such as the brain. This is where man meets his environment.

The Bible says that **"you were dead in your transgressions and sins" (Eph. 2:1)**—that is, before you came to Jesus. When you come to Jesus, your spirit is quickened, and your human spirit is alive unto Christ and dead to sin. The Holy Spirit comes to take up residence in your spirit. In the human spirit, prior to being born again, the person is able to meet another person and assess if that person will be "good" or "bad." When a person is born again, the Holy Spirit comes to sanctify that human spirit and teach it the ways of God. Now the human spirit makes connection with others who have the Holy Spirit residing in their human spirit.

As the Holy Spirit has more encounters with man, the human spirit begins to **"walk by the Spirit" (Gal. 5:16).** The Holy Spirit encounters man through prayer, Bible reading, friendships with other Christians, and many other ways.

The human soul begins to be converted, or changed, thus sending out change signals to the mind, the will, and the emotions. The way we think has a huge effect on the way we feel and the choices we make. The way we think, act, and feel has an enormous effect on the way we meet circumstances in our lives. As the human spirit is converted, our personality begins to be converted or changed. Thus, the environment where we live will be affected as our spirit and soul is converted. This is change from the inside out. Some call this a heart change. It is a belief system change.

Since we are one person with three distinct parts—spirit, soul, and body—nothing happens to us that touches only one of these parts. If it is a problem at all, it is a spirit, soul, and body problem. Man meets God in the human spirit. He meets circumstances through his soul, and, with his body, he meets the environment.

Addiction, one of life's toughest issues, is not limited to just the physical body, although it does affect the physical organs of a person. But physical disorders, such as cancer, don't simply destroy the body. They affect the soul and spirit as well. Addiction is called "a brain disease or disorder" because addiction changes the physical chemistry of the brain and changes the pathways of those chemicals. Addictions are not limited to the emotional part of mankind either; they change the way a person feels, what he thinks, and what he chooses. Addiction is said to be a mental illness and is listed in the *Diagnostic and Statistical Manual of Mental Disorders IV*. Addiction is not limited to the spiritual aspect of man, but it does separate the addict from God and from others. Addiction is sometimes called "a curse or spiritual problem." Diseases and other mental disorders cause issues in the spiritual realm of a person, as well as the soul areas. You are complex in your design, and treatment is complex for you. With the sin/disease concept, a person can be treated as a spiritual being, a physical being, and an emotional being.

The Bible tells us in **1 Corinthians 15:46, "The spiritual did not come first, but the natural, and after that the spiritual."** We understand much by first understanding the natural order of things. As we understand natural order, we can see how this applies to the spiritual order of life.

In any treatment process for life change, start first with the physical. It is good to begin with a checkup by a doctor to determine if there are any physical issues that need to be addressed. High blood pressure, thyroid issues, chronic headaches, and stomach issues are relative to most soul issues and spiritual issues. Such physical issues can reduce the desire for true lifestyle changes and can sap the energy it takes physically to maintain change.

The soul, as we are discussing it today, is a person's mind, will, and emotions. Added into the soul is the personality. I believe personality is hardwired; while thoughts, feelings, and decisions are choices we make throughout our life. Once the physical body is up to speed, you can begin working on the soul. Treating the soul requires work. The mind must be changed from a negative mindset to a positive mindset. When the mind changes, choices improve. With improved choices or decisions, the emotions eventually come in line with the truth of recovery. Meditation, studying the Word of God, and memorizing

Scripture or other positive declarations speeds the healing of the soul and forms a positive backdrop for the mind to believe the truth.

The spirit of a person is the first part of a human being to be formed. I believe when the egg meets the sperm, the spirit is planted. This human spirit is not in direct contact with God at this time because of our fallen nature. But the human spirit is alive. Paul also said we are alive in Christ at salvation (Eph. 2:5).

Treating the spiritual aspect of the person wounded by life calls for prayer, counseling, church or positive meeting attendance, fellowship with like-minded people, and accountability. As you become sober, the spirit, soul, and body become more at peace. A sober life is a balanced life.

Since obsession is such a large part of a negative lifestyle, it is important to work in a balanced way on all three areas. The enemy of your life would like nothing better than to get you so obsessed in one area, it could drive you back to your old life. Changes come through persistence and the determination not to be distracted by anything. It is a lifestyle change. Everything you do must be reevaluated in light of lasting change.

In this diagram you see the soul, spirit, and body as they relate to life. The soul is the mind, will, and matter of a person. The human spirit is the breath of man and the spirit, which we are born with. As a person comes to Christ, the human spirit, **"dead in trespasses and sin" (Eph. 2:1),** is made alive in Christ. God meets man; man meets God. Prior to being born again, the human spirit has been affected by the human spirits of others. The human spirit of one man meets the human spirit of another. Often the human spirit is wounded prior to redemption. After redemption, the human spirit is made alive to God and is able to be healed from any former wounding. The personality or soul of a man is affected by the conversion of the soul. As the Holy Spirit permeates the human spirit, it spills over into the soul, and man's personality softens and begins to produce a loving nature. As the soul changes, the body is then renewed and healed as the faith of the man or woman grows.

TODAY'S SCRIPTURE

"Commit your way to the LORD; trust in him and he will do this: He will make your righteous reward shine like the dawn, your vindication like the noonday sun" (Ps. 37:5-6).

TODAY'S PRAYER

"The Bible says if I commit my way to You, that You will act if I trust in You. Some of the affairs of my life are in a really bad place. I am choosing today to trust You to bring Your righteousness and Your justice to all the problems in my life."

TODAY'S JOURNAL QUESTION

What can you commit to God today?

DAY FOUR

FEELINGS

Emotions and feelings have tripped me up in life. So many times, I have stuffed in a feeling and did not know how to get it out. I have learned a few lessons about emotions and feeling. I have learned my emotional self needs to understand my true feelings. All of us have emotions. Even the most stoic are emotional. I have a friend who has told me for years she was stoic, but I have never agreed with her. Her emotional self is supercharged with emotions, but she attempts to show no external actions which we relate to feelings.

Crying is a type of action related to feeling in our culture. Laughter is a feeling action. In other cultures, the actions of feelings are minimized and often ridiculed. Therefore, I believe emotions and feelings are two slightly different things. For example, you don't say a person hurt your emotions, but that they hurt your feelings.

Let's look at what I call the emotional self. The emotional self is developing at birth. There are classic emotions that belong to each one of us, simply because we are made in the image of God—emotions such as love, a sense of belonging, satisfaction, anger, hatred, loneliness, and others. As babies, our emotions are God-given. We are meant to experience emotions through a God-filter, but we don't because we live in a lost and fallen world. Our emotional self gets hidden behind a myriad of explosive external actions of feelings. I have raged when my emotional self was afraid. I have cried when my emotional self was angry. I have laughed when my emotional self was embarrassed.

Jeremiah said, **"The heart is deceitful above all things and beyond cure. Who can understand it" (Jer. 17:9).** I interpreted this verse to mean that feelings are fickle. They are changeable and unsteady. Feelings can be interpreted according to the circumstances of life. I can be angry one minute and happy the next. My feelings cannot be trusted, especially in a season of growth or change. My emotional self may be my true self; but with my feelings being so fickle, I do not know what my emotions are. Am I content or discontent? Am I loving or hating? I have learned to examine my feeling actions to determine my emotions. We have to get to know our emotional self.

Back to my stoic friend. She refused to let her emotional self-emerge because of fear of vulnerability. She had learned as a child to protect herself by showing no outward sign of her internal feelings. But her "truth-lie" had surrounded her for most of her life; and, to face God, the truth would cause her to sometimes release a tear because she is emotional, or her body would shake with anxiety because she had for years hidden her true, emotional self. We must know our emotional selves and make our feelings line up with that self, or we will have a breakdown—a breakdown in self-communication and a breakdown in communication with God and others.

Feeling Action Phrase	Emotional Self Words
I hate you.	Lonely, selfish
I love you.	Fearful, abandonment
I am mad.	Selfish, needy

These are just examples of the "feeling action phrases" we use, but they do not reflect our true emotional self. Take some time to review the "feeling actions" you have experienced this week and ask yourself if this the way you truly feel. Is this representative of your real emotions? You may find that your feelings are fickle and cannot be trusted until you are sanctified to God for full restoration.

TODAY'S SCRIPTURE

"The Lord saw how great the wickedness of the human race had become on the earth, and that every inclination of the thoughts of the human heart was only evil all the time" (Gen. 6:5).

TODAY'S PRAYER

"Lord, I am finding out I don't know my emotional self. I am also finding out my feelings are fickle and that I can't trust them. Please open the eyes of my heart, so I can see myself and know my true emotions."

TODAY'S JOURNAL QUESTION

What are some of the most common feelings you have in a day? Are these feelings reflective of your true emotional self?

DAY FIVE

DELIVERANCE

"But because my servant Caleb has a different spirit and follows me wholeheartedly, I will bring him into the land he went to, and his descendants will inherit it" (Num. 14:24).

Moses led the Israelites to the edge of Canaan, or the Promised Land, after the exodus from Egypt. Moses chose twelve spies from the tribes to go and see what the land looked like and to bring back a report to the people. All of the spies gave a good report about the land. They all agreed that the land was flowing with milk and honey. They brought evidence of the vast wealth of the Promised Land. There was no doubt that the land they were headed to was better than where they were, but there was one problem—there were giants in the land. The giants were so big, the spies said that it made them look like grasshoppers to the giants.

Caleb and Joshua agreed with the report, except Caleb had a different spirit. He followed God wholeheartedly. He and Joshua tried to convince the people that the Promised Land was worth the fight, but the people would not fight. They did not believe that God could help them, so they rebelled and refused to go.

God told Moses that only two people from that generation would enter the Promised Land. Caleb and Joshua would enter into what God promised because they believed God would continue to deliver them from their enemies.

But what can go into the Promised Land? Two things can get you to the Promised Land of remission from drugs and alcohol. That is a saving faith and a call for help. *Joshua* means "salvation." Joshua himself could not save the people, but his faith in Jehovah saved himself and others many times. This must go into the Promised Land. *Caleb* means "yelping." A yelping dog will bring its owner running, and Caleb's yelping brought God to his side immediately. Faith in Jesus Christ will sustain you through the many battles of claiming a new life for yourself, along with your continual crying out for help from Him.

NAMES OF GOD

I AM

When Moses was in the desert tending to sheep, the Lord appeared to him in a burning bush. Moses was instructed by God to go to Egypt and bring His people out of bondage. Moses wanted to know who was sending him into Egypt. What was God's name? God told Moses to tell Pharaoh that He was "I AM," and there was no other god before Him (Exod. 3:14).

When you come to the Old Gate and work to restore your belief in God, you, too, must know Who it is that is sending you and Who it is that will be taking care of your life. Who is this God that you must turn your will and life over to? The answer is the **I AM**, the Alpha and the Omega, the Beginning and the End. He is the source of all life. He was the beginning, and He will consume the end. This is the God Who sent Jesus, His only Son, to redeem you from the weight of sin.

PRAYER FOR THE I AM

"You are the great I AM—all that I need. You were the great I AM when I started this journey. You were the great I AM when I needed Your help to continue this journey. You are still the great I AM in my life today, and I thank You for that. Praise Your Name that You are the great I AM."

TODAY'S SCRIPTURE

Whoever dwells in the shelter of the Most High will rest in the shadow of the Almighty. I will say of the LORD, "He is my refuge and my fortress, my God, in whom I trust." Surely he will save you from the fowler's snare and from the deadly pestilence. He will cover you with his feathers, and under his wings you will find refuge; his faithfulness will be your shield and rampart.

You will not fear the terror of night, nor the arrow that flies by day, nor the pestilence that stalks in the darkness, nor the plague that destroys at midday. A thousand may fall at your side, ten thousand

at your right hand, but it will not come near you. You will only observe with your eyes and see the punishment of the wicked. If you say, "The LORD is my refuge," and you make the Most High your dwelling, no harm will overtake you, no disaster will come near your tent. For he will command his angels concerning you to guard you in all your ways; they will lift you up in their hands, so that you will not strike your foot against a stone. You will tread on the lion and the cobra; you will trample the great lion and the serpent.

"Because he loves me," says the LORD, "I will rescue him; I will protect him, for he acknowledges my name. He will call on me, and I will answer him; I will be with him in trouble; I will deliver him and honor him. With long life I will satisfy him and show him my salvation" (Ps. 91).

TODAY'S PRAYER

"You are my Refuge and my Fortress. I trust in You, God. You will deliver me from the snare of the fowler and from any deadly disease. I will not fear for the terror at night nor the arrows that fly by day. Though a thousand will fall by my right hand, I will not fear because You will keep me standing. No evil will ever befall me, and no disease will come near my house. Because I hold fast to You, You will deliver me. You will be with me in trouble; You will rescue me, and I will be satisfied with a long life."

TODAY'S JOURNAL QUESTION

What is it that you fear most about believing in God?

DAY SIX

RESTORING A RELATIONSHIP WITH GOD
THROUGH YOUR BASIC BELIEFS

The Old Gate of the city of Jerusalem was on the western side of the city. It was thought to be the oldest gate of the city and may have been originally built by the Jebusites, who occupied the city before King David made it the Holy City. The city represented the heritage of the peoples of Jerusalem. For hundreds of years, people from every tribe and nation came into Jerusalem. There would have been no reason for King David to destroy the gate. He used what was there as part of his defense system.

The Old Gate was also called the Jeshanah Gate. It had stood for many years. Rebuilding it would remind them that their heritage was important, bringing protection to the city instead of destruction. The sons of the original builders of the gates of Jerusalem helped in rebuilding this gate. They were the sons of Levi—the first group of priests to minister to God. Biblical traditions, morality, and humanity were rebuilt here.

Restoring a relationship with God will include rebuilding your basic beliefs. Basic beliefs are those beliefs that are central to your makeup. Such beliefs will include what you believe about God, family, community, yourself, and others. At this gate, you need something to hold onto. It is where faith in God is established, and your will or decisions are turned over to God's care. At this gate, you must restore the things of God to your life. At this gate, you must restore truth—the never-changing truth of God.

This is week three of your restoration plan. You may be feeling a little overwhelmed with the newness of recovery. This reminds me of the story of the children of Israel as they began to walk over the sands of the desert in search of a new home. They were hot, tired, and scared of the new enemies they faced. They had little water, and they were struggling. The memory of Egypt was so tempting. They forgot the hardness of the life of brick-making and building for Pharaoh. All they could remember was the taste of onions and sweet water. They only remembered the times when the families celebrated with feasts. The Israelites wanted the familiar, regardless of the cost. They wanted to go back to where they came from.

You may want to go back. Nobody ever told you that the way to freedom was hard. They only told you that freedom was good. Well, it doesn't seem so good right now, stuck in the limbo of the desert. So, what can you do to continue the journey? You can submit.

You have got to be kidding, you may be thinking. You may still be in the pre-contemplation stage of thinking about thinking about changing. That sounds redundant, but reread that statement. "Thinking about thinking about changing" is a very real stage of change. Somebody else has thought about you changing, but now you are being forced to think about it.

The one thing about the gates of Jerusalem that many forget is that all the gates were being rebuilt at the same time. It took fifty-plus days to rebuild all the gates. The rebuilders worked side by side and took no breaks until the work was completed. They did whatever it took to get their city protected. It is the same thing that must be done as you work to rebuild your life. You must be willing to work diligently on the restoration plan until recovery is well-established.

A new lifestyle cannot be segmented into individual areas to work on at one time. The parts of our lives intersect and overlap. While we are trying to correct one area, that area affects other areas. For example, when a person goes on a diet, she stops eating certain things and begins eating different foods. While she is dieting, she will notice her moods change. How much time is left on her hands changes. She may notice her wardrobe needs to be adjusted. With the wardrobe change comes financial considerations. The diet has affected every area of her life. Such is the way of recovery. You will want to be mindful of these effects. The heart change is one example of the lifestyle changes which can become overwhelming to the early recovering person.

This heart change comes to you as you meet God through Jesus Christ. In your heart or spirit, you decide, and then the remaining restoration is restoring yourself to yourself, to others, and to the community. The feeling of excitement may hit you as your heart lifts from accepting Jesus, but everybody will not feel the same as you do. You will face distractions and obstacles. This will force you to look at your old values, traditions, and new values. So, with the heart change will come decisions to change to God's morals.

With the restoration of the Old Gate, traditions, values, and morals are restored. Considering God's morality, His traditions, and His values help you to restore a broken relationship with Him. Through the belief in Jesus Christ as your Savior, you are now open to building a trusting and caring relationship with Him through accepting and participating in the traditions of God, rather than the traditions of man.

TODAY'S SCRIPTURE

> **"The LORD is with me; I will not be afraid. What can mere mortals do to me? The LORD is with me; he is my helper. I look in triumph on my enemies. It is better to take refuge in the LORD than to trust in humans. It is better to take refuge in the LORD than to trust in princes" (Ps. 118:6-9).**

TODAY'S PRAYER

"Are You really on my side? Can I really trust You? Man has done a lot of terrible things to me. Were You there to help me then? Can I really take refuge in You? Speak to me in a way that I can understand. I want to believe."

TODAY'S JOURNAL QUESTION

What are the questions about God that hinder your belief?

DAY SEVEN

WORSHIP/STYLES OF MUSIC

Music is a tool for entering into the worship of our Lord. There are many genres of music for Christians to enjoy. The style is basically a personal preference.

Contemporary style is the current popular Christian music. I believe we base a lot of what we listen to in contemporary services by hearing music on the radio stations. Secular styles are often copied in the Christian music industry to increase familiarity. However, the similarity of styles may be a hindrance to really worshipping God. The mind can associate the rhythm of the song with a past memory, and you can end up thinking about the past, instead of concentrating on the Lord.

Southern Gospel is a type of country music with Christian words. Again, the rhythm and the style can carry you back to other times if country music is what you are accustomed to. The same thing is true of Gospel or Blues.

Christians can choose Christian rap, Christian rock, and even Christian heavy metal. All of these styles will depend on your personal listening preference. Listening to Christian music in your vehicle, at work, or during other times will not always mean you are worshipping the Lord.

One current trend is to use standard hymns with a new musical style. The words are the same, but the arrangements are more current for this generation.

When I discuss worship music, I include any style which takes you into the presence of the Lord, away from the past life mistakes, and brings about healing of the mind, the body, or the spirit. Worship should always point you toward Jesus. It is a time set aside to embrace an intimate knowledge of Jesus as the real and living God.

Once again, worship puts you in the presence of God. Isaiah described his encounter with God in the Temple in Isaiah chapter six. He said the Lord's train **"filled the temple" (Isa. 6:1)**. Isaiah was overcome with the glory of God and fell face first to the floor. The reverence of the holiness of God is a part of worship. Worship music must point us to His reverence and holiness and not just be a feel-good moment of relaxation.

Experiment with various genres and arrangements until you find a musical tool for meeting Jesus in an intimate relationship.

TODAY'S SCRIPTURE

"In that day you will say: 'I will praise you, LORD. Although you were angry with me, your anger has turned away and you have comforted me. Surely God is my salvation; I will trust and not be afraid. The LORD, the Lord himself, is my strength and my defense; he has become my salvation'" (Isa. 12:1-2).

TODAY'S PRAYER

"I will give thanks to You, O Lord, for though You were angry with me, Your anger has turned away, and You comfort me. I will trust and will not be afraid, for You are my Strength and my Song."

TODAY'S JOURNAL ASSIGNMENT

Write a prayer to God about what you believe.

CHAPTER SEVEN

INSPECTION GATE: GATEWAY TO RESTORING SELF

"Next to him, Malkijah, one of the goldsmiths, made repairs as far as the house of the temple servants and the merchants, opposite the Inspection Gate, and as far as the room above the corner" (Neh. 3:31).

"Examine yourselves to see whether you are in the faith; test yourselves. Do you not realize that Christ Jesus is in you—unless, of course, you fail the test? And I trust that you will discover that we have not failed the test. Now we pray to God that you will not do anything wrong—not so that people will see that we have stood the test but so that you will do what is right even though we may seem to have failed. For we cannot do anything against the truth, but only for the truth. We are glad whenever we are weak but you are strong; and our prayer is that you may be fully restored" (2 Cor. 13:5-9).

DAY ONE

GRACE AND CHOICES

"In the paths of the wicked are snares and pitfalls, but those who would preserve their life stay far from them" (Prov. 22:5).

Life has a way of teaching us lessons. We don't have to be rocket scientists to learn these lessons; we only have to pay attention. One such life lesson came to me not too long ago. Actually, it is a lesson that has been ongoing for the past several years, except part of the saga ended, and the other part continues. I just want to tell you the facts of the story and then, perhaps, relate the story with a spiritual understanding. You may not even agree with my conclusions, but that's okay; this is my lesson.

Two women were born into southern families and were taught southern values. These southern values translated into Protestant church attendance, gracious manners, and hospitality to everyone. They attended their local high schools, fell in love with their high school sweethearts, got pregnant, and had babies. If you think this sounds like a Lifetime movie theme so far, well, you haven't heard anything yet.

Both babies—one a boy and one a girl—were with their mothers at first, and then the story changes. Both women were estranged from their southern values, except for the hospitality, and both adopted new values, which included drugs and alcohol. Both were looking for acceptance. Both hard-working women tried to regroup from the feelings of rejection and loneliness. Each nurtured her baby—one not quite as often as the other, but still nurturing, still loving.

Both in their mid-twenties, still searching for love, they dropped a little deeper into the alternative values that were so different from their southern values. Both went deeper and deeper into the drug culture. One chose street drugs; one chose prescription drugs. Both types of drugs were deadly, and both drugs were capable of robbing a woman of her husband, her dignity, her child, and herself.

That is when I met them. They both ended up at my door in 2002 looking for something. They were looking for some way to keep using drugs and hold onto all they had—children, husband, lover, home, self. That is what every addict is looking for, by the way. None of us ever really wants to give up the drug. The drug has become everything to us—our best friend, our day-to-day existence. Once we are hooked, it takes something extremely powerful—something like a new love, something like change—to unhook the hook of drugs.

In 2002, both these women showed up at Bethesda Recovery. It is amazing that, as I look back at the pictures, the women were not only emotionally similar, but their body structures were, too. They even both wore their hair in a short cut. You may say this means nothing, but, remember, this is my lesson. We were doing some street ministry at the local park, and both women came forward at different times to repent and give their lives over to Jesus Christ. They both sang. After submitting to the rules and getting sober, they would sing to the crowds at the park on Fridays and, sometimes, on Sunday at church. Everything looked good.

Both of the women left about the same time from Bethesda—one living there about eleven months and the other only three. The one leaving after eleven months told me she had "done her time" at Bethesda. That was a prison term, "doing time." You see, this woman had been in prison and had chosen it for her lifestyle. She had gotten caught in her mess, the mess of living for drugs. She felt she had paid her debt herself. Grace and mercy, the new love which we often talked about, was foreign to her. The other woman I sent home. She was so afraid that she would lose everything if she went home too soon, but she had three little children and a husband at home to care for. She wanted to go home—don't get me wrong—but did she have enough of this new love to keep her from the old hook?

One laughed. One cried. One packed all her stuff in the car of her boy-friend, took her kitten and said, "See you later." One cried all the way home, wondering if she and her husband would make it.

Both of these women had the same life issue. They both had to decide to stay sober, but the truth is that sobriety is hard to get. Paul says that we should want to apprehend what has apprehended us—namely the love of God—but the truth of this Scripture was perverted by the devil. **Philippians 3:12 (KJV)** says, **"Not as though I had already attained, either were already perfect: but I follow after, if that I may apprehend that for which also I am apprehended of Christ Jesus."** These women were, indeed, trying to apprehend what had apprehended them (drugs), but that would never work. They would have to learn the difference of apprehending love or life and apprehending evil or death. You can apprehend death because it will wait for you to catch up and even turn and overtake you. Love will apprehend you; but the apprehension of love builds you, while the apprehension of evil kills you.

It wasn't long before the apprehension of evil showed up. It just showed up in different places. One of the women went to work; another went back to jail. The one in jail got out of jail, and then back again, and, finally, she went to prison once more. The one thing I've learned about prison is nobody wants to stay there. She got out of prison, vowing never to return.

The one at home went back to work with a friend, who was safe from drugs. She went to her home church and faced the music of what she had done to herself, her friends, and her family. She asked for forgiveness and, somehow, she got it. She never had to pay her debt to society. She let Jesus do that for her, and, somehow, He did. Somehow, though, she forgot it.

Four years after they left Bethesda Recovery, I heard from both women. Finally, I heard from both women's families. One woman's son, whom I had never met face to face, showed up on Sunday afternoon. He asked if I was Cathy Sweat, and I said yes. He told me his mother had been killed in an automobile accident and asked if could he come in for a moment. With tears and extreme grief, he said, "I want you to know that she was clean and sober. The coroner said there were no drugs of any kind. I wanted you to know that. Thank you for all you did for my mother; you meant a lot to her. I always thought I would find her in a ditch somewhere or killed by a dope dealer or dead of an overdose. I believe my mother finally got it right. They say she was baptized a few days ago and had asked Jesus into her heart. I believe God was waiting on her to get sober before He took her."

What do you say to that? Of course, I know all the appropriate pastoral comments to make. But what do you really say to that, knowing what I know? More than once, I have heard these comments about a mother—a family so hurt by past behaviors that when the mother died of anything other than suicide or a drug overdose, their immediate relief was that God waited until He saved them from that awful fate.

Grace is a strange commodity. What I learned that day is that even in death, grace is present. This young man was so full of grace for his mother because God was full of grace for him. In his heart, the Lord had given him an answer to prayer. That prayer was that his mom would not die high. And he was right. God had been full of grace for his mother, too. His mom did not want to die high, and, in the moment of death, she wasn't. She had a chronic habit and only very short times of abstaining from her drug of choice. Grace . . . Grace . . . Grace . . . .

A few days later, my husband ran into the father of the second woman. He, too, had news of his daughter. She was in a poor, foreign country, helping to build churches with her husband and daughter, when her husband fell from a ladder and broke his arm. He returned to the United States, while she and her daughter stayed to complete the assignment for the poor churches there.

How can this be? Two women, similar backgrounds, similar problems, almost equal in gifts and talents that end up with two entirely different legacies? What happened to the one? What happened to the other? How can the stories be so alike and, yet, so different? Grace happens because it was His marvelous grace operating in a third-world country that helped the other woman, too.

The second came by to see me, and I let her read this story. "Do you really think we are that much alike?"

"Yes. This what I believe the Lord showed me."

It was only later that I really knew how much they were alike in their addiction, too. The other woman's husband stopped in to see me one afternoon. His wife was using again. How could this be? She was just in a foreign country, sharing Jesus. I have learned that your heart can be in one place and your addictions in another. You can love Jesus and pills. Addiction does not care if you are in ministry. Addiction doesn't care if you love Jesus. Addiction cares about addiction.

Grace and choices—it is God's grace which keeps our choices from death. We make our own choices each day to attempt to define our independence, but it is God's grace that keeps us alive long enough to meet Him and really choose Him. Choices are good if they are the right choices moving us toward love and life; but when we make bad choices, thank God for His grace.

KEY TO RESTORING SELF

You choose self-control. It is true that you have lost control over your drug of choice, but you still have control over your choices. Use this key to develop self-respect and responsibility.

ACTION STEPS

- Complete a timeline of the major events of your life. The timeline of where you have been will show you the person you have been. Making choices to grow will expose the new you to yourself and others.

- Set goals for the next ninety days. Break the goals into three major time frames. These goals should relate to your emotions and your spiritual growth.

  1. Set short, attainable goals with measurable results. These goals need to be simple and related to your new identity. For example, set a goal to learn Scriptures concerning who God says you are.

  2. Set a one-year goal, a second-year goal, a third-year goal, and a fourth-year goal. The goals for one year should be related to your identity and new lifestyle.

  3. Set a five-year projected goal for your future. This goal should be a picture in your mind of how your new life should be.

- Write a letter to yourself to encourage yourself as to where you are in your life plan.

PRAYER FOR RESPONSIBILITY

"I have refused to accept responsibility. I have chosen my own path. I have neglected my responsibilities to myself, my family, and my friends. I have not listened to anyone, except the ones I chose. Today, I know that those I chose to listen to were wrong. I need authority in my life, so I can learn responsibility. Help me to choose to come under authority in my life today. As I pray for the authority over me, soften my heart and make me pliable in Your hands.

"Help me to respect those who have taken responsibility for their lives and who have authority. I choose to pray for leaders in government because they have responsibility to do the next right thing for You and Your people.

"The government of our land needs Your help today. The powers You have set in place are as they should be. No one has power, except You give it. Today, give those in power over me wisdom and knowledge in all the decisions they make.

"Today, I especially ask You to bless our President, the Cabinet members, those in the House of Representatives, and the Senate. Give them understanding of every bill before them. Help them to always honor the Ten Commandments in their decision-making. Protect the judicial branch of our government from corruption, O Lord. Help the Supreme Court judges to see Your ways.

"Bless the judges who have authority over the cases pending in my life and the lives of my loved ones today. Give them wisdom to know when to give mercy and grace and to whom mercy should be given. I pray for mercy in the lives of those in recovery as they face court decisions. Bless the mayor and the city and county commissioners as they go about their daily lives. Give wisdom to the schoolboard as they administer rules over our children. Place those who have been saved and who know Your voice in positions of leadership in the schools. Make me to be a person of honor and responsibility like Daniel in this day."

IDENTITY

Restoration to self or self-recovery is difficult, at best. For one thing, self-recovery is convoluted because you only have the self you have now. But the self that is to be recovered is the self God intended for you to be from birth. You will have to search for that self. You do not know that self. In fact, if you ever thought of that self, it was long ago. The recovery of self is not going to be instantaneous. It may take a long time. You will begin to recover the first part of the self God wants you to be by honestly getting to know the self that you are now.

Identity starts with personality. No two people are alike, but all of us have similarities. So many studies of personalities divide humanity into four or five categories. Sometimes I think we put too much emphasis on the manmade theories of personality and not on what the Bible says. **"For just as each of us has one body with many members, and these members do not all have the same function, so in Christ we, though many, form one body, and each**

member belongs to all the others. We have different gifts, according to the grace given to each of us. If your gift is prophesying, then prophesy in accordance with your faith" (Rom. 12:4-6).

Paul says we are all individuals with many different gifts. We may have similar gifts, but there will be a uniqueness to each one of us as we begin the recovery of self. These personal preferences are a part of the basic person. Some like to be outspoken, some soft-spoken. Some like reading; some like working with their hands. What do you like? Don't be surprised at this question. We often don't know what we like.

In recovery, you have to learn your preferences. Sober likes are not the same as the preferences you have when you are sick, sad, lonely, or depressed. Also, your tastes change. You begin an adventure of discovery of likes and dislikes. You try different things. You experience different things. You learn about different things. As you do these things, you are learning about your personhood and developing your personality.

Emotions make up our personhood. In a negative lifestyle, emotions can be supercharged or lulled to sleep. I have known many women in both situations. Both types of emotional development can stunt the growth of the new self. Emotions are not to be in charge. They are a thermometer, determining the temperature of your passion. The temperature can then be evaluated to allow your emotions to simmer down. What you have thought about yourself may be totally wrong because your emotions have not been checked.

The mind is also a part of your personality or identity. What you think about is very important. As you think about your thoughts, you can determine if the thoughts are helping you find yourself or helping you bury yourself. Think on things that are positive and are of a good report to change a negative brain (Phil. 4:8). Focus on the positive, and the brain will change.

"Before I formed you in the womb I knew you, before you were born I set you apart; I had appointed you as a prophet to the nations" (Jer. 1:5). God speaks to Jeremiah in this verse to let him know He had designed him for a specific task. Since God is not a respecter of persons, we surmise God designs us all for a specific task. Our personalities and our identities are made for the tasks we are assigned to. How important it is that we know ourselves, so we can get ready to fulfill our tasks.

TODAY'S SCRIPTURE

"Whoever conceals their sins does not prosper, but the one who confesses and renounces them finds mercy" (Prov. 28:13).

TODAY'S PRAYER

Prayer of St. Francis of Assisi

"Lord, make me an instrument of Your peace.

Where there is hatred, let me sow love;

Where there is injury, pardon;

Where there is doubt, faith;

Where there is despair, hope;

Where there is darkness, light;

Where there is sadness, joy.

"O Divine Master, grant that I may not so much seek to be consoled as to console,

To be understood as to understand;

To be loved as to love.

For it is in giving that we receive;

It is in pardoning that we are pardoned;

And it is in dying that we are born to eternal life."[22]

TODAY'S JOURNAL QUESTION

List the authority figures in your life today. How do you show these people respect?

---

22 "Peace Prayer of St. Francis of Assisi." In Catholic News Agency, http://www.catholic-newsagency.com/resources/saints/saints/peace-prayer-of-st-francis-of-assisi (accessed July 23, 2017).

DAY TWO

SELF

Self—what do we know about it? It is indeed mysterious. "Who am I?" is a question people have asked throughout time. Knowing self is part of the very first sin of Adam. When the serpent tempted Adam and Eve, the temptation hinted that they could be someone else other than who they were. "You can be like God," the serpent promised. This timeless question centers on accepting so much about God, about others, and ultimately about what your role in life is.

Discovering who you are takes inspection. It is an inspection of your failures, accomplishments, your pasts, and your futures. You will explore the design of God for your life and build boundaries to protect self that will allow you to grow to be the person you were intended to be. The boundaries that you have allowed in your life have not accomplished very many good things. At this junction, you will tear down and build up. You will tear down those walls that have kept you bound to negativity and build up the walls and gates for positive and healthy lifestyles.

The Harvest Gate was also known as the Miphkad Gate. *Miphkad* in the Hebrew language means "numbering, a mandate, and an appointed place."[23] You now begin numbering or naming your achievements and failures. This is a mandate if you wish to move forward in recovery. At the appointed place, which in the Word of God implies a specific place for a specific purpose, you will offer these achievements and failures to not only be recognized but also to be surrendered. When you have completed your inventory of your gifts and flaws, you will find someone to share these with. As an act of contrition, you can burn them and symbolically destroy these flaws.

Remember when the walls and gates of Jerusalem were being rebuilt that everyone was working on all the walls and gates at one time? You may focus on one at a time for rebuilding, but do not lose what you have gained, or your life will be ravaged by the enemy at your weak spot.

---

23   Fountaingate Loaves and Fishes. "Destiny of the Church: The Gates of the City (Part II)." Churchlink.com. http://www.churchlink.com.au/churchlink/bible_studies/dotc/dotc6.html (accessed October 25, 2017).

It is so important to continue to stay in reality as you inspect your life. As you say "I need help," looking to God because God can help, you can say, "I can believe the truth about myself in my past and in the future." Without the help of God, you will not be able to honestly look at where you have been and where you are going. As your relationship with God builds from reality to authority to a new belief system, you can say, "I can look at myself with forgiveness, having received the forgiveness of God." There will be no need to look at self until you have admitted that you need help, committed your life to God, and submitted in belief. Without God, you will see your achievements with pride and refuse to look at your failures. Or you will look at your failures and be stuck there forever. These gates of reality, authority, and beliefs need to be well-established as you try to inspect self.

Let's look at the accomplishments of your life to begin with.

- What would you say is the greatest good that you have ever done?
- When have you known that something in your life was really good?
- Who has contributed the most to these accomplishments and good things?
- What are some of the good things you like to do which don't cost any money?
- Where have you travelled?
- What schools have you completed or attended?
- What rewards have you received?
- What do you like about yourself?
- What is one thing that you would like to change about yourself that is in your power to change?
- What is the one single thing you have done that haunts you?
- What is the one thing that someone has done to you that haunts you?

AN HONEST EXAMINATION

No matter how terrible your life has been, there have been some good times. You must make an inventory of the good as well as the bad. You must look at what can be salvaged and what must be thrown away.

Again, this will take some time, so don't get in a hurry. If you start, you will soon discover the inventory evokes emotions and memories that sometimes have been lulled to sleep by addiction. The period of time when the emotions are half-asleep and half-awake can be very uncomfortable. When your physical leg has fallen asleep and begins to awaken, you feel all the nerve endings and almost wish the leg would remain asleep. But, of course, you know better. You can't walk with your leg asleep. You allow the leg to get fully awake in order to better utilize the leg.

TODAY'S SCRIPTURE

"When I was a child, I talked like a child, I thought like a child, I reasoned like a child. When I became a man, I put the ways of childhood behind me" (1 Cor. 13:11).

TODAY'S PRAYER

Prayer to Restore Basic Trust

"Lord, I confess I do not trust. The lack of trust has permeated my life and hindered me. I know I must forgive. I choose to release the anger and bitterness I have toward You, Lord, for putting me in the family that You did. Heal the wound that my distrust of You has caused to our relationship. Help me see You and know Your faithfulness. Touch my eyes that I may see clearly. I ask You to build in me what has not been there. I forgive my parents, Lord, for the wounding they caused me. Heal those places in my spirit so that I can be free to have a relationship with them again. I forgive my siblings, authority figures, and friends who hurt me. Even though some of these wounds were made in ignorance or innocence, they still hurt. Finally, please forgive me for judging You, Lord, and my family for determining not to trust. I confess my need for trust and my inability to build it myself. I need Your help. Help me not to run or hide when love comes close. I ask You to build and restore and, with it, restore the years the locust have eaten."

TODAY'S JOURNAL QUESTION

What do you have authority over in your life today?

DAY THREE

THE MIND, BODY, AND SPIRIT IN ADDICTION

The brain is made of cells, and, for our purposes, we will look at nerve cells, or neurons. Nerve cells communicate in the brain through synapses. At each synapse, communication takes place when one cell releases a chemical called a neurotransmitter. This impulse is received in another cell known as a neuroreceptor. Neuroreceptors are also sensitive to chemicals that circulate through the bloodstream. The delicate balance between the cells is critical, and, when the balance of one group is affected, this affects the larger systems of the brain. The actual physical chemistry changes in the cell in addiction (any type of habitual behavior, including repetitive thoughts) as the cells adapt to whatever chemical is introduced to the body. As a very simplified example, we will look at what happens when a person takes a sedative.

Cell A has a primary function of stimulating Cell B whenever more alertness is called for. To do this, Cell A releases neurotransmitter chemicals to Cell B's neuroreceptors, which will, in turn, send the message out to other cells. When you are ready to rest, Cell A calms down, transmitting less, and so Cell B is receiving less and also calms down. Everything is in balance at this point. Something happens in your life—some type of stressor occurs—which causes your agitation levels to increase. Cell A is working overtime and keeps sending transmitters when you are ready to sleep because it has been over-stimulated. Cell B will send some type of feedback to Cell A, realizing it is time to rest, and, eventually, Cell A will decrease in activity.

If you decide to help this process along by taking a sedative, the ability of Cell A to transmit is interfered with. Cell B, realizing there is something wrong, sends feedback to stimulate Cell A. The sedative has done its work, however, and Cell A cannot respond in its natural way, and so sleep comes. If this occurs only infrequently in someone, the body will correct itself, return to its natural balance, and adjust. However, if you continue to take the sedative, Cell A begins to adapt and quickly builds tolerance.

In the meantime, since Cell A is sending out less neurotransmitters, Cell B adapts by building more receptors and increases the sensitivity of them. This creates a whole new balance. Cell A, used to large amounts of the chemical, now has none and begins to go crazy. It begins to manufacture and release excessive amounts of the neurotransmitter that has been stifled and sends them raging to Cell B. Cell B has grown numerous sensitive receptors and is totally overwhelmed, sending all sorts of insane signals on to the other cells. This, in essence, is withdrawal. Agitation is greatly increased; the heart beats faster; body temperature rises; muscles tighten; and there are cramps, twitching, and a racing mind. The battle of the will has begun.

DETOX

Detox is a shortened form of the word *detoxification*. The body goes through detoxification through a natural process of elimination, when a person makes a decision to get clean of certain chemicals, foods, or poisonous substances. Typically, we think of detox from sugar, alcohol, drugs, or allergens. However, detox is more than a physical aspect of recovery. Detox occurs in the thought patterns and also in the spiritual realm.

Let's consider the aspects of detox from the soul and the spirit in this section. If you consider detox as elimination, then detoxing the soul will be eliminating certain thoughts, feelings, and choices. When you eliminate your thoughts and change your choices, a space occurs. This space must be filled with new and positive information and experiences. While you are detoxing your thoughts, there will be a war in the mind—a struggle, if you will, which has both victory and defeat.

The old way of thinking is very difficult to break. The struggle will come in the form of loneliness, agitation, and frustration. It may also take the form of misdirected anger and confusion. Soul detox requires reading and studying new affirming materials. Watching and listening to positive television and radio will shorten the time of the soul detox. Like any other detox, the possibility of relapse is strong. The cycles of detox are three days, seven days, twenty-one days, and twenty-eight days. During a cycle, you can expect more intense negative thoughts and negative actions, which will carry you back to old patterns of behavior unless identified and dealt with.

Spirit detox is more about switching the headship of your life from self to God. This is a process of eliminating selfish activities. The problem with this is most of us don't know when we are being selfish. We have an idea that the things we do are special and loving. Expect spiritual detox to come in stages as you grow and develop your Christ-like walk.

TODAY'S SCRIPTURE

> **"Whoever conceals their sins does not prosper, but the one who confesses and renounces them finds mercy" (Prov. 28:13).**

TODAY'S PRAYER

> "Lord, Your Word says that my life can be transformed by the renewing of my mind, so help me to change my mind about authority. I have been rebellious toward Your Word and Your ways. Forgive me. Help me to establish boundaries that will restore my trust in myself."

TODAY'S JOURNAL QUESTION

How can you establish trust in yourself?

DAY FOUR

SIN/DISEASE CONCEPT

The New Testament has a list of deeds done in the "flesh," which are considered to be against the Holy Spirit of God; therefore, these things are sins done in deed.

> **The acts of the flesh are obvious: sexual immorality, impurity, and debauchery; idolatry and witchcraft; hatred, discord, jealousy, fits of rage, selfish ambition, dissensions, factions and envy; drunkenness, orgies, and the like. I warn you, as I did before, that those who live like this will not inherit the kingdom of God" (Gal. 5:19-21).**

Sexual immorality means to have sex outside of marriage, including before marriage. Sex with anyone or anything other than your spouse is often referred to as adultery. In today's society, pornography is such a common occurrence that we must add this to the list of sexual immorality. Cybersex is also sexual immorality.

Debauchery refers to unacceptable behavior—such as pornography, inappropriate language, or just moral filth. Debauchery is an old-fashioned word for lust or sensual desires.

Idolatry includes the worship of idols; it is a blind or excessive devotion to something or someone.[24] Sorcery is the use of power gained from the assistance or control of evil spirits, especially for divining or consulting of spirits.[25]

"Hatred or hate is a deep and emotional extreme dislike."[26] It can be directed against a certain object or class of objects. The objects of such hatred can vary widely from inanimate objects to animals, oneself or other people, entire groups of people, people in general, your existence, or the whole world. Hatred is often associated with feelings of anger and disposition toward hostility against the objects of hatred. Actions after a lingering thought are not uncommon upon people or oneself. Hatred can go as far as war or just a simple verbal outrage to even oneself committing suicide for they hate the world or

---

24   *The King James Bible Page, s.v.* "idolatry," accessed August 15, 2017, http://av1611.com/kjbp/kjv-dictionary/idolatry.html.

25   *The Free Dictionary, s.v.* "sorcery," accessed August 15, 2017, http://www.thefreedictionary.com/sorcery.

26   *Wikipedia, s.v.* "hatred," accessed November 10, 2017, https://en.wikipedia.org/wiki/Hatred.

whatever is bothering him/her enough to push the envelope. Hatred can be considered a disease and has been known to be a key when diagnosing anxiety, depression, and sex addiction.[27]

Contention is an act or an instance of striving in controversy or debate. It can include a striving to win in competition or a rivalry as well as an assertion put forward in argument.[28]

Jealousy is a secondary emotion and typically refers to the negative thoughts and feelings of insecurity, fear, and anxiety over an anticipated loss of something that the person values, particularly in reference to a human connection. Jealousy often consists of a combination of presenting emotions such as anger, sadness, and disgust. It is not to be confused with envy. Jealousy is a familiar experience in human relationships. It has been observed in infants five months and older. Some claim that jealousy is seen in every culture; however, others claim jealousy is a culture-specific phenomenon.[29]

Fits of rage, or *wrath*, is also included in this Scripture. *Thumos* is translated as "outbursts of wrath" (NKJV), "wrath" (KJV), and "fits of anger" (ESV) and is defined as "passion, anger, heat, anger boiling up and soon subsiding again."[30] William Vines defines *thumos* as "hot anger, passion."[31] This, too, is being condemned by the inspired apostle Paul in his letter to the Galatians. Are you ever guilty of this work of the flesh?

Selfish ambition is being too concerned with one's own welfare or interests and having little or no concern for others. It is a form of self-centeredness. Dissensions are disagreements, especially when leading to a quarrel.[32]

---

27   *Simple English Wikipedia, s.v.* "hatred," accessed October 25, 2017, https://simple.wikipedia.org/wiki/Hatred https://en.m.wikipedia.org/wiki/hatred.

28   *Merriam Webster Unabridged, s.v.* "contention," accessed August 15, 2017, https://www.merriam-webster.com/dictionary/contention.

29   *Dictionary.com, s.v.* "jealousy," accessed August 15, 2017, http://www.dictionary.com/browse/jealousy.

30   Carl Ludwig Wilibald Grimm, Joseph Henry Thayer, Christian Gottlob Wilke, Christian Gottlob. *A Greek-English Lexicon of the New Testament, Being Grimm's Wilke's Clavis Novi Testamenti*, tr., rev. and enl. by Joseph Henry Thayer. New York: New York American Book Company, 1889. 339. https://archive.org/details/greekenglishlexioogrimuoft.

31   William Edwy Vines, M.F. Unger, and W. White. *Vine's Complete Expository Dictionary of Old and New Testament Words*. Nashville: Thomas Nelson, 1984. 688.

32   *Bible Hub, s.v.* "selfish ambition," accessed August 15, 2017, http://biblehub.com/greek/2052.htm.

Heresy is the rejection of one or more established beliefs of a religious body or the adherence to other beliefs. Christian heresy refers to non-orthodox practices and beliefs that were deemed to be heretical by one or more of the Christian churches. Various Christian churches have also used the concept in proceedings against individuals and groups deemed to be heretical by those churches.[33]

Envy, also called invidiousness, is best defined as an emotion that "occurs when a person lacks another's *(perceived)* superior quality, achievement, or possession and either desires it or wishes that the other lacked it."[34] Envy can also derive from a sense of low self-esteem that results from an upward social comparison threatening a person's self-image; another person has something that the envier considers to be important to have. Bertrand Russell said, "Envy is one of the most potent causes of unhappiness. It is a universal and most unfortunate aspect of human nature because not only is the envious person rendered unhappy by his envy, but also wishes to inflict misfortune on others."[35]

Murder is the unlawful killing of another human being with "malice aforethought,"[36] and, generally, this state of mind distinguishes murder from other forms of unlawful homicide, such as manslaughter. As the loss of a human being inflicts enormous grief upon the individuals close to the victim, as well as the fact that the commission of a murder is highly detrimental to the good order within society, most societies both present and past have considered it a most serious crime worthy of the harshest of punishment. In most countries, a person convicted of murder is typically given a long prison sentence, possibly a life sentence where permitted; and in some countries, the death penalty may be imposed for such an act.

Drunkenness or *alcohol intoxication* is a physiological state that occurs when a person has a high level of ethanol (alcohol) in his or her blood. Common symptoms of alcohol intoxication include slurred speech, euphoria, impaired balance,

---

33   *Bible Study Tools, s.v.* "heresy," accessed August 15, 2017, http://www.biblestudytools.com/dictionary/heresy/.

34   Bertrand Russell. "Envy." *The Conquest of Happiness.* New York: Liveright, 1996. 67.

35   Ibid.

36   *Wikipedia, s.v.* "murder," accessed November 12, 2017, https://en.wikipedia.org/wiki/Murder.

loss of muscle coordination (ataxia), flushed face, reddened eyes, reduced inhibition, and erratic behavior. In severe cases, it can cause coma or death.[37]

All of these above actions or "works" are addictive in nature. The evil aspects of these behaviors can be habitual, thus causing your flesh or human nature to continue doing the behaviors past their intended results. You might say you "have" to continue doing these behaviors as a compulsion, or you do them impulsively, looking back and wondering how you could ever have done such a thing.

We contrast these works with the fruit of the Spirit. Fruit is produced by mature trees planted in a specific place, at the right time and for the right purpose. When you accept Jesus, a seed is planted by the Holy Spirit in your human spirit. By allowing the Holy Spirit to grow up in you, He produces His fruit of "love, joy, peace, patience, kindness, goodness, faithfulness, gentleness, self-control" (Gal. 5:22-23). These characteristics are produced by the Holy Spirit working in and through your life.

The works of the flesh are work-related. The flesh yearns to do what it wants to do and will therefore work diligently to get it.

TODAY'S SCRIPTURE

"May these words of my mouth and this meditation of my heart be pleasing in your sight, LORD, my Rock and my Redeemer" (Ps. 19:14).

TODAY'S PRAYER

"Taking responsibility and accepting authority are very difficult for me. I choose today to accept my responsibility for my actions and choose to submit to Your authority in my life."

TODAY'S JOURNAL QUESTION

Who do you trust and why?

---

37 *Wikipedia, s.v.* "alcohol intoxication," accessed August 15, 2017, https://en.wikipedia.org/wiki/Alcohol_intoxication.

DAY FIVE

DELIVERANCE

The twelve spies who were called out to take a look at the land of Canaan were representatives of each of the twelve tribes of Israel. Israel was the new name that God gave to Jacob after he wrestled with the angel of God and was forever changed. Jacob, once known as "the deceiver," would from that day forward be known as Israel or "God perseveres." God will persevere in taking Israel into Canaan despite flawed thinking.

One of the spies who was afraid to go into Canaan was Shammua, which means "renowned."[38] Fame is a more modern term for his name. A fame-seeker is self-centered, always seeking to find a way to become more famous. Shammua must have been so proud that he was chosen to go to spy out Canaan. He would be assured of fame because of that trip. He was a fame-seeker.

Fame must die before you can enter into the Promised Land. Some women come to Bethesda thinking that once they are sober, their story will be the one everyone wants to hear. What they do not understand is that almost every story is the same. Fame cannot be an avenue for sobriety. A few may become famous, but only a select few. This walk of deliverance is not for the fame-seeker, who wishes to get his or her name on the front of some clinic or recovery house. Fame won't enter into the Promised Land.

Shaphat means "judge."[39] Judging the intentions of others is one of the easiest things the recovery community falls into. How one dresses, talks, walks, behaves, or seeks God is no one's business but the one doing it. Judgment is God's business. Unforgiveness in the lives of people in recovery will not enter into the Promised Land of full deliverance. Judging those that hurt, harm, or show indifference by passing sentence on them in one's mind will only stop progress. As you continue in recovery, you will find that judging and notoriety are two character defects to eliminate from your life.

---

38   *Strong's Exhaustive Concordance, s.v.* "Shammua," accessed October 9, 2017, http://bible-hub.com/hebrew/8051.htm.

39   *Abarim Publications, s.v.* "Shaphat," accessed October 25, 2017, www.abarim-publications.com/Meaning/Shaphat.html.

NAMES OF GOD

Jehovah means "Lord Almighty." He is the Lord, and He must be your Lord. He is Master and Leader.

He is "Master of my righteousness," *Jehovah Tsidkenu*.[40] He becomes my Righteousness as I believe in Him. His righteousness is imputed to me by the death and resurrection of Jesus.

Jehovah Mekoddishkem means "He is Lord and master of my sanctification."[41] I am sanctified, or set apart, for God through believing in Jesus.

NAMES OF GOD PRAYER

"You are *Jehovah Tsidkenu*, my Righteousness. And I praise You that no matter how I have messed up in the past, Your righteousness became mine when I received the Lord Jesus Christ as my personal Savior. I praise You that today I don't have to measure up to anyone or anything but You. I praise You that You see the Blood as You look at me today.

"You are *Jehovah Mikaddesh*, my Sanctifier, and I praise You that you are setting me apart for Your service. I thank You, Lord Jesus, that You sanctified me with Your blood and Your death. I praise You that no longer do I have to seek the approval of men because You have sanctified my very being, and every action now is set apart by Jesus."

TODAY'S SCRIPTURE

> **"Who were building the wall. Those who carried materials did their work with one hand and held a weapon in the other, and each of the builders wore his sword at his side as he worked. But the man who sounded the trumpet stayed with me" (Neh. 4:17-18).**

---

40   *Hitchcock's Dictionary of Bible Names, s.v.* "Jehovah Tsidkenu," accessed October 25, 2017, https://www.biblestudytools.com/dictionary/jehovah-tsidkenu.

41   *Blue Letter Bible, s.v.* "Jehovah Mekoddishkem," accessed October 25, 2017, https://www.blueletterbible.org/study/misc/name_god.cfm.

TODAY'S PRAYER

"I choose to trust You, Lord Jesus. I do not understand Your ways because Your ways are above my ways. I do not have to understand to trust. I can choose to trust You, and I do choose to trust You now."

TODAY'S JOURNAL QUESTION

In what ways can you respect God's authority in your life?

DAY SIX

RESTORING A RELATIONSHIP WITH SELF

William Shakespeare said, "To thine own self be true" (*Hamlet*, 1.3.78). The Inspection Gate was known as the Miphkad Gate or "the place of the appointment." Temple servants and merchants restored this gate. They were well-acquainted with the need for a gate which held merchants accountable. It was here that the temple materials were counted during King David's reign. King David was the greatest king of all Israel.

As you might expect, the people at this gate inspected all the wares, materials, and items used in the temple. They were accountants. The temple servants may have helped to repair this gate.

In your spiritual life, you inspected or took account of what was going into your life and what was going out. After a few weeks of detox, your mind begins clearing from the fog. Most of the hardest part of detoxification is over, but you may not be ready to face all the reality that sobriety brings.

In the recovery work of restoring a relationship with God, you have to look at something outside yourself to help get your mind back. That something turns out to be God. He began a work that He will continue until you reach heaven. Now you must look inside yourself for restoration. First, you look up; now, you look in. It may be more difficult to look in than it was to look upward.

When I say "restoring you to yourself," I am really referring to the work of forgiving yourself. If you will be honest, the first three gates helped you let go of the anger and bitterness you have felt toward God for not being Who you wanted and expected Him to be. You have always wanted God to be the God of your understanding, and then you find out that in order for Him to really help you, you need to see Him as the God of the Bible. You must "forgive" or let go of your preconceived ideas of Him and then ask Him to forgive you for thinking that you know better than He does.

You have to forgive yourself for being a "bad" person and accept yourself for the "good" person that you are. This can take some time, so be prepared for a few days of inward inspection and a few days of emotional upheaval. It may take more than a week to really look at yourself. It may take years. Nevertheless, let's begin now.

When I say "good person," I mean the good behaviors, not the ability to be "good" like God. The "bad" person means the bad behaviors that are done. The Bible doesn't use the term "self-forgiveness." In fact, the Bible only refers to self when speaking of God. Self-forgiveness is a manmade term and has become a major focus for recovery. I believe the self-forgiveness comes from repentance. Godly sorrow, the deep knowing that your sin has cost others, brings change from your sin. That means you don't do it again. Repentance removes the shame. Restitution removes the guilt feelings.

You may feel as though you can't make up for the things you have done, but you can. Forgiveness is a gift you receive from God and then give yourself, but it is not a gift you constantly need to look at. Receive it; give it; and let it go. Turn your attention to others, and soon you won't remember what you have done in the past.

Doing a moral inventory, therefore, begins as you make a list of your good morals, as well as bad. Morals are another way to express boundaries. Boundaries are how far we have gone, or how far we won't go. As you make a list of your boundaries, you are also taking an inventory of your gifts, your talents, your abilities, what you have wasted, what you have abused, and the things you have failed to use.

No matter how terrible your life has been, there have been some good times. You must make an inventory of the good, as well as the bad. You must look at what can be salvaged and what must be thrown away. It is so important to continue to stay in reality as you inspect your life. As you say, "I need help," looking to God because God can help, you can say, "I can believe the truth about myself in my past and in the future." Without the help of God, you will not be able to look at where you have been and where you are going in an objective way. As your relationship with God builds from reality to authority to a new belief system, you can say, "I can look at myself with forgiveness, having received the forgiveness of God."

There will be no need to look at self until you have admitted that you need help, have committed your life to God, and have said, "God can help." Then you submit by saying, "I can believe." Without God, you will see your achievements with pride and refuse to look at your failures. Otherwise, you will look at your failures and be stuck there forever.

As the gates of Jerusalem were being rebuilt, there was unrest from the enemies of the city. Nehemiah faced continual assault from Sanballet and Tobiah. The assault was so oppressive that the people had to hold a weapon in one hand and work laying bricks with the other. Nehemiah refused to come down off the wall. Determine for yourself that you will not stop rebuilding your life until it is secure. Many people will not understand your determination. Some will even try to stop you, but you must continue the inspection and continue to rebuild each area of your life until you have a new life.

TODAY'S SCRIPTURE

"My son, keep your father's command and do not forsake your mother's teaching" (Prov. 6:20).

TODAY'S PRAYER

"Lord, I accept my family for the gift that You meant them to be. I forgive them because they did not do the things I thought they should do for me. I pray that You will forgive me for dishonoring my parents. I pray that You will forgive me for not listening to them when they knew best for me. I ask You to help me forgive my parents for all that they did against what the Bible says parents should do. Today, I choose to forgive my parents for the things that I believe caused me to turn to drugs and alcohol. Although I do not believe they are responsible in my logical thinking, my emotions seem to believe that they could have done something to prevent this from happening. I am choosing to take full responsibility for my addiction and my recovery. By forgiving my parents, I take the blame off them and place it where it belongs—on me. I choose to honor them from this day forward by not cursing them with my words or disrespecting them to my friends and family members."

TODAY'S JOURNAL QUESTION

Describe your relationship with your parents. Do you trust them?

DAY SEVEN

WORSHIP LEADERS

Worship leaders lead worship. They are not to be idolized or worshipped. They are just like the rest of us, except they have a gift to lead worship, and we have other gifts. Congregations look to the worship leaders to get them revved up for the service, but the truth of the matter is that that is not their job. Their job is to worship God themselves. Satan looks for ways to distract congregations from entering into worship. He will cause the worship leader to appear in a way that makes the people fall in love with the worship leader instead of God. It is our responsibility to turn our eyes to Jesus and follow the leading of the worship leader. Prepare yourself for worship by focusing on Jesus. Of course, we can admire the gift the worship leaders have, but the admiration of the gift should never turn into worship of a man rather than Jesus. Praise teams are extensions of the praise leader. Again, they are pointing us to Jesus and not to themselves.

TODAY'S SCRIPTURE

"Do not take revenge, my dear friends, but leave room for God's wrath, for it is written: 'It is mine to avenge; I will repay,' says the Lord" (Rom. 12:19).

TODAY'S PRAYER

"Lord, today I choose forgiveness. I choose to forgive those who have hurt me, and I choose to forgive myself for hurting others and myself. I choose to begin fresh today with hope and a clean slate. Let there be nothing between You and me. Thank You for the authority figures in my life. Thank You for everything they have tried to teach me. Thank You for rules and boundaries. Thank You for law enforcement. Thank You for judges and lawyers. Thank You for Your authority in my life. Thank You that You are helping me to surrender to the authority in my life."

TODAY'S JOURNAL QUESTION

What have you learned this week about taking authority and accepting responsibility?

CHAPTER EIGHT
FOUNTAIN GATE: GATEWAY TO RESTORING TRUST

"The Fountain Gate was repaired by Shallun son of Kol-Hozeh, ruler of the district of Mizpah. He rebuilt it, roofing it over and putting its doors and bolts and bars in place. He also repaired the wall of the Pool of Siloam, by the King's Garden, as far as the steps going down from the City of David" (Neh. 3:15).

"Therefore confess your sins to each other and pray for each other so that you may be healed. The prayer of a righteous person is powerful and effective" (Jas. 5:16).

DAY ONE

THE CHASE

The crimson pool was real blood. The face of the man was her husband. The shrieks, shrills, and wails of unbelief were coming from her. It was her voice, her husband, his blood. The knife belonged to her lover. Her lover stood over the lifeless body of her husband. This could not be happening. She had never meant it to go this far. She had only longed for the chase. She had only longed for the excitement of being the object of two men's affections. But now, slumped over the body of her dead husband and carrying a child by one of the men, she turned her thoughts to herself and her pain. She was the victim here. What was she to do now?

As the sirens blared louder and louder, she began to drown in her sorrow. Blood was everywhere—on the ground, on him, on her protruding stomach. The scene was burned on the wrinkles of her brain. She was the victim. It was their fault. They both had left her standing in the middle of the parking lot, alone and pregnant.

She (names are always withheld to protect the source) loved the idea of pursuit. She even loved the idea that God pursued her. She often romanced the Song of Solomon as a song to a "lover" that God pursued. She was the one that God would rescue. "God loves to rescue us," she would tell me. It was just such a love of being chased that ended the life of her husband that dreadful day in the parking lot of the community store.

She had let it out of the bag, so to speak, that she might be carrying another man's child. "It simply slipped out," she confessed. She never really meant for her husband to try to find the man. But he did. It was that fateful day when she sent her husband to the store. Her husband had threatened to kill the man. That was so exciting for her. She never really believed that he would kill the lover, and she was right. The lover killed her husband.

The two saw each other on the highway. Their anger raged, and one car passed the other, almost drag racing. That is what witnesses said. Finally, they both ended up at the community convenience store. Both jumped out of their cars—one with a knife and one with only his fists. Her husband probably intended to teach this guy a lesson and then let it be. But the lover was not in the mood to take a beating. He came ready to take care of business.

The fight lasted only seconds, both men stunned at the reality of death. The eyes of the dead man told of his surprise, and the frozen shock of the lover told of his surprise.

The chase ended badly. She was left the victim of their refusal to continue to chase. She never really wanted to be caught because the chase was so much fun.

I chased her once. She had fled her home, left her children, and disappeared, leaving just enough clues for me to pursue. She knew I would chase her. She had worked her spell on me. I saw so much talent, so many gifts that could be used for the Kingdom of God. She knew my weakness for pursuing people for God's kingdom.

I took the bait. Brokenhearted for her, I chased her into a drug-infested area. I narrowed down the house she was in and made contact with the people inside. But to be caught was not enough for her. To be pursued by God's messenger and to be apprehended by His love was not enough. She ran, thinking I would continue the pursuit, but I did not. It was enough for me to find her. It was enough for me—and God—to let her go.

She told her story; she verbalized her life. She never confessed. She never agreed that her life was caused by her sin. She was the victim. In her life story, she said, "Why did God let this happen to me?" No amount of explaining that confession means to acknowledge sin and to own that sin would convince her to stop this insanity of wanting to be chased. She would tell her story over and over and never get relief.

She would share the gory details of her life and blame her lover or her husband for dying. I talked to her not long ago, and she begged me to chase her again. I told her no. "I need you," she said. But I told her no because deep down I knew that I would have to chase her. Chase her to stop using a different drug than what she said she was using. Chase her to comply with the rules of recovery. Chase her to tell the truth. I just couldn't chase her. She would have to continue her run with someone else. My chasing days ended that day in the trailer park when she hid herself in the trunk of a car, laughing at us as we desperately tried to save her life.

I learned the lesson of telling and not confessing. You see, you can tell your story and never confess your wrongdoing. You can tell it for many different reasons. You can tell it to get sympathy or support. You can tell it to manipulate or control. You can tell it to get money or drugs or to get out of trouble or many other reasons. But you can only confess it for one reason, and that reason is to lay it down. Once true confession is made for the wrongdoing in your life, you will never want to pick it up again. True confession is simply lining up with the Word of God that sin is sin, and you are the sinner.

ACTION STEPS

Decide to deliberately obey. Choose at least one difficult act of obedience and do it with all your heart.

Write on an index card how you are making changes.

For example: I see change in me in this area:

1.

2.

3.

Make a thanksgiving prayer journal. In this journal, list all the things you have to be grateful for today.

PRAYER AT THE FOUNTAIN GATE

DAILY PRAYER FOR THE WEEK

"By Your stripes, I am healed, and it is only by Your stripes, Lord, that I receive true healing. So many of my friends and family members need spiritual healing, physical healing, and emotional healing. I am realizing more and more that You alone can bring this healing to them.

"My heart needs healing today from the emotional trauma of my life. Like the Bethesda pool, trouble the waters so that I might find healing here today. Stir up those things that I have held pressed down in me that others see and I feel but won't admit. Heal my heart today.

Help me to remember the things that need to be confessed to You and to another human being. I need to confess the sins of my past, so I can be free to change. Heal those wounded from incest in this community. Heal those scarred by rape in this community. Heal those physically sick in this community. Heal those hearts who feel abandoned in this community today. Heal those who have pain."

TRUST RESTORED PRAYER

"Lord, Your Word declares You are trustworthy and faithful. The heavens declare Your power and majesty. The works of Your hands are made known to all mankind. I declare to You, Lord, and to myself, that You are trustworthy and dependable to me. I can count on You. I have not been able to count on myself, but I choose today to count on You. Honestly, Lord, I don't know what trusting You will look like, but I am, by faith, believing You will show me. Lord, help my unbelief."

TODAY'S SCRIPTURE

"When anyone becomes aware that they are guilty in any of these matters, they must confess in what way they have sinned" (Lev. 5:5).

TODAY'S PRAYER

"Lord, I confess to You that I am afraid. I have been afraid for a long time. Fear is always near. I am learning that to trust, I must have someone in my life that is trustworthy. Help me today to know who is trustworthy and who is not."

TODAY'S JOURNAL QUESTION

Why is it important to confess your faults to another human being?

DAY TWO

CONFESSION

The trust factor blocks your way and stands as a major hurdle to overcome in recovery. You have broken trust with others, and others have broken trust with you. Trust is healed by confession. You may be wondering how trust can be restored through confession. After all, doesn't confession mean telling all your dirty secrets? Confession seems, at first, the very opposite of restoring trust. However, as you study confession and basic trust, you will begin to realize that open and honest confession heals the emotions and opens the door to building trustworthy relationships. Basic trust is a feeling of security.

Basic trust is built into a child by nurturing love given by both parents. The father's love forms the foundation for trust in a child. Babies who are swaddled and then cuddled by loving parents rarely find it hard to freefall into the arms of the father or mother. This freefalling exhibits the security felt by the child with the adult. It is only after that trust is broken by another that the secure child or adult feels emotionally spent. You may have seen or experienced a trust exercise by allowing another adult to catch you as you fall backwards. This is just one example of trust-building. If a baby has limited nurturing by both parents or if a parent is absent for any reason, basic trust will most likely be an issue for life, unless, as an adult, basic trust is restored.

> "Basic trust is first built into a child by nurturing love given by both parents, but especially by the father."

When basic trust is a problem for a child, many emotional issues will develop as he grows older. Poor self-esteem, inferiority, superiority, poor relationship-building skills, and many other problems can develop as a result of broken trust. At this point in recovery, there is a desperate need for healing of the emotions.

Let's talk about this Fountain Gate and its historical location to help us get a picture of the healing process. It was at this gate that the Pool of Siloam was located. Jesus healed a blind man by telling him to wash in the pool of Siloam. This pool at the Fountain Gate was the only fresh supply of water inside the city. This spring, which fed the pool, was called the Virgin Spring and would supply the drinking water for the city in times of enemy attack. Jesus said that "rivers of living water will flow from within [our hearts]" (Jn. 7:38). The emotional healing you receive would be a fountain, or life stream, for others. Symbolically, as the truth of God flows into you, you get the watering of the Word of God. As the Word churns around in your mind, it begins to cleanse you. Over time, the watering transforms you, and you are to go and share the Good News.

TODAY'S SCRIPTURE

"'Only acknowledge your guilt—you have rebelled against the LORD your God, you have scattered your favors to foreign gods under every spreading tree, and have not obeyed me,' declares the Lord" (Jer. 3:13).

TODAY'S PRAYER

"Lord Jesus, I want to acknowledge my sin. I have sinned against You. I have failed. I desire to be free from the guilt of my sin. Help me, Jesus, to have the courage to look at my life."

TODAY'S JOURNAL ENTRY

Write about a time when you know that you sinned against God and give details.

DAY THREE

SIN/DISEASE CONCEPT: HOW THE PHYSICAL BODY IS DAMAGED

It is true that the brain is diseased in addiction. Other organs, as we have seen, are harmed by various drugs, alcohol, and other behavioral addictions.

Drinking too much alcohol can lead to three types of liver conditions: fatty liver, hepatitis, and cirrhosis. For all types of liver disease caused by alcohol, the main treatment is to stop drinking alcohol completely. The following is a list of various physical problems caused by drinking too much. (Drinking too much would be considered drinking more than one drink for women or two drinks for men a day.)

- Serious liver problems, as well as some stomach disorders
- Mental health problems, including depression and anxiety
- Sexual difficulties, such as impotence
- Muscle and heart disease
- High blood pressure and damage to nerve tissue
- Accidents (About one in seven road deaths are caused by drinking alcohol.)[42]
- Some cancers—such as the mouth, liver, colon, and breast
- Obesity (because alcohol has many empty calories)
- Damage to an unborn baby in pregnant women
- Pancreatitis, which is severe inflammation of the pancreas
- Acute Pancreatitis: this condition occurs when the pancreas becomes quickly and severely inflamed. The major causes are heavy alcohol ingestion, drugs, and other factors. Binge alcohol drinking is a common cause of acute pancreatitis.
- Kidneys: Both acute and chronic alcohol consumption can compromise kidney function, particularly in conjunction with established liver disease. Investigators have observed alcohol-related changes

---

42   National Institute on Alcohol Abuse and Alcoholism. "Alcohol Facts and Statistics." NIH.gov. https://www.niaaa.nih.gov/alcohol-facts-and-statistics (accessed August 15, 2017).

in the structure and function of the kidneys and impairment in their ability to regulate the volume and composition of fluid and electrolytes in the body. Chronic alcoholic patients may experience low blood concentrations of key electrolytes, as well as potentially severe alterations in the body's acid-base balance. In addition, alcohol can disrupt the hormonal control mechanisms that govern kidney function. By promoting liver disease, chronic drinking has further detrimental effects on the kidneys, including impaired sodium and fluid handling and even acute kidney failure.[43]

- Esophagus: Alcoholism damages the mucous membranes (mucosa) at the junction of your stomach and esophagus. Even small amounts of alcohol can increase the production of gastric acid. When alcohol is abused, these increases in acid can damage the mucosa of your stomach, which leads to a condition called gastritis. The list of potential problems in the stomach and intestines is a long one, mainly because alcohol acts as a poison to the human body in anything over the recommended dose of one drink a day for a woman or two drinks a day for a man.[44]

WORD STUDY

Confession

Confession means to agree with the word of God about sin. *Homologeō* is the Greek word, which is translated in Acts 24:14 as "confess or admit."

"However, I admit that I worship the God of our ancestors as a follower of the Way, which they call a sect. I believe everything that is in accordance with the Law and that is written in the Prophets" (Acts 24:14).

As you begin to write out your confession and then decide to share it with someone else, it will be good to learn the foundational truths about sin in the

---

43   Murray Epstein. "Alcohol's Impact on Kidney Function." NIH.gov. http://pubs.niaaa. nih.gov/publications/arh21-1/84.pdf (accessed August 15, 2017).

44   Drug/Alcohol Abuse Rehab Centers. "The Effects of Alcohol Use." Drugabuse.com. http://drugabuse.com/library/the-effects-of-alcohol-use/ (accessed August 15, 2017).

Word of God. You will not be able to completely confess until you know the whole counsel of God. Do not be dismayed with this. You will simply find that as you grow in the knowledge of what the Word of God says about sin, you may need to confess again and again. No one can understand the magnitude of sin or the role it has in everyday life at the beginning of recovery. You can confess only what you recognize as wrong. As you grow in the love of God, you will begin to recognize other sins you may have committed but did not realize that they were wrong at the time.

Confession is necessary now, and it will be necessary in the future. I have heard it said that we should keep "short tabs" with God. This is a great way to keep everything upfront between you and God. This gateway to restoration of trust can only be rebuilt through vulnerability. "Vulnerability refers to the susceptibility of a person, group, society, sex, or system to physical or emotional injury or attack. The term can also refer to a person who lets their guard down, leaving themselves open to censure or criticism. Vulnerability refers to a person's state of being liable to succumb to manipulation, persuasion, temptation, etc."[45] This definition may seem harsh and unappealing, since much of addiction has put you in a very vulnerable state already. Vulnerability, in the sense of confession, is, in reality, a state of honest openness.

One great benefit to honest confession of sin is the reduction of guilt and shame. Personal hiding with the shame of the past sets a person up for emotional, physical, and spiritual pain. Those suffering from shame caused by real guilt or false guilt can be riddled by depression, mood swings, fear, anxiety, and other mental disorders. They can also have back pain, stomach ulcers, and several other physical manifestations which are directly or indirectly linked to the guilt. Spiritually speaking, a person who is burdened down with guilt will often stay away from others who are seemingly more spiritual or who are "right" with God. The personal guilt drives a wedge between man and God.

Adam and Eve, when they felt guilt, covered what they considered their sin and hid from God. God came near to them, regardless of their shame, but they were reluctant to face God. That is the way it is with us when we have

---

45   *SensAgent. s.v.* "vulnerability," accessed November 12, 2017, http://dictionary.sensagent. com/Vulnerability/en-en.

something in our lives we know God would not be pleased with; we begin hiding immediately. Then, after the hiding, when God comes near to us by sending others, we push them away, driving a greater wedge between us and God. Confession removes the wedge and clears any barrier that exists between us and God.

TODAY'S SCRIPTURE

> **"And they will go to others and say, 'I have sinned; I have perverted what is right, but I did not get what I deserved. God has delivered me from going down to the pit, and I shall live to enjoy the light of life'" (Job 33:27-28).**

TODAY'S PRAYER

"I confess my sin of lying today. In my addiction, I have lied about everything. I have lied about who I was going to be with, where I was going to be, and how much drugs or alcohol I was doing. I have lied to my parents, my friends, my family members, and, mostly, myself. I confess today that I am a liar."

TODAY'S JOURNAL QUESTION

What will change as you begin now to tell the truth about everything?

DAY FOUR

THE MIND, BODY, AND SPIRIT IN ADDICTION

In this week's work, we will attempt to show how the negative choices become death to us and how, without a complete change, the drug will creep up again and again in our lives. Many of us have said that something was calling our name. That something could be chocolate, alcohol, even a former boyfriend. How can this be when the natural part of the drug has long since left our bodies? Some have even admitted that a trip to a supermarket with beer and alcohol on the shelf could result in a mental battle for control. Some say that it is almost like a magnet pulling them to the aisle.

One woman said that on a trip to a local supercenter, she found herself just staring at the beer and almost reached to put some in the buggy before she realized what she was doing. An addict in open group said she was walking down the street and spied a bag of crack just lying on the ground. The woman decided to pick it up but declared that it would not cause her to fall. An explanation of this is the spiritual effect the negative lifestyle has on the individual. There are three aspects to this lifestyle, in my opinion, which make recovery very difficult. These are physical effects, emotional effects, and spiritual effects. Unless we accept the spiritual effects of the negative choices, we are all in for more trouble.

The first aspect is the physical, which has been examined in previous weeks. The second part is emotional, which is covered by the brain and the body at work together. There are emotional triggers of lifestyle, such as the love and friendship aspect of the choices. This is almost unexplainable. The spiritual aspect is the unseen and unexpected calling, the requiring and expecting to return to old habits. This hidden snag robs us of restoration.

Consider the meaning of the word *spirit*. For most people, the picture that comes to mind is ghostly, or something unseen. For the religious, a picture of something evil or something holy may find its way into your mind. Either picture is something obscure; you just can't put your finger on it. You must believe or not believe because a spirit cannot be touched with the human hand. The spirit of negativity can't be touched by human hands either. For example, a person may sit down in my office and say, "I am really serious about change, but something keeps taking me back." The negative spirit has a heavy weight still lodged inside of them.

When the urge or the "jonesing" starts, all the logical information, all the physical force, all the human thinking in the world will not stop you. Why? The spirit of the drug is overwhelming. There is nothing in the room that you can put your hands on, nothing physical anywhere close, but you "feel" the pull so strongly that nothing will stop it. For lack of a better illustration, a ghost of the past in thought takes hold of you and carries you back to that which you know. The familiar spirit has control. The only thing that will stop this spirit is a more powerful spirit within you. This is the Holy Spirit. Without Him, you can expect to lose, because negativity has a will of its own.

The will of a human being is the strong desire to do or be something, anything. When a person says, "I will," their every intention is to accomplish whatever it is which is willed. When a person becomes a Christian, his will has been given over to Christ. In a more concrete term, a written will gives the receiver rights to property once owned by someone else. The writer of a "Last Will and Testament" gives what he chooses to another. The writer of the will can only give what belongs to him away; he can't give something he doesn't own to anyone else.

In the same way, your will is given over to the negativity. The drug—some say without consent—takes over your spirit or will and becomes your center. The will of the drug is thus in place—driving, guiding, manipulating, and controlling your life.

A drug enters the body through the physical first, affecting the body with different symptoms as determined by the type of drug used. The body begins to feel the effects and begins to exhibit symptoms such as slurred speech, red eyes, or extra energy. Then the emotions get involved. Life seems to feel better. Depression leaves; anxiety is changed; the emotions react according to the type of drug being used. Finally, the spirit is affected. You lose your willpower, and a new power has found a resting place. The loss of will is quite subtle, almost sneaky. It is usually not until many years down the road that you have an idea that you can't just stop. You discover something is driving and pulling at you all the time. Though you may want to stop with your whole mind and heart, you will find that once a negative lifestyle has taken over your spirit, a fierce battle must ensue to stop the addiction.

"The spirit of man seeks to know the higher Spirit Which created him."

The spirit is the last major stronghold. You may white-knuckle the treatment and practically lock yourself in your room for a period of abstinence. Your emotions may be relieved by a change of people, places, and things, but your spirit can only be relieved by the one, true Jehovah God through His Son, Jesus Christ.

In every man, woman, and child is a desire to find the meaning of life. From infancy, in every culture known to mankind, there is a desire to find our Creator. Simply speaking, every baby wants his daddy and his mama. An adopted child seeks his or her true identity or their family of origin. The spirit of man seeks to know the higher Spirit Which created him—his Creator.

Because of the sinful nature of man and because of a separation from the truth of God since the Garden of Eden, man has tried various avenues to find the Spirit from which he came. If you consider this for a moment, the spirit of a negative lifestyle often becomes the substitute for God because this lifestyle is an instant relief for problems at hand. So, if the spirit of man, which contains what I have learned to call a "God-hole," is empty, why not begin to fill it with whatever spirit is available?

The only problem with filling the God-hole with drugs is that when that hole is not satisfied, the drugs have become a god to the addict and, therefore, hard to get out of the place where Jesus needs to be. This is where the spiritual fight continues. Often, people get the outer understanding of God in the physical. They attend church, pray, preach, and do all the things good Christians do. They often get emotional under submission and change their love for one thing to the love of another, but the spirit of the very thing that continues to haunt them has not changed. How in the world can a person with the spirit of a drug controlling their God-hole ever expect to get relief?

The ability to become free of anything is in the belief of a Spirit Who is able to do more than that thing can. The spirit of negativity works in the dark hole of lies and half-truths. It has no power in the open or in the light of truth. Once you expose the drug's spiritual hold on you to God or to another person, the hold diminishes.

There is a practical way to live as an overcomer. Each morning, each moment sometimes, remember what Paul said, **"I have been crucified with Christ and I no longer live, but Christ lives in me" (Gal. 2:20a).** Say to yourself each step of the way, "I am dead to the demands of my flesh and the spirit of this drug and alive unto Christ, who is not bound by chemicals or addiction."

There is a war going on in your God-hole once you have decided to change. The person you want to be is yelling at the old person you don't want to be. The old versus the new. The war intensifies when you accept Jesus because the spirit of the drug knows what you do not—that Jesus is stronger than any negative source. When He is completely allowed to fill our lives with His love and mercy, there is no place left for the negativity. To change your will requires total submission to the will of God.

When a foreign spirit has taken over your will, you must regain your own will from the drug or behavior of choice by submitting to God and then giving over your own will to God for redemption. We say no to the desire to stay the same and yes to the new idea of being different.

The way to change results is through salvation. Confess that you are a sinner and that the sins you have committed have been against man and against God. Repent of your sins, and stop running *from* God and start running *to* Him. Believe in the changing power of Jesus, and you will begin the long road to recovery.

You may have a hard time surrendering because you don't know what your new life will look like. During a meeting one night, I looked at the group and asked, "What does recovery look like to you?"

One man said, "I do not know what it looks like because I have never been recovered."

I have thought of this man often. How can he get to where he is going without a clue or picture of what it looks like? It will take a blind faith to make a change for him because he sees what a life of addiction looks like. Like it or not, it is something he recognizes. I think this man was hopeless to the possibility of change. Can we draw a positive picture of recovery for those who have no picture? What does recovery look like? What does change look like?

TODAY'S SCRIPTURE

"Then Joshua said to Achan, 'My son, give glory to the Lord, the God of Israel, and honor him. Tell me what you have done; do not hide it from me'" (Josh. 7:19).

TODAY'S PRAYER

"Lord, hiding things from people has been a way of life for me. Help me today not to hide my negative ways and the evil things I have done to You."

TODAY'S JOURNAL ENTRY

Write a story about a time in your life when you lied and hid something from someone because of drugs or alcohol.

DAY FIVE

DELIVERANCE

Our minds are filled with misconceptions about God—from the idea that God is a Santa Claus, Who gives good little boys and girls toys, to the harsh Judge who is waiting to strike a death blow for some unknown offense; these misconceptions make deliverance from life's hard issues almost impossible.

The church is filled with varying opinions about deliverance. Some groups are offended to think that one of "theirs" would need deliverance. Some groups think all of "theirs" need deliverance. Some think that only those who are not in their group need deliverance. Some are looking for demons behind every bush, and others are not looking for demons at all. Some believe that the only deliverance the Bible talks about is the deliverance from the influence of Satan's imps. Some believe the deliverance found in the Bible was only for that time. The church has no true consensus about deliverance. In recovery, there is not a single, indisputable answer about deliverance either. Some groups believe "once an addict, always an addict." Some groups believe that addicts are changed and healed and never return to their addictions.

After being with many women in addiction and watching the changes that come, I do believe there is a deliverance from addiction which is much like the deliverance from Egypt the Israelites experienced. Here's what I mean. When the Israelites were in Egypt, they were enslaved by a very strong and powerful force called the Pharaoh. That Pharaoh controlled every aspect of life for the Israelites. He employed Egyptians to keep that control enforced day by day and moment by moment.

The Israelites realized the need to break free from the power and cried out to God for help. God sent a deliverer named Moses, and the work of breaking free began. Moses did not just walk into Egypt and tell the Israelites to pack up their belongings and leave the Pharaoh. Moses had a specific plan of action, which included convincing the Israelites to follow him out of Egypt and breaking the stronghold of Pharaoh.

After the Israelites left Egypt and the power of the Pharaoh, Pharaoh pursued them. With the wisdom and power of their new, God-ordained leader, Moses, the Israelites crossed the Red Sea and entered into the wilderness.

What happened in the desert is very important. Leaving Egypt is only the beginning of deliverance; getting to the Promised Land is the final chapter of deliverance. So many Israelites never made it to the Promised Land. Groups announce that to stop drugging or drinking is deliverance, but the work of true deliverance has only begun.

There are many reasons the Israelites didn't make it to their promised destination. As we have looked in past weeks at the twelve spies, we have discovered just some of the reasons why they didn't make it. These same problems exist in the lives of addicts who will never make it to the land of freedom from addiction.

In your life, a very strong and powerful force takes control of every aspect of life. That strong and powerful force is negative. You employ many things to keep your life in control. Attitudes, life values, friends, and normal life issues are all employed by the addiction to keep you in control. This is a very powerful force, which makes it very hard to resist the power of the addiction.

Igal and Palti were two more spies who didn't think they could face the problems of going into the Promised Land. *Igal* means "He will redeem" or "He will liberate."[46] In our day, we think that if we do enough right things that God will liberate us. This is bargaining. Bargaining cannot enter into the Promised Land. Bargaining with God by doing good does not work because we cannot do enough good to make up for the wrong we have done. Bargaining partners with perfectionism. As we bargain with God, we attempt to be perfect, but our efforts fall short. When this happens, we strike another bargain, and the cycle continues. Trying to do everything perfectly will never be good enough. That is why Jesus died for us. He was the only perfect Lamb.

Palti means "whom Jehovah delivers."[47] If you dig a little deeper you find that the suggestion of running is implied or the thought of slipping out. They

---

46   *Strong's Concordance*, s.v. "Igal," accessed October 25, 2017, http://biblehub.com/hebrew/3008.htm.

47   *Hitchcock's Bible Names Dictionary*, s.v. "Palti," accessed October 25, 2017, https://www.biblestudytools.com/dictionary/palti.

who run away from God will never enter into the Promised Land. They must run to God and never away from responsibility or accountability.

NAMES OF GOD

"So Gideon built an altar to the Lord there and called it The Lord Is Peace" (Judg. 6:24a).

Build an altar in your heart today, for the Lord is Peace. In a frightening time, Gideon recognized that God could give him peace. Gideon lived during a time of war. He hid in order to have food for his family. In fact, the angel of the Lord found him threshing wheat in a winepress, fearful for his life. The angel told Gideon he was a mighty man of valor, but Gideon didn't feel very courageous. When Gideon finally realized who it was who spoke to him, he built an altar and received peace that God had his back.

The names of God revealed His character. He was *Jehovah Shalom*[48] to Gideon in a time of war and later revealed Himself as "the God who is there" to Ezekiel.

"And the name of the city from that time on will be: 'THE LORD IS THERE' (Ezek. 48:35b).

NAMES OF GOD PRAYER

"You are *Jehovah Shalom*, my Peace, and I thank You that in the stormiest times of my life, You have been peace to me. I thank You that You are my peace today—no matter what things look like, feel like, taste like, or smell like. No matter what people say, You are Peace to me.

"You are *Jehovah Shummah*, my God of now and my God Who is here in the midst of everything—both good and bad. You are here, and now, when the bills need paying, You are here. And now, as I go about my daily chores and take care of my business and my relationships, I thank You that You are here."

---

48   *Easton's Bible Dictionary, s.v.* "Jehovah-Shalom," accessed August 16, 2017, http://www.bi-blestudytools.com/dictionary/jehovah-shalom.

TODAY'S SCRIPTURE

"Whoever conceals their sins does not prosper, but the one who confesses and renounces them finds mercy" (Prov. 28:13).

TODAY'S PRAYER

"Jesus, I want to prosper. I want to have Your mercy. I am choosing to not cover my sins, and I am choosing today to forsake them one by one."

TODAY'S JOURNAL ENTRY

Write about the times you received mercy and did not deserve it.

DAY SIX

THE BRAIN ON DRUGS

This is a personal testimony of how I learned that drugs affect the brain. My sister had a stroke. It was a mild stroke, which happened one afternoon at her work. She began acting strangely, and I was called to see if I could tell what was happening to her. She was very agitated and very confrontational. Her personality was changed. She had a terrible headache. She calmed down when I began talking to her and trying to convince her that she needed help. She refused. I was convinced that something was going on with her physically, but I could not convince her to go to the doctor.

She, evidently, began to "feel better," but her personality and the way she walked were different. She ran into doorways; she talked out of her head; she had significant mood swings. After a few days of this, she finally was diagnosed as having had a stroke in the midbrain area.

What I noticed in my sister's behavior was very similar to what people experience as they begin to get sober. Norma Jean, my sister, had to relearn some vital and important activities. She had to, as I learned later, reroute her brain around the injury.

In prayer, I asked the Lord to show me if this was what happened to those in addiction. A few weeks passed, and a community-wide seminar on drugs came to Waycross. I attended the seminar called "Hijacking the Teenage Brain," sponsored by the Georgia Council on Substance Abuse and conducted by Merrill Norton R.PH, NCACII, CCS. After the training of that seminar, I continued to study, via video, *From Disgrace to Grace: Contempt Prior to Investigation*, also by Dr. Norton and the Georgia Council on Substance Abuse.[49]

The brain is a complex organ. It controls every part of the body from breathing to kidney function to the feeling in your little toe. The brain is the head of the nervous system, including the peripheral nervous system. The central nervous system includes the brain and the spinal cord. The neuron is the basic communication unit of the nervous system. Neurons receive information from

---

49 Merrill Norton. "Clinical and Administrative Pharmacy," University of Georgia College of Pharmacy. UGA.edu. http://cap.rx.uga.edu/index.php/people/faculty/norton/chemicalhealthassociates.press (accessed November 10, 2013).

cells in the body, thus communicating to the brain what is actually going all over the body. Neurons are what help us to react to external changes. Dendrites are like little fingers that receive information from the body, and axons carry information from the neuron.

Let's talk about my sister's stroke again. She learned that her brain had become damaged by the stroke. She also learned that throughout her recovery, she would have to retrain her brain to work correctly. Her circuit pathways had been interrupted by the stroke, and now she would have to teach her brain to tell her body what to do and her brain how to think correctly by building a new pathway.

My sister found this out through her own stroke. She also found out more details as she helped her son recover from a massive brain bleed. When a person uses drugs, the normal pathway of the reward center is supercharged with dopamine. This dopamine is what causes a person to feel good. The brain is a quick learner. After just a few supercharged runs around the reward center with a drug boost, the brain forms a path of least resistance. The brain not only likes the new chemical boost, but it also demands it to make the run around the reward center pathway.

At one of the "curves" in the reward circuit is the brainstem. The brainstem is the place in the brain where all the involuntary activity of the body begins. The brainstem controls breathing, among other things. As the strong chemical boost continues, the brain not only demands the boost and enjoys the boost, it moves the memory into the involuntary brainstem. When this happens, the drug of choice becomes the drug of "no choice," and you don't seem to be able to feel or act normal without it.

Just like a stroke victim, you must learn a new way of life. You must teach your brain a new pathway around the reward circuit. In the meantime, while recovery is happening, about a million other things are going on in the brain. A brain that has been saturated with drugs or alcohol or behaviors that increase or deplete the dopamine will take much longer "sober" to create the pathways of recovery than it did to make the first "no choice" pathway.

How will this new rerouting of the brain be accomplished? It will be accomplished with intentional dedication to change. The stroke victim must learn to reroute the brain to carry on normal activities, such as walking, talking, and remembering. You must make a conscious decision daily to help the brains circuitry be rerouted. Relapse returns the brain to the old route, and, thus, the process must start all over again. The longer the drug use, the more entrenched the pathway becomes or the deeper the rut. The brain can develop new pathways, but it takes time and determined work. In other words, old habits die hard.

Did you know that the body has a bonding hormone? This hormone is what enables mothers to bond with babies and couples to bond together in a relationship. It is the feeling you get when you first meet somebody and know immediately they are "good people." This hormone is suspected to be the same hormone that causes us to love ourselves, love others, and love God. Isn't it just like God to hardwire us to be able to fulfill His commands to us? The Bible teaches us that we are to love God with **all [our] heart and with all [our] soul and with all [our] mind and with all [our] strength** and to **"love [our] neighbor as [ourselves]" (Mk. 12:30-31)**. This is just another example of science catching up with the Word of God.

In recent studies, according to Norton, scientists have discovered that we have a personal intrinsic pheromone (PIP) which is depleted in twelve months or less by abuse of drugs and alcohol. This is the first to go and the last to be restored.[50]

Because we are triune beings with body, soul, and spirit, this study helps us to understand the complexities of addiction and why we have not been able to pinpoint the exact cause and cure of this disease. People who have depleted their PIP are anti-social and anti-God and do not care enough about themselves to want to change. The physical aspect has affected the personality and spiritual components of the person. It may take as many as seven years for PIP to be restored. This is one of the problems in the church today; people are so altered by the misuse and abuse of their bodies that they cannot possibly have good relationships.

Norton says that Americans like chemicals so much that about fifty percent of us could be considered abusers of such chemicals if the *DSM-IV* criteria were

---

50   Merrill Norton. "Hijacking the Teenage Brain." Seminar, Georgia Council on Substance Abuse, Waycross, accessed February 7, 2008.

to be used.[51] This applies to those who are in church as well. **Psalm 139:14** says that we are **"fearfully and wonderfully made."** We are also told that our bodies are **"the temples of the Holy Spirit" (1 Cor. 6:19)**. It is time to recognize the importance of mind, body, and spirit in the healing process. You must learn how to take care of your soul, body, and spirit to be forever changed.

TODAY'S SCRIPTURE

Although our sins testify against us, do something, Lord, for the sake of your name. For we have often rebelled; we have sinned against you. You who are the hope of Israel, its Savior in times of distress, why are you like a stranger in the land, like a traveler who stays only a night? Why are you like a man taken by surprise, like a warrior powerless to save? You are among us, Lord, and we bear your name; do not forsake us (Jer. 14:7-9).

TODAY'S PRAYER

"Lord, even though I have sinned so very much against You, I know now that You have had great mercy on me. I do not deserve Your great mercy. Help me to remember the mercies of my life."

TODAY'S JOURNAL ENTRY

Write about a time when you wanted to turn back to the sins of the past. Tell how you made it through that time.

---

51   Ricky Boggs. *Alcohol and Addiction: How It Affects the Brain.* YouTube video, 54:39. Posted [January, 2012]. https://www.youtube.com/watch?v=e9F5wpvq2ho.

DAY SEVEN

WORSHIP STYLES

In our church culture, we use words in a common way, but each person may have a different understanding of the words. *Worship* is one such word. The church uses *worship* to mean a type of song, a kind of service, or a physical demonstration. We can be confused as to what the culture of a particular church means when we have been exposed to a different style.

Biblical definitions are also diverse. The word *worship* is used over a hundred times in the Scriptures.[52] With various meanings, the word *worship* is an example of how we get caught up in a form of religion instead of a personal relationship. Coming to a conclusion of what true worship is may be confusing at first, but you can be sure that worship will include sacrifice of your personal desires, prayer, singing, sharing, and surrendering your choices.

We hear many explanations of worship throughout the body of Christ. Some say it is an atmosphere, so they attempt to recreate an ambience to force that atmosphere. Some say it is an expression of feeling, so they attempt to find songs which touch the emotions. Some say it is respect and admiration, so they will demand a "holy quiet." Some say it is how much time and money we spend on God, so they will dedicate lots of money to the church and give all their excess time to Him.

TODAY'S SCRIPTURE

> **"For the sake of your name, Lord, forgive my iniquity, though it is great" (Psa. 25:11).**

TODAY'S PRAYER

For the director of music. A psalm of David. When the prophet Nathan came to him after David had committed adultery with Bathsheba.

> Have mercy on me, O God, according to your unfailing love; according to your great compassion blot out my transgressions. Wash

---

52   *Bible Hub. s.v.* "Worship," accessed August 18, 2017, https://www.blueletterbible.org/search/search.cfm?Criteria=worship&t=KJV#s=s_primary_0_1.

away all my iniquity and cleanse me from my sin. For I know my transgressions, and my sin is always before me. Against you, you only, have I sinned and done what is evil in your sight; so you are right in your verdict and justified when you judge. Surely I was sinful at birth, sinful from the time my mother conceived me.

Yet you desired faithfulness even in the womb; you taught me wisdom in that secret place.

Cleanse me with hyssop, and I will be clean; wash me, and I will be whiter than snow. Let me hear joy and gladness; let the bones you have crushed rejoice. Hide your face from my sins and blot out all my iniquity. Create in me a pure heart, O God, and renew a steadfast spirit within me. Do not cast me from your presence or take your Holy Spirit from me. Restore to me the joy of your salvation and grant me a willing spirit, to sustain me.

Then I will teach transgressors your ways, so that sinners will turn back to you. Deliver me from the guilt of bloodshed, O God, you who are God my Savior, and my tongue will sing of your righteousness. Open my lips, Lord, and my mouth will declare your praise. You do not delight in sacrifice, or I would bring it; you do not take pleasure in burnt offerings. My sacrifice, O God, is a broken spirit; a broken and contrite heart you, God, will not despise. May it please you to prosper Zion, to build up the walls of Jerusalem. Then you will delight in the sacrifices of the righteous, in burnt offerings offered whole; then bulls will be offered on your altar" (Psa. 51).

TODAY'S JOURNAL ENTRY

Write a prayer to tell God how you feel about the confessions you have made this week.

CHAPTER NINE

HORSE GATE: GATEWAY TO RESTORING EMPOWERMENT

"Above the Horse Gate, the priests made repairs, each in front of his own house" (Neh. 3:28).

"James, a servant of God and of the Lord Jesus Christ, To the twelve tribes scattered among the nations: Greetings. Consider it pure joy, my brothers and sisters, whenever you face trials of many kinds, because you know that the testing of your faith produces perseverance. Let perseverance finish its work so that you may be mature and complete, not lacking anything" (Jas. 1:1-4).

_____

DAY ONE

NEW LIFE

With a simple physical description in hand, Janice waited for the "new girl." "New girl" was the label given to each woman who came to Bethesda for recovery. It wasn't meant to be disrespectful; it was just a way to identify one of the women as one who had just arrived for treatment. This "new girl" was coming to the bus station via a detox center in Atlanta.

I am not exactly sure how this happened, but Janice could always spot the "new girl." She has picked them up at the airport, bus stations, and train stations and never missed one. Call it a "God thing" if you want to, but Janice always got her "girl." And so it was this day. The woman stepped from the bus, and Janice approached her with, "Hi, I'm Janice from Bethesda."

She was nice enough. But she was in physical trouble, which was easy to see. She had been given a drug in detox to help her, and that drug was not completely out of her system. She also was physically wasted because of a long and deep addiction to heroin and methadone. On top of all that, she was coming out of an alcoholic binge that had taken her further than she wanted to go and kept her longer than she wanted to stay. At the emergency room, prior to detox, she had almost died. Emotionally, she was dead. She had lost her daughter. She had lost her husband, her home, her everything. The thing that mattered most was the loss of her daughter.

Many in addiction lose their children. It is just part of the plan of addiction to take everything of value from a person. Since one of God's gifts to us is children, it is easy to see how addiction is determined to get that gift. The problem is that only rarely can a child make a difference. Usually by the time a woman has gone that deep into addiction, she is not interested in getting her children back, except for the purpose of destroying the guilt she feels for losing that gift of God.

But this woman was different. Her family intervened on her behalf, removed the child from her, and presented a plan of accountability to get her back. Of course, she was angry, physically sick, and emotionally spent. She said, one day, that her "issues had patience." She meant that all the emotions she had numbed for years had waited on her to get sober. In other words, now was the time to deal with those areas of her life that needed healing.

In less than a week, this woman was having severe stomach pains. She was doubled over with pain, which scared me. I am not one to "baby" a woman in recovery, but this pain seemed very real, so off we went to the emergency room. She was hospitalized for three days. I offered to send her home, but she refused, saying that she had to get healed and get off all drugs, so she could get her daughter back. She came back to Bethesda with determination.

Thinking back on the situation today, I am glad I didn't second-guess God. I believed I was hearing from Jesus, so I kept telling her that she was in Waycross to be healed. "God did not spare you for you to come here and die. You will live, and you will feel better. Just give it a month."

Every day during our walking program, this woman would drag herself around the track. She walked and sat to rest only occasionally. Once, she questioned me about this "God thing." She said, "I thought you said I would feel better."

"You can't put a limit on God. Keep on doing what you have been doing, and you will be healed."

She had great issues to heal. Her mind was ravaged by the pain of addiction. Some folks think that addicts don't have pain because they are numb, but that isn't true. They have pain; they just don't feel it at the time. When they are getting sober, the pain is very intense, and, because of using pain killers, both physical and emotional pain is harder to handle.

This woman was like that, but, by faith, she would be healed. Gradually, her stamina increased. As she walked to build her physical strength and talked to open up her emotions, she began to show signs of healing. It has been many years now, and this "new girl" is really a "new girl." She told me of her life with her family—not only with her daughter she fought to get back but also with additional children as well. She also shared with me of her relationship with a wonderful man, her restored parental relationships, and her business.

I said, "Hey, girl, it sounds like you are living your dream."

"You bet I am," she said, "and it all started right there in Waycross."

There is empowerment in Jesus Christ; there is a healing, cleansing fountain that flows from Jesus to us all. This young woman took advantage of the empowerment she found and now is restored and living the abundant life.

TODAY'S PRAYER

"I am ready now to have my defects of character removed, but I can't do it myself. Please take the defects from me and show me how to walk in new life. I surrender (lying, manipulation, unfaithfulness, laziness). We cannot survive without industry in our town. Lord, I ask You to send Christian industry to our town and the surrounding area. Give those already here the insight to provide a clean and safe environment for the workers. Let there be more and better jobs provided for people here. I pray for these businesses: (List businesses in your town here.)"

KEY TO EMPOWERMENT

You can choose. Choice is a free gift from God to every person. Free will allows choice. Use this key to encourage yourself with making right choices.

ACTION STEPS

- Determine to set boundaries for particular areas of your life. For example: Determine to stop romancing the old life. Determine to stop gossiping, having sex outside of marriage, and cursing.
- Write these boundaries on an index card and begin practicing the boundaries today.

THE HORSE GATE

"The whole valley where dead bodies and ashes are thrown, and all the terraces out to the Kidron Valley on the east as far as the corner of the Horse Gate, will be holy to the Lord. The city will never again be uprooted or demolished" (Jer. 31:40).

The Horse Gate was near the king's house. The horse symbolized power. Men were not to look to horses but to God for true power for change and direction. It takes power, God's power, to change. In this society, we think that the power is within us to change, but it is not. The power to change is in God, and God alone. He enables us, encourages us, and helps us to make changes, which alone we cannot. We need God's power and help to look at ourselves and then to change our course of direction in life.

"The freedom that God preserves in us has a double edge. On one hand, it means God's love and empowerment are always with us. On the other hand, it means there is no authentic escape from the truth of our choices," says Dr. Gerald May in his book *Addiction and Grace.*[53]

Grace and choices, when in line with God's will, empower victory. The head and heart must be right with God and get in line with the will of God to make lifelong changes. If a person's only desire is to stop an addiction, they will not be interested in giving their life to God in order to stop any behavior. A spiritual journey that will shake every foundational belief will be too difficult for the one who simply wants to stop drinking. Almost everyone starts recovery with the idea of simply changing the addictive or negative behavior. An attempt is made to reform the destructive behavior by substituting constructive behaviors. But, according to May, a person will continue to struggle until he or she gets the opportunity to see the spiritual significance in the struggles.[54]

Every time you begin the behavioral modification plan of swapping one behavior for another, you will get an opportunity to choose God. Often, however, you will say no to God and attempt on your own to simply stop the behavior. Failure to stop brings God closer to you, but does not necessarily bring you closer to God. It is your desire that needs to change. Your desire is stubborn. Once it knows the "love" of addiction, the desire clings to it. This is an inward knowing—a question, a thought, an idea that God has a better way.

God is in the desert places of your life. "Because openness with God is threatening, and because our desire is more to overcome an addiction than to calm our deeper desire for God, we will fill the space with something else," says May.[55] When you stop any habitual, addictive behavior, there is so much time left on your hands. This is the time when "idle hands become the devil's

53   Gerald May. *Addiction and Grace.* New York: HarperCollins, 2009. 123.
54   Ibid.
55   Ibid.

workshop." This time is what you might call "the desert." That desert feels void, but only in a void can we hear the call of God to surrender. Also, it is during this time that the call from God comes. If you say yes to God, the struggle takes on a new direction and becomes consecrated to God. At that time, God fills the void. Left alone without God to fill that hole, you will fill the hole with something else. It is only through God's grace that your "want to" begins to be transformed. For the sake of the love of God, you are no longer dedicated to relieving your pain but become dedicated to a greater good, according to May.[56]

When your desire is consecrated to God, this consecration breaks through self-deception. Self-deception is very hard to break through because it is just what it sounds like—self being deceived by self. It takes God to open your eyes and reveal the motives of the heart. When you see the ugliness of your motives and the beauty of the grace of God, you will give up things. You can and will drop your grasp on the things which do not reflect the grace and love of God.

TODAY'S SCRIPTURE

"I can do all this through him who gives me strength" (Phil. 4:13).

TODAY'S PRAYER

"Take, Lord, and receive all my liberty, my memory, my understanding, and my entire will, all I have and call my own. You have given all to me. To you, Lord, I return it. Everything is Yours; do with it what you will. Give me only Your love and Your grace, that is enough for me."—Saint Ignatius Loyola.[57]

TODAY'S JOURNAL QUESTION

In what ways do you need to be empowered?

---

56   Ibid.
57   "Suscipe Prayer of St. Ignatius of Loyola." *Loyola Press*, http://www.loyolapress.com/our-catholic-faith/prayer/traditional-catholic-prayers/saints-prayers/suscipe-prayer-saint-ignatius-of-loyola (accessed July 25, 2017).

DAY TWO

WORD STUDY

"I have told you these things, so that in me you may have peace. In this world you will have trouble. But take heart! I have overcome the world" (Jn. 16:33).

Overcome

In the preceding verse, the word *overcome* means "to conquer or to get the victory." In the *Merriam-Webster Dictionary*, *overcome* means "to get the better of."[58] Jesus, in talking to His followers, wants them to know troubles are common in this world. He assures them that, even though troubles come, His followers can take heart because He has gotten the victory.

Hannah Hurnard in *Hinds Feet on High Places* describes the very private ascent to the High Places with the Good Shepherd. In this beautiful allegory of the Song of Solomon, Hurnard helps the reader take a look at what must happen for change to happen in a person's life. The main character, Much Afraid, struggles to go the distance to be transformed by the love of God. The story of Much Afraid is a metaphor of what it could be like for us to make the changes necessary to overcome the past. In one of the scenes in the book, the birds seem to chirp, "He's gotten the victory, hurrah" over and over as Much Afraid climbs to the top of the Precipice of Injury and surmounts the difficult mountain to enter the High Places with Jesus. Throughout the pages of her book, Hurnard reminds the reader that Much Afraid must face these life challenges while being opposed by her Fearing relatives.[59]

It is so much like that for us. To overcome fear, to surmount life's steep places, and to dare to try drain us of all of our energy. Like Much Afraid, our love for the Good Shepherd is the only thing that can help us overcome.

Victory

Victory is defined as "the overcoming of an enemy or antagonist, achievement of mastery or success in a struggle against odds or difficulties, or the state of having

---

58   *Merriam-Webster Dictionary, s.v.* "Overcome," accessed August 18, 2017, www.merriam-webster.com/dictionary/overcome.

59   Hannah Hurnard. *Hinds Feet on High Places.* Carol Stream: Tyndale House, 1979.

triumphed."[60] When Much Afraid won the victory over fear, she reached the High Places of the Kingdom of Love. Her name changed to Grace and Glory. Throughout her difficult journey, she collected stones of remembrance. Once on the High Places, she took the Stones of Remembrance, which reminded her of the past times when she had almost given up, and gave the stones to Jesus, or the Good Shepherd. He, in turn, took the stones and transformed them into jewels, which He made into a crown. All the trials, all the problems, all of the hurts and disappointments were turned into beautiful character traits when the victory had been won.[61]

Before the complete victory is won, there are many smaller victories. One such victory is ninety days of abstinence, then one year of abstinence, and then five years of sobriety. Other victories include forgiving wounds, getting and maintaining a career, restoring family relationships, and developing a new personal self-worth. All of the daily victories should be celebrated and enjoyed.

TODAY'S SCRIPTURE

"For sin shall no longer be your master, because you are not under the law, but under grace" (Rom. 6:14).

TODAY'S PRAYER

Selfie's Prayer

"Dear Lord, I admit that I am a selfie. I have been trying to get my needs met by my own inadequate efforts. I realize this is wrong and will never truly work. I now give up all my rights and acknowledge You as my Lord. You have permission, as far as I am concerned, to do with me anything You choose.

"I now begin to see that when Christ died, I died with Him; when He was buried, I was buried with Him; and when He arose, I arose with Him and was made new. I thank You that, in the Spirit, I now sit with Him at Your right hand in heavenly places.

---

60 *Merriam-Webster Dictionary*, s.v. "Victory," accessed August 18, 2017, http://www.merriam-webster.com/dictionary/victory.

61 Hurnard, 99.

"I choose now to trust You, Lord Jesus, to live Your life in and through me by Your power. I will not try to perform for You. I trust You to perform through me. I also trust You to teach me more each day of what it means to know You in my life. Amen."[62]

TODAY'S JOURNAL QUESTION

What are some of the victories of recovery you have experienced? Write about how you celebrate your victories in recovery.

---

[62]   Source unknown.

DAY THREE

CRAVINGS, CYCLES, AND CONNECTIONS

What is a trigger? A trigger is something that is associated, sometimes unconsciously, with our negative lifestyle. A trigger can be accompanied by sweaty palms, a fast pulse, or severe agitation. It could be a song, a smell, a person, a movie, or even a book. It is anything which causes what is in the subconscious to come to the conscious and, thereby, causes an action. Certain foods can be triggers, such as the association of pizza and beer, a good meal with fine wine, etc.

There is a common saying in recovery circles: "A person needs to change his playgrounds, playthings, and playmates." What are playgrounds? Anywhere that is associated specifically with the old lifestyle. A rock concert, a sporting event, a bar, or perhaps even an office or car can be playgrounds. Areas of your home can be triggers. First, there must be a thorough housecleaning. Someone from your support system must be involved in the housecleaning. It is too dangerous for you to do this alone.

"There must be a thorough housecleaning."

After cleaning house, new routines need to be established. Obviously, the places that are strongly associated with old habits must be avoided. New routines need to be established: change the furniture; paint; get new curtains. If you used first thing in the morning, you need to find something to fill that void that is created by change. Pray and meditate instead. Most people get so deep in their negative behaviors that they basically have no life that does not revolve around negativity. There is a whole world out there to be discovered. If you have some time on your hands, you can go to the zoo or to a museum. Find a state park nearby, and take family and friends there for an afternoon of relaxation. Get involved in several areas of the life of a church; many have activities all during the week. Become a volunteer at a nursing home or hospital or any number of places in the community. There are things that you can do to remove yourself from the line of fire.

Romancing the old lifestyle leads to trouble. So often our minds take us down memory lane, showing only the few fun times in a life filled with negativity. You cannot afford to fantasize the "good ole days." It is easy when talking with an old friend to talk about the good and bad times. War stories are a real problem. Romancing can quickly lead to craving. Instead of focusing on the past, you must always go forward.

New relationships are also a real danger for those in recovery. Your emotions are pretty unstable for at least the first couple of years. It is not the time to try to begin a new love relationship. It is especially dangerous for two recovering people to be together because one can always pull the other down at some point. Any relationships that were ongoing when treatment began need to be reevaluated and possibly put on hold. You are not the same person when you become sober, and the basis of the relationship may be nonexistent once you have some clean time. Wait at least a year, preferably more, before trying to form one.

TODAY'S SCRIPTURE

"For the Spirit God gave us does not make us timid, but gives us power, love and self-discipline" (2 Tim. 1:7).

TODAY'S PRAYER

Anima Christi

Soul of Christ, sanctify me;

Body of Christ, save me;

Blood of Christ, inebriate me;

Water from the side of Christ, wash me;

Passion of Christ, strengthen me;

O good Jesus, hear me;

Within Your wounds hide me;

Separated from You let me never be;

From the evil one, protect me;

At the hour of death, call me;

And close to You, bid me; That with Your saints,

I may be praising You, forever and ever. Amen

—St. Ignatius Loyola[63]

TODAY'S JOURNAL QUESTION

What causes you to lose self-discipline?

---

63   "The Anima Christi." Catholic.org, http://www.catholic.org/prayers/prayer.php?p=1140 (accessed July 25, 2017).

DAY FOUR

DELIVERANCE

Deliverance enables us to make a change in our behavior. It does not, however, necessarily remove the problem. A total work of grace brings deliverance. Deliverance empowers us to exercise personal responsibility simply, gently, and effectively. That grace of deliverance is what lifts the weight of addiction. Deliverance can come in a moment or over time. It represents extraordinary grace, which allows us to move forward and to develop discernment.

Discernment is the ability to tell right from wrong. It is a spiritual application of living prayerfully, seeking direction from God, and faithfully following that direction.

Deliverance must bring honesty. This honesty does not just affirm that something is wrong but admits or acknowledges that the problem exists. With this honesty comes a certain calm assurance and lack of hysteria. This honesty requires facing the truth of self, regardless of how ugly, threatening, or unpleasant the truth is.

You must never use failure as an excuse to quit trying. You must learn to "get up quickly" from any "fall" or failure. At the point of failure, you must begin at that moment to do the next right thing.

Dignity is restored, and truth comes to you. You must reach outside yourself for grace and then act in accordance with the grace we find. This responsibility requires living a dedicated, consecrated life. All of your actions should reflect that dedication and consecration.

THE TWELVE SPIES

In the attempt by the Israelites to go into the Promised Land, there were twelve spies sent into the land. The following is a list of those spies and the tribes to which they belonged:

Shammua, son of Zaccur, was from the tribe of Reuben.

Shaphat, son of Hori, represented the tribe of Simeon.

Caleb, son of Jephunneh, was from the tribe of Judah.

Igal, son of Joseph, was from the tribe of Issachar.

Hoshea (Joshua), son of Nun, was from the tribe of Ephraim.

Palti, son of Raphu, represented the tribe of Benjamin.

Gaddiel, son of Sodi, came from the tribe of Zebulin.

Gaddi, son of Susi, was from the tribe of Manassah.

Ammiel, son of Gemalli, represented the tribe of Dan.

Sethur, son of Michael, was from the tribe of Asher.

Nahbi, son of Vophsi, represented the tribe of Naphtali.

Geuel, son of Maki, was from the tribe of Gad.

Each one of these names represents a character trait, which must be dealt with in order to live in the Promised Land. All of these men walked through the Red Sea on dry land, but when they went into the Promised Land, all but two came back with a fearful report of the giants in the land.

This can happen to any of us. Though the "Promised Land of Recovery" may have its "giants," once a person makes it through the "Red Sea," experiencing complete recovery is possible. It is up to you to be willing to face forward and, if a fall occurs, to fall forward, not backward.

NAMES OF GOD

"He said, 'If you listen carefully to the Lord your God and do what is right in his eyes, if you pay attention to his commands and keep all his decrees, I will not bring on you any of the diseases I brought on the Egyptians, for I am the Lord, who heals you'" (Exod. 15:26).

In Exodus, the Israelites form a picture of what it is like to leave slavery and try to get to destiny. Time and time again on their way to the destiny of the Promised Land, the Israelites murmured and complained. They refused over and over to be satisfied with the provision of God in the new place. In Exodus 15:22-26, God provided water and promised healing, even during these times of complaining. When the people complained to Moses about their plight, he cried out to God. God then showed Moses a tree to cast into the bitter waters of Marah. The tree made the waters sweet. God tested the people with difficult circumstances to educate them on His healing character. He made a promise to them—and, likewise, to us—that if we listen to the voice of the Lord and do what God tells us to do, He will let none of the diseases of the world come upon us. This is where God reveals himself as *Jehovah Rapha*, "the Lord that heals."[64]

This revelation of healing leads a recovering person to pay attention and follow the pathway of wisdom that God has laid out through others. If you will do what you are told to do in recovery and diligently seek the ways of God, you can expect full and complete healing.

PRAYER

"You are Jehovah Rapha, my Healer. I thank You that You heal when I expect it and when I don't expect healing. I thank You that You started healing my emotions long before I realized it. I thank You that You are healing me now of old patterns and old thoughts. I thank You, Jesus, that You bore the stripes and the punishment, which heals me physically."

TODAY'S SCRIPTURE

What, then, shall we say in response to these things? If God is for us, who can be against us? He who did not spare his own Son, but gave him up for us all—how will he not also, along with him, graciously give us all things? Who will bring any charge against those whom God has chosen? It is God who justifies. Who then is the one who condemns? No one. Christ Jesus who died—more than that, who was raised to life—is at the right hand of God and is also interceding for us. Who shall separate us from the love of Christ? Shall trouble or hardship or persecution or famine or nakedness or danger or sword? (Rom. 8:31-35).

TODAY'S PRAYER

"Most High, glorious God, enlighten the darkness of my heart and give me true faith, certain hope, and perfect charity, sense and knowledge, Lord, that I may carry out Your holy and true command. Amen"—St. Francis of Assisi.[65]

TODAY'S JOURNAL ENTRY

Describe what your life will look like in full deliverance.

---

64 *Bible.org*, s.v. "Jehovah-Jireh-Rapha-Nissia," accessed August 23, 2017, https://bible.org/seriespage/60-compound-names-jehovah-jireh-rapha-nissi.

65 St. Francis' Prayer Before the Crucifix." In National Shrine of Saint Francis of Assisi, Shrinesf.org, http://www.shrinesf.org/franciscan-prayer.html (accessed July 25, 2017).

DAY FIVE

SPIRIT, SOUL, BODY

When people come to Bethesda Recovery, there is at least a twofold reason. First, they come to get off of drugs. That is the most evident reason. Each one has some inkling of hope that they can learn to live sober lives. The second reason they come is that they are on a quest for God.

People want to know Who God is and how they can find Him. The problem comes when they fail to realize that addiction is a body, mind, and soul (or spirit) issue. God Himself is a triune God. He is three-in-one. He is Father, Son, and Holy Spirit. A person cannot fully understand this concept, but he or she must accept this truth by faith. Man is a triune man. He is body, soul, and spirit.

"May God himself, the God of peace, sanctify you through and through. May your whole spirit, soul, and body be kept blameless at the coming of our Lord Jesus Christ" (1 Thess. 5:23).

According to this verse, God wants to sanctify each of us through and through. The word "sanctify," *hagiazo*, means "to make holy or to free from the guilt of sin."[66]

The body is easily identified because the body is how one person identifies another. The body includes all the physical attributes of a person. The soul usually refers to the personality aspects of a person. This personality is made up of the mind, the will, and the emotions. The spirit—that is, the human spirit—is the part of mankind which is formed first and includes all the basic instincts of man, including the drive to survive, the drive to know the Creator, and the drive to be independent.

One example of the distinction of the trinity of man is a man in a coma. The body is present, and the spirit is present, but the soul or personality is not present. The spirit leaves the body when the body dies, but the soul can die long before the spirit leaves.

The body of a person relates to the world at large. The body touches the environment, and the soul of a person relates to other people. The spirit of a

---

66   *Bible Hub, s.v.* "hagiazo," accessed August 18, 2017, http://biblehub.com/greek/37.htm.

person, the human spirit, is where God touches man and where man touches God. The Scriptures say that we **"were dead in your transgressions and sins"** **(Eph. 2:1)**. The body was not dead; the soul was not dead; but the spirit was dead. When God touches man, his human spirit is then made alive in Christ.

Let me say, without any reservation, that God is God, and He can do whatever He wants to do. He can, if He so chooses, reach down and zap a person, and, in a moment, the person can be changed in body, soul, and spirit. But that usually doesn't happen.

What does usually happen in the lives of those I have worked with is that God touches the spirit, making it alive, and then the spirit affects the soul, which in turn affects the body. A person meets God, and his or her spirit is made alive to the "new life." The spirit begins to be fed with the Word of God spilling over into behaviors, and the soul is affected.

Last, but not least, feelings change. The soul starts changing first in the mind with its patterns of thoughts, then by the way decisions are made, and finally by the way the feelings react. The body follows with a new way to do things. The spirit brings life, personality refined, and those things work out into the hands and feet. We don't touch what we once did, and we don't walk where we once did.

Let's go back to the addicted person looking for God. The mind is a negative place when we are using. It is twisted to believe the only thing in life that is worthwhile is the drug of choice. The human spirit is broken and has little or no concept of the true and living God. The only god that it knows is the drug of choice. Since the human spirit has accepted that false god, it has been able to make its way into our personality. The drug of choice helps us think, make decisions, and tells us how to feel.

In my opinion, this is why we have so many who have "jailhouse religion." This is a term used for those who go to jail, seek Jesus, seem to be really changed, and then get out of jail and "lose" their faith. When the spirit is made alive in Christ, the war starts in the spirit of the man or woman for total control.

Before the "new birth" (which, by the way, is spiritual), the dominating principality was drugs. That drug "lord," who has set up his kingdom in your spirit, is not very happy to give up his rule and reign. That drug "lord" lost his authority in your spirit when Jesus entered. Scriptures tell us about Someone Who is stronger and able to overcome the strongman. **"Or again, how can anyone enter a strong man's house and carry off his possessions unless he first ties up the strong man? Then he can plunder his house" (Matt. 12:29).**

If the drug "lord" is not able to rule in the spirit after salvation, he will take up lordship in the soul and the body. Let's think about that for a moment. How confusing it is to see someone who one day "gets saved" and wants to be sober and the next day is out doing drugs again. If it is confusing for you, the one looking at it from the outside, how much more confusing is it for the person who is actually living it?

Instead of reaching out to the one struggling, the church will often toss the person aside as hopeless or not worth helping. This leaves them even more confused about what has happened. With no church or Christian support, they continue to surrender their mind, will, and emotions (soul) over to the drug "lord." So many have told me that they are more confused and unhappier, and now the drugs do not really work as well as they should. The human spirit, which once was friends with the soul and body, is now at war. This is what Paul calls **"the war against the law of my mind" (Rom. 7:23).** If the spiritual battle raging inside is to be surrendered to Jesus, we must learn about the Christian disciplines.

Richard Foster was not talking about addiction in his book *Celebration of Discipline* but it fits addiction so well. He said, "Superficiality is the curse of our age. The doctrine of instant satisfaction is a primary spiritual problem. The desperate need today is not for a great number of intelligent people or gifted people, but for a deep people." He went further by saying, "The purpose of the disciplines is liberation from the stifling slavery to self-interest and fear."[67]

Richard Foster also said in the same book, "Willpower will never succeed in dealing with the deeply ingrained habits of sin." He continues to say that the disciplines help us to put ourselves before God so that God can transform us. According to Foster, "We must always remember that the path does not

67   Richard Foster. *Celebration of Discipline: The Path to Spiritual Growth.* New York: Harper-Collins, 1988. 1.

produce change; it only places us where the change can occur. This is the path of disciplined grace."[68]

The inner disciplines are meditation, prayer, study, and fasting. Meditation is to faith as worry is to fear. Meditation fuels faith, while worry fuels fear. Worry focuses on the negative aspects of life, while meditation focuses on the Word of God, which we must learn to meditate on. **"Keep this Book of the Law always on your lips; meditate on it day and night, so that you may be careful to do everything written in it. Then you will be prosperous and successful" (Josh. 1:8).**

TODAY'S SCRIPTURE

"Jesus looked at them and said, 'With man this is impossible, but with God all things are possible'" (Matt. 19:26).

TODAY'S PRAYER

You are holy, Lord, the only God, and Your deeds are wonderful.

You are strong.

You are great.

You are the Most High.

You are Almighty.

You, Holy Father are King of heaven and earth.

You are Three and One, Lord God, all Good.

You are Good, all Good, supreme Good, Lord God, living and true.

You are love.

You are wisdom.

You are humility.

You are endurance.

You are rest.

You are peace.

You are joy and gladness.

---

68   Ibid, 2.

You are justice and moderation.

You are all our riches, and You suffice for us.

You are beauty.

You are gentleness.

You are our Protector.

You are our Guardian and Defender.

You are our courage.

You are our haven and our hope.

You are our faith, our great consolation.

You are our eternal life, Great and Wonderful Lord, God Almighty, Merciful Savior.

Amen

—St. Francis of Assisi.[69]

TODAY'S JOURNAL QUESTION

How has God empowered you this week?

---

69 "Saint Francis's Prayer in Praise of God, Given to Brother Leo." In National Shrine of Saint Francis of Assisi, Shrinesf.org, http://www.shrinesf.org/franciscan-prayer.html (accessed July 26, 2017).

DAY SIX

AN EXERCISE IN MEDITATION

STRETCH YOUR IMAGINATION

Paul said to **"take captive every thought to make it obedient to Christ"** **(2 Cor. 10:5)**. Maybe he was letting us know that our imaginations are important. He could be saying to us today to use our imaginations but not let vain or worthless imaginations take the place of Jesus. Perhaps we should use our imaginations for good instead of to promote ungodly acts in our minds.

The following is an exercise in stretching the imagination for good. Set aside about fifteen or twenty minutes for this exercise.

- Find a relatively quiet place where you won't be interrupted.

- Get in a comfortable position.

- Begin to visualize or imagine a lake, taking time to see the lake in detail. Notice the ripples of the water; feel the gentle breeze stirring the leaves of the trees along the shore. Notice the moss on the trees swaying in the wind. Take time to see the occasional fish jumping and hear the birds singing.

- Notice a small rowboat bobbing in the water at the edge of the lake. See yourself at the edge of the water, then stepping carefully into the boat. (Take a moment to settle into the boat, feel the movement, find your seat in the center. Take the oars.)

- Row your boat out into the lake, noticing the rhythm of the boat and the water.

- Now look up and see that Jesus is in the boat with you. He has been there all along. He nods his head to acknowledge you. Take time to examine your feelings. Are you startled to find that He is in the boat? Are you relieved? What is going on in your feelings?

- See Jesus reach for the oars of the boat. Can you release the oars to Him, or do you feel reluctant to let go? Are you feeling afraid, happy? Take a moment to feel the feelings through.

- Make a decision to give the oars to Jesus. See His kind expression as He takes the oars of the boat and turns the boat back toward shore.

- Choose to feel relieved as you watch Jesus take the boat safely to shore. If you have questions to ask Him, ask them of Him. This is your meditation, and He is present in this meditation.

You can end the exercise in a variety of ways. As you see Him take the oars of your boat, the Holy Spirit will begin to lead you into thoughts which will compel you to deal with issues of control, fear, and trust. As you begin to see Jesus in control and choose to give Him control, a peace will come to you. One ending of the exercise is to allow Jesus to row your boat back to dry land and to lead you gently out of the boat to shore. You may want to see Jesus take you safely through a storm or any other issue you may have.

One thing is critical, and that is that the meditations are Holy Spirit-driven. You may be surprised at the reactions you have to the exercise, but at the end, you should have a sense of rest and peace.

TODAY'S SCRIPTURE

"May my meditation be pleasing to him, as I rejoice in the LORD" (Psa. 104:34).

TODAY'S PRAYER

"Lord, teach me to meditate on Your Word and be filled with the gifts You so freely give those who earnestly seek You. Thank You for meeting me in my times of prayer and meditation as I grow to know You more and more."

TODAY'S JOURNAL QUESTION

When was a time when you truly felt the presence of God?

DAY SEVEN

WORSHIP

Seven Hebrew words can help us understand worship and praise a little better. The first such word is *halal*. This is the primary root word for "hallelujah." Halal references meanings like "to be clear, to shine, to boast, show, to rave, celebrate, to be clamorously foolish."[70] When we say "hallelujah," we are being clamorously foolish in our praise and worship of God.

> **"Praise the LORD. Praise the LORD, you his servants; praise the name of the LORD. Let the name of the Lord be praised, both now and forevermore. From the rising of the sun to the place where it sets, the name of the LORD is to be praised" (Psa. 113:1-3).**

Yadah is another word for "praise," dealing with the wringing of hands or the extended hand.[71] We yadah, or praise, God with our hands tightly together or extended out, signifying our heartfelt worship, which includes not just our intellect but our emotion. **"I will declare your name to my people; in the assembly** I will praise **you" (Psa. 22:22).**

> "Seven Hebrew words can help us under-
> stand worship and praise a little better."

Towdah also deals with the hands, but this is more in submission as we raise our hands to surrender.[72]

> **"Sacrifice thank offerings to God, fulfill your vows to the Most High, and call on me in the day of trouble; I will deliver you, and you will honor me" (Psa. 50:14-15).**

Shabach means "to shout out our praise."[73]

70   *Blue Letter Bible*, s.v. "Halal," accessed August 18, 2017, https://www.blueletterbible.org/lang/lexicon/lexicon.cfm?t=kjv&strongs=h1984.

71   *Strong's Concordance*, s.v. "yadah," accessed August 18, 2017, http://biblehub.com/hebrew/3034.htm.

72   Global World Ministry. "Praise-Yadah and Towdah." Globalworldministry.org. https://www.globalwordministry.org/worship/praise-yadah-and-todah (accessed August 18, 2017).

73   CLMNWA Family Church. "7 Hebrew Words for Praise: Shabach." Christlikeministriesnwa.com. https://christlikeministriesnwa.com/2013/02/21/7-hebrew-words-for-praise-shabach/ (accessed August 18, 2017).

"For the director of music. Of the Sons of Korah. A psalm. Clap your hands, all you nations; shout to God with cries of joy" (Psa. 47:1).

Barak means "to kneel down in worship."[74]

"Come, let us bow down in worship, let us kneel before the LORD our Maker" (Psa. 95:6).

Zemar addresses the musical instruments of praise.[75] The word also means "singer."

"Praise Him with timbrel and dancing, praise him with the strings and pipe" (Psa. 150:4).

Tehillah means "to sing praise."[76]

"Be exalted in your strength, Lord; we will sing and praise your might" (Psa. 21:13).

Whenever you worship God, it opens your spirit to receive healing like nothing else can. This healing is not just for the body, but for the soul as well. In the depths of our soul lies emotional unrest and confusion. When we enter worship with our spiritual being, the emotional part of us connects with God for the healing we sometimes so desperately need.

The seven different words I listed above give us a sort of picture of praise and worship. They celebrate the wonders of God with the wringing of hands and heart while surrendering our lives to God. Then, with a shout of excitement, we kneel in worship while instruments of praise lead us in singing.[77]

TODAY'S SCRIPTURE

"Finally, be strong in the Lord and in his mighty power" (Eph. 6:10).

---

74 *Strong's Concordance*, s.v. "barak," accessed August 18, 2017, http://biblehub.com/hebrew/1288.htm.

75 *Strong's Concordance*, s.v. "zemar," accessed August 18, 2017, http://biblehub.com/hebrew/2171.htm.

76 *Strong's Concordance*, s.v., "tehillah," accessed August 18, 2017, http://biblehub.com/hebrew/8416.htm.

77 Abounding Love Bible Ministry. "Seven Hebrew Words for Praise." Albministry.org. http://www.albministry.org/pdf/HebrewandGreekWordsforPraise.pdf (accessed August 18, 2017).

TODAY'S PRAYER

"Have mercy on me, my God, have mercy on me, for in you I take refuge. I will take refuge in the shadow of your wings until the disaster has passed. I cry out to God Most High, to God, who vindicates me" (Psa. 57:1-2).

TODAY'S JOURNAL ENTRY

Write about the things that make you feel strong.

❦ CHAPTER TEN ❦
PRISON GATE: GATEWAY TO RESTORING FREEDOM

"Over the Gate of Ephraim, the Jeshanah Gate, the Fish Gate, the Tower of Hananel and the Tower of the Hundred, as far as the Sheep Gate. At the Gate of the Guard they stopped" (Neh. 12:39).

"Therefore, say to the Israelites: 'I am the LORD, and I will bring you out from under the yoke of the Egyptians. I will free you from being slaves to them, and I will redeem you with an outstretched arm and with mighty acts of judgment. I will take you as my own people, and I will be your God. Then you will know that I am the LORD your God, who brought you out from under the yoke of the Egyptians'" (Exod. 6:6-7).

FREED BUT NOT FREE

The law determines the prisoner's sentence. Sentence is imposed by a judge and overseen by law enforcement. Our shortcomings are prisons inflicted on us by the sins we continue to commit. We need deliverance from prison and from the sentence of the law. We need to accept that Jesus exchanged His sinless life for our sinful life and gave us His life in exchange. We are delivered and can walk a new lifestyle, step by step, by turning away from the sins that have bound and imprisoned us. Some of us are freed in this life and others in the next. Some are freed but not free.

The first day I met her, I knew that she was going to be interesting. There she was on my front porch with her lacy socks and overall shorts. She was appearing in my life for the first time to check out things and see if she was going to stay with us. It was the Fourth of July, and she was ready to start a new life. I asked her to come back at her appointment time because we were taking a holiday. She did.

When we met for her appointment, she told me she was sure I was going to be trouble for her because I was a Pentecostal preacher. She just knew it, she said. I told her that I wouldn't be trouble for her; it was God she would have the trouble with because it is His Word that we use here at Bethesda.

I really don't know why she stayed with us that first day, unless it was because she was hungry, angry, lonely, and tired. She was weary of battling with life, and her battle scars were showing. After a few days, she and I became friends. She wasn't at all sure of why she was in my life, but, after a few weeks, I was very sure.

Since I am a preacher, one of the very first things I encourage when someone comes to stay with me is that they read the Bible for themselves. "Don't take my word for it; read it yourself," I would say. And she did. She read, and she read. She went to her makeshift office, which consisted of a plastic lawn chair under the shade of a pecan tree in the yard, and read her Bible. And one day, quite against anything we preachers are told to do to lead people to Christ, she had her own theophany. That is, she met God while reading her Bible in a new and real way. She told me she had heard about God and that she had gone to church, but never before had she had an experience like the one she had there. Jesus Christ became real to her in Waycross. Now, I can't explain what she had to go through to get to Waycross, but I know that Jesus was waiting for her. I know that, in the time that I knew her, she exhibited the qualities of a Christian in many real and tangible ways.

I have a tremendous picture in my head of her sitting on the side porch at Bethesda Fellowship with two babies and Skoshi, our dog, singing children's hymns to them, smiling and loving every minute she was down on that floor. I see her standing at the whiteboard, writing trivia for the children to guess on Sunday afternoons. I hear her concern and passion for the victims in the Gulf who were hit by Hurricane Katrina and watched as she left Waycross to go on a missionary trip to help those people. I see her coming up out the waters of the baptismal pool in Waycross, changed and forgiven. She shed tears over our friend Hawk, whose disease snuffed out his life. I can hear her voice on the answering machine, saying, "At the tone, leave your number, and you know I'll call you back." So often, the reason she had to call me back was she was talking to her family; she was always telling me how happy she was that her family was back together. She told me—more than once—that she was living her dream. So, what could have happened to take her life so suddenly? What made her dream turn into a nightmare?

Drugs. Addiction. Sin. Denial. Too much too soon. All of that and so much more robbed this world of a loving, caring person, and all of that and so much more robbed her of her life.

One hot July afternoon, she drove up to the backyard at Bethesda and asked me a very difficult question. She said, "What is the sin unto death?" I hesitated, and that made her ask again, "Cathy, what is the sin unto death?"

I answered, "I don't think you want me to answer that."

"Yes, I do. I found it in the Bible, and I don't understand it."

"There is a line that can be crossed with God, I believe. That line is when God knows there will be no evidence of change in a person's life, and He takes that person on out of this world. I believe that people cross that line in addiction sometimes."

"Do you think I have crossed the line?"

"I can't answer that question; only God can. First John 5:16 says, 'There is a sin that leads to death.'"

"I know," she said. "I read it this week."

"I think that this is a warning to stop committing known sin."

The truth is that after that day, things went downhill quickly. She tried really hard to pick up the pieces of her life that were shattering around her, but she couldn't.

One other day, weeks prior to this July afternoon, she had exploded into my space and definitively stated, "I'm giving God one year, and if my life is not completely better by then, I am through."

She was going through a difficult time in her marriage, and she wanted God to fix the problem. She was giving God an ultimatum. Ultimatums are presumptions, and presumption on God doesn't work—at least that is what I have come to understand.

She fell dead at her outside trash can in the middle of the night. She was cleaning out her car after picking up her husband from the hospital. She had had her husband's prescriptions filled and started taking them. At first, she felt on top of the world, but then her world was upside down. Oxycontin®—her favorite drug, which had been her friend, now had ended her life. Her neighbor discovered her body when she took out her trash the next morning.

"Nobody really knows how far drugs can take the body before it is too late."

Something is wrong here. How did it happen? Nobody really knows how far drugs can take the body before it is too late. Nobody really knows how far one can go before they cross the line and commit "the sin that leads to death." She never planned to die that morning, but it was enough of a mistake to take her life. She taught me that nothing is easy in this life. To be changed forever is a gradual thing, not something that can be scheduled. The heart can be turned to God, but the mind must be transformed by continual renewing.

KEY FOR FREEDOM

You can walk away. You are free from your past when you walk away. Use this key to remind yourself that freedom is in moving forward.

ACTION STEPS

- Make a list of the areas of your life in which you are bound.
- Find a Scripture that relates to those areas and which spell out how to get freedom from them.

- Make a notecard of the Scripture. Memorize the Scripture.
- Find a positive activity to replace the activity which binds you. Do it.

PRAYER AT THE PRISON GATE

"Some of my friends are behind physical bars today—some because of what they have done and some because of what others have helped them to do. I pray that You have mercy and grace on them today. Your Word says that Your mercy endures forever and that Your mercy is renewed every morning. Renew Your grace in their lives today. Make them to grow where they have been planted. Give them strength to survive their imprisonment with You as the center of their world. Touch them today with Your compassion. Only Your tender mercy will comfort them.

"I pray for those in prison who have children. Keep the children from the cycle continuing in their lives. Grant the children peace about their parents. I pray for spouses of those in prison. Help them to continue to encourage those behind bars.

"I pray for new prison ministries to minister to all inmates because everyone needs soul recovery. I pray for honesty in our local law enforcement. Bless our sheriff, our police chief, our deputies, and our policemen. Give the detectives new and revealing insight into the crime in our city. Bring home to us those who are in prison and should be here today and those who are held captive in foreign countries.

"I have been imprisoned by my sin and character flaws. I can't seem to get past the past. I have some habits that I can't break. Please show me the areas that I need to begin to work on. These are the flaws or sins you have shown me so far in my work in recovery: (List your flaws or sins.)"

We were under great pressure, far beyond our ability to endure, so that we despaired of life itself. Indeed, we felt we had received the sentence of death. But this happened that we might not rely on ourselves but on God, who raises the dead. He has delivered us from such a deadly peril, and he will deliver us again. On him we have set our hope that he will continue to deliver us (2 Cor. 1:8b-10).

TODAY'S PRAYER

"Teach me to pray, Father, because I do not know how. Teach me to ask in Jesus' name for the things that I need. Teach me to pray for myself and others in a way that will change my life and theirs. Give me a kind personality. Make me real today. Be real to me, Father. Make me more like You and less like me. Teach me to pray."

TODAY'S JOURNAL ENTRY

Write about what you think God has been too slow to answer in your life.

DAY TWO

SIN/DISEASE CONCEPT: THE MIND IN ADDICTION

Negativity attacks the mind. It is in the mind that the will, the decision-making part, initiates all behaviors. Out of the mind and the will, self-esteem develops. As negativity begins to take hold of the mind, the will is split into two parts. One part of the will wants to quit the negative behavior, while the other part wants to continue.

In order to keep this split of the will from causing greater emotional problems, the mind creates patterns to deceive itself. This form of deception acts as a camouflage, which convinces you that you are really attempting to quit when, in actuality, you are finding ways to continue your negative behavior. During this deception, your self-esteem is destroyed through repeated failures to change. Even though you are deceived, there seems to be a knowing deep inside that something is not exactly right. This duplicity is a self-esteem destroyer. The mind is masterful in deceptive strategies. The mind resists change and desires to keep the status quo.

Repression is another strategy to keep negativity alive. The mind rejects any information about the formation of the habit. The mind rejects the ideas and refuses to think about the possibility of a habit being formed. The behavior is obvious to others, but not to you. As evidence of negative behavior increases, the mind works harder and harder to keep the truth from the rational part of the brain and out of consciousness. In denial, the mind must be always occupied or dulled, so there is no time for a conscious realization of the truth.

Where denial or repression fails, rationalization begins. Rationalization makes excuses for the behavior. The behavior is justified. The behavior started or continues because...and we begin to blame something or someone for our problem.

As the will continues to split more and more, self-alienation occurs. The true self, the one God intended the person to be, is being smothered by the new, self-destructive self. You are separated from yourself due to a lack of internalized truth. You believe the lies. Because man is created in the image of God and God is truth, you are divided inside yourself as you continue to believe more and more untruths.

As the negativity becomes stronger and stronger, it becomes more and more impossible to avoid the truth. You know the problem exists because all the denial, repression, and rationalization fail to keep the problem hidden from ourselves. As a result, you begin to hide the problem from others. You will keep secrets, lie, and isolate from others. The revelation of the problem to others would be unbearable. You are riddled with guilt, have great depression, and begin to mask any incompetence. By this time, all self-esteem is destroyed.

You may make a resolution to master the problem. You may even say, "I really need to stop." But the more creative or intelligent you are, the longer the process will take because the mind then begins to use "logic." The timing won't be right. It will be somebody's birthday, a holiday, a job. You will plan your recovery for another time. Tomorrow, tomorrow—there will always be tomorrow. At this point, terror arises at the thought of giving up the behavior.

The prison of the mind is a horrible place to be. Over and over, the mind will stop us from finding help. So many times, the battle is won or lost in the mind.

Another mind trick is the "I can't handle it" mode. Self-hatred takes over because of shame, remorse, and guilt over destructive behaviors and relapse. In this mode, many often surrender completely to the addiction. "I can handle it" creates tricks and strategies if you temporarily succeed at stopping the behavior. You will think you can do it because you *have* done it. The joy of the success fuels pride. The slippery slope of pride lets you think that just one time you can indulge, and the unconscious desires explode into relapse. Even after relapse, the trickster mind says, "I am moderating it. It was a little slip."

When all the mind tricks fail, the fall is inevitable. At this point, all self-respect disappears. Bizarre forms of rationalization take over, and all reason is gone. This is called "a breakdown." Not all reach this point, but many do. The Bible says in **Romans 12:2, "Do not conform to the pattern of this world, but be transformed by the renewing of your mind."** Renewing the mind is based on knowing the truth. No matter how ugly the truth is, you must be willing to face it. Truth is always positive.

It is important to remain in reality. It is very important to stay in the present. The present realities may be difficult, but they will not be as difficult as trying to make it back from some endless fantasy. Positive, truthful friends, who are dedicated to accountability, are important in relationships that help a person get out of the negative mind strategies.

TODAY'S SCRIPTURE

"Then you will know the truth, and the truth will set you free" (Jn. 8:32).

TODAY'S PRAYER

"Dear God, grant me the ability to reject the things about me that are not true, the humility to accept the things that are, and the discernment to know the difference. Thank you for hearing and answering my prayer. Gratefully, in Jesus' name, amen"—Billy Joe Vaughn.[78]

TODAY'S JOURNAL ENTRY

Write about a time when you repressed your memories and lived in denial.

---

78 "Another Serenity Prayer." In Acts International, by Billy Joe Vaughn, http://www.acts-web.org/articles/article.php?i=322&d=2&c=4 (accessed July 26, 2017).

DAY THREE

CYCLES

Cycles and connections are integral parts of addiction. The first cycle is a cycle for change. Over and over again, a thousand times, you have vowed to quit; but, before an hour goes by, a friend comes by, or the telephone rings, and the cycle begins again. It may take a blue light or the glaring lights of an emergency room to slow or stop the cycle. Nothing can happen until the negative cycle is stopped by either choice or death. To determine to change from a cycle of destruction to a cycle of reconstruction is not an easy choice to make. You must be willing to change the entire focus and direction of your life. The first step is to survive.

Day One: You are totally convinced that you have everything under control; no negative behavior is going to control you. You are tired and desperate for change—whatever form it takes.

Day Two: After having slept or not slept, you may question your motives to change. As the day wears on, your mind begins to remember. Restlessness and irritability begin to set in.

Day Three: The plan unfolds. The mind becomes a seething mass of screaming neurons. Any opportunity will be quickly seized to return to the negative behavior, unless there is intervention. Intervention must be quick and decisive, or you will outthink, outsmart, and outmaneuver the intervener.

At Bethesda, we have discovered that this third day is the first, most critical juncture in the recovery process. You must have a prior agreement to be still on the third day, no matter what. You must be willing to do whatever it takes and to agree to be in submission. This three-day cycle will be repeated throughout the entire recovery process.

"Change is a frightening thing, even in the best of circumstances, so many of us will return to those things that are most familiar."

Seven days is another critical period. Having survived the first three days, you will begin to miss the familiar fabric of your life, however painful it may have been. Change is a frightening thing, even in the best of circumstances, so many will return to those things that are most familiar.

You will return to old behaviors, unless you recognize the need for stability. Again, this is a cycle, and no matter how much you want to stop the behavior, you will slide into old habits, unless you carefully monitor the situation. Pay attention to the warning signs. Such signs include fidgeting, irritability, pacing, withdrawal, scheming, imagined illnesses, or exaggerated injury. You must be confronted with careful reality, and you must be willing to accept the confrontation.

Three weeks into the program, you will begin to feel better about things. The family is excited that two of the hardest cycles have been broken and, sometimes, encourage you to feel too safe. If, in fact, the cycle has been repeated, it will be at this time that you will think you can save the world. This is very serious. A false sense of security is very dangerous. The cycles may be difficult to manage.

Twenty-eight days is also critical. If you do not rethink your position and again recommit to whatever it takes to continue abstinence and gain sobriety, the cycle will begin again.

TODAY'S SCRIPTURE

"When hard pressed, I cried to the LORD; He brought me into a spacious place" (Psa. 118:5).

TODAY'S PRAYER

I love You, LORD, my strength. The LORD is my rock, my fortress and my deliverer; my God is my rock, in whom I take refuge, my shield and the horn of my salvation, my stronghold. I called to the LORD, who is worthy of praise, and I have been saved from my enemies. The cords of death entangled me; the torrents of destruction overwhelmed me. The cords of the grave coiled around me; the snares of death confronted me. In my distress I called to the LORD; I cried to my God for help. From his temple he heard my voice; my cry came before him, into his ears" (Psa. 18:1-6).

TODAY'S JOURNAL ENTRY

Write about why you are in recovery.

DAY FOUR

WORD STUDY

Transformed

According to the *Merriam-Webster Dictionary, transformed* means

"to change in composition or structure";

"to change the outward form or appearance of";

"to change in character or condition; convert."[79]

In **Luke 22:32**, Jesus tells Peter that when he is converted he will **"strengthen [the] brothers."** Jesus had been with Peter for three years. Peter had walked on water. Peter had given up a fishing business for Jesus. What could Jesus mean by this, that when He was converted or transformed, He would strengthen the others?

I believe Peter was in recovery. Recovery is not just for those in some debilitating addiction or some dreaded sin/disease. Recovery is for all of us who seek God's fullness in our lives. Recovery, as we know it from addiction, is certainly a transformation, a conversion. We must be changed in character and condition. All people must be changed from a sinful, lustful, worldly character to a Christ-like character.

At this gate of restoration, character reformation must begin. In order to have your life restored to others, there must be a conversion experience. This conversion is similar to what I think about when I think of a "conversion van." The van is already a van. The original van will work, but when the van is converted, it will be useful for a new purpose.

This is the way with transformation and conversion for a person in recovery. The person already exists. He is not being created. At the salvation experience, Jesus creates a new person. That newborn spirit is ready for heaven at any time, but may not be ready for life here on earth. This is why we need to be converted. As Jesus spoke to Peter at the Last Supper, He was saying to Peter, "I need you to help others. I need you to be changed from selfishness

---

79   *Merriam-Webster Dictionary, s.v.* "Transformed," accessed August 23, 2017, www.merriam-webster.com/dictionary/transformed.

to selflessness." That would take a conversion experience. That would take transformation of character.

Character is the sum total of all your habits. Habits are formed by every choice you make in life, and Peter's character needed to be converted. The character of every one of us needs this conversion and transformation, including those in recovery in the traditional sense.

How did Peter have this conversion experience? He came to the end of himself. He met the real Peter as the rooster crowed the third time. Jesus warned him that his character would not stand up to a test at this time. He warned Peter that he needed to be converted. But Peter, full of himself, felt that Jesus was wrong. When the rooster crowed the third time, Peter knew that he was not who he thought he was. He needed transformation.

TODAY'S SCRIPTURE

"Search me, God, and know my heart; test me and know my anxious thoughts. See if there is any offensive way in me, and lead me in the way everlasting" (Psa. 139:23-24).

TODAY'S PRAYER

"Keep your servant also from willful sins; may they not rule over me. Then I will be blameless, innocent of great transgression. May these words of my mouth and this meditation of my heart be pleasing in your sight, Lord, my Rock and my Redeemer" (Psa. 19:13-14).

TODAY'S JOURNAL ENTRY

Write about your thoughts on transformation.

DAY FIVE

DELIVERANCE

When the twelve spies or observers were selected to go spy out the Promised Land, each tribe sent a representative. Keep in mind that the tribes were organized in the wilderness and set forth for specific works by God to fulfill His purpose. God's purpose was to make for Himself a people who loved and worshipped Him. Their purpose was to get out of Egypt. Their hope was that since slavery was so burdensome, the new life they had received would be without those same burdens. It was true they no longer had to make bricks or build pyramids, but they did have work to do. God was transforming the Israelites into a people who could defend themselves with His help and who would never go back into slavery again. He was preparing the way of Jesus, so His people must be ready for their final deliverance in Him.

The tribe of Benjamin sent Palti, son of Raphu. It might be assumed that the only type of leadership the Israelites had known was the leadership of Pharaoh. Imagine, if you will, what the leadership of Pharaoh looked like. It was dictatorial, demanding, and relentless. Pharaoh had only to speak, and things were accomplished for him. He did not have to fight battles; he had warriors who led his troops. The spies went into the Promised Land and were happy to find the provision but were not so happy to find out that they must fight giants.

Palti means "whom Jehovah delivers."[80] But if you dig a little deeper, you will find that the suggestion of running is implied, too, or the idea of slipping out. Those who run away from God will never enter into the Promised Land. They must run to God and never away from responsibility or accountability. Running from God's deliverance can cost a person their life; that is exactly what it cost Palti and all his tribe. For the next forty years, they would be wandering until death overtook all those whose minds were stuck in Egypt. Their bodies may have been out of slavery, but their minds remained.

80   *Bible Hub, s.v.* "Palti," accessed August 18, 2017, http://biblehub.com/topical/p/palti.htm.

Gaddiel, son of Sodi, was from the tribe of Zebulon. *Sodi* means "secrets." [81] Perhaps these names mean more than we can imagine, since Zebulon was one of the tribes which refused to drive out the natives of Canaan. They took tributes or taxes from the people of the Promised Land. The idol worship remained in their lives throughout history. These things will never be successful in the full recovery of Canaan.

Gaddiel means "the fortune of God" and represents the blessings of God, but not necessarily Jehovah's blessing.[82] The spies knew the blessings of other gods and, even in the wilderness, worshipped idols. In Egypt, the Israelites are thought to have idols in their homes.[83] Idols of any kind cannot be in deliverance. The idol of self-love is the implied idol here. Self-love and self-centeredness must not be brought to the Promised Land.

NAMES OF GOD

In Exodus seventeen, Moses and the children of Israel were forced to fight the Amalekites. This battle was won by Joshua as Aaron and Hur held up the arms of Moses. At the end of the battle, when they had won the victory, Moses built an altar and declared that God was his Banner and would go before them in battle. It was common practice in that age for warriors to carry a banner into battle, much like the American flag symbolizes our nation. The banner of Jehovah represented God as the source of strength for the Israelites.

PRAYER

"You are *Jehovah Nissi*,[84] my banner, and I thank You for that. Thank You that You have been the Banner that goes before me into every day of my life. Thank You for being the Banner to give favor, to win battles, to overcome the enemy. Thank You for being my Banner today."

---

81 *Hitchcock's Bible Names Dictionary*, s.v. "Sodi," accessed August 18, 2017, http://www.biblestudytools.com/dictionary/sodi/.

82 Headcoverings by Devorah. "Names of Men in Torah." Headcoverings-by-Devorah.com. https://headcoverings-by-devorah.com/NamesMenTorah.htm (accessed November 10, 2017).

83 Michael Alan Stein. "The Religion of the Israelites in Egypt." JBQ.JewishBible.org. http://jbq.jewishbible.org/assets/Uploads/393/jbq_393_religioninegypt.pdf (accessed August 18, 2017).

84 *Easton's Bible Dictionary*, s.v. "Jehovah-Nissi," accessed August 18, 2017, http://www.biblestudytools.com/dictionary/jehovah-nissi.

"Moses built an altar and called it The Lord is my Banner" (Exod. 17:15).

TODAY'S SCRIPTURE

"It is for freedom that Christ has set us free. Stand firm, then, and do not let yourselves be burdened again by a yoke of slavery" (Gal. 5:1).

TODAY'S PRAYER

I hate those who cling to worthless idols; as for me, I trust in the LORD. I will be glad and rejoice in your love, for you saw my affliction and knew the anguish of my soul. You have not given me into the hands of the enemy but have set my feet in a spacious place. Be merciful to me, Lord, for I am in distress; my eyes grow weak with sorrow, my soul and body with grief. My life is consumed by anguish and my years by groaning; my strength fails because of my affliction, and my bones grow weak. Because of all my enemies, I am the utter contempt of my neighbors and an object of dread to my closest friends—those who see me on the street flee from me.

How abundant are the good things that you have stored up for those who fear you, that you bestow in the sight of all, on those who take refuge in you. In the shelter of your presence you hide them from all human intrigues; you keep them safe in your dwelling from accusing tongues. Praise be to the LORD, for he showed me the wonders of his love when I was in a city under siege. In my alarm I said, "I am cut off from your sight!" Yet you heard my cry for mercy when I called to you for help. Love the Lord, all his faithful people! The Lord preserves those who are true to him, but the proud he pays back in full. Be strong and take heart, all you who hope in the Lord (Psa. 31:6-11, 19-24).

TODAY'S JOURNAL ENTRY

Write about the things you have been set free from.

DAY SIX

STRONGHOLDS

A stronghold is an automatic and practiced way of thinking that has developed a life of its own. An individual stronghold is shaped by events in a person's life. Corporate strongholds are ways of thinking for a society which hold minds captive and pressures everyone in that society to believe the idea is a truth or is morally right. Corporate strongholds could be societal ideas on life, sexuality, marriage, or family structure. Such clichés as "the one with the most toys wins" or "women must be married to be happy" could be born from corporate strongholds or mindsets. An individual stronghold could be the idea that women are weak; men are stupid; or that "children must be seen and not heard." Other individual strongholds are ideas in an individual such as "I am stupid" or "I can't change."

Some have referred to strongholds as habits, fantasies, or persistent ideas that occur over and over again. Whatever the strongholds are, they are formidable obstacles to the process of healing, restoration, and recovery. Strongholds are deeply embedded in a person's mind and block the relationship one has with God and others.

"The weapons we fight with are not the weapons of the world. On the contrary, they have divine power to demolish strongholds. We demolish arguments and every pretension that sets itself up against the knowledge of God, and we take captive every thought to make it obedient to Christ" (2 Cor. 10:4-5).

God has created us with lives and wills of our own. Because we are made in the image of God, we have creativity, and, thus, what we create can have a life of its own. When I worked in sales, I had a particular route that I drove to work every day. I am a routine person. I like structure, so I make my life as simple as possible by keeping a routine. After several years of working at this job, I was called into ministry. I left the job and began a new life in another part of town. I had very little occasion to travel the "job route."

One day, after several years of doing my new ministry job, I found myself on the street where my old job was. I did not consciously think about it, but, before I knew it, I was about to turn my vehicle into the parking lot. I had created a structure in my mind that took over. This is a very simple example of a stronghold. This stronghold had little consequence, except a feeling of embarrassment for almost turning into the parking lot. The person in my vehicle said, "Where are you going?" I laughed an embarrassed laugh and said, "I guess I was going to work."

Before a person comes to Jesus Christ, there are many such structures of thinking in our minds. We are made new creatures in Christ at the new birth, but these old ways of thinking can resurrect and maintain lives of their own.

"Paul tells us that the mind set on flesh is not our friend; it is death."

In Romans, Paul tells us that the mind set on flesh is not our friend; it is death. The mind set on the spirit is life, according to Romans 8:6. The mind set on flesh is hostile toward God, according to Romans 8:7. **The mind governed by the flesh is death, but the mind governed by the Spirit is life and peace. The mind governed by the flesh is hostile to God; it does not submit to God's law, nor can it do so"** (Rom. 8:6-7).

The mind can be your worst enemy. The mind sets up a throne and will not come off the throne without a fight. Some believe the first sin was a mental sin as Eve thought about what Satan said. If you think about the brain as a computer, the physical brain is the hard drive, and the physiological brain is the software. If the brain has been sinfully programmed, the only remedy is to wash those programs out of the computer. That is why we must be born again. **"Do not conform to the pattern of this world, but be transformed by the renewing of your mind. Then you will be able to test and approve what God's will is—his good, pleasing and perfect will"** (Rom. 12:2). In other words, we must change our minds. I have told countless people that my job is to change their minds about addiction, sin, and God.

The mind can only focus on a few things at a time. It processes a lot of data, but the thinking brain blocks out a lot of sensations. As you walk into a room, there are countless details, but you focus on the things your mind doesn't block out of the conscious realm. This is why two people can enter a room and see different things about the room. This ability to block out sensations may also cause the mind to block out the Holy Spirit. The mind set on flesh rebels against the Holy Spirit. In recovery, a person must learn to war against his or her own mind. This is not chasing demons; this is destroying every lofty thing raised up against the knowledge of God. It is taking every thought captive to the obedience of Christ.

> **For though we live in the world, we do not wage war as the world does. The weapons we fight with are not the weapons of the world. On the contrary, they have divine power to demolish strongholds. We demolish arguments and every pretension that sets itself up against the knowledge of God, and we take captive every thought to make it obedient to Christ (2 Cor. 10:3-5).**

The Word of God is the greatest weapon against the strongholds of the mind. The truth of God's Word breaks down the walls of the stronghold and forces the stronghold to be destroyed using the Word of God. To break down these strongholds, you must first recognize that you have a mind of your own. There may be a little truth in it, but there is always a lie behind the stronghold that can mask and cloud the real issues. You must then repent or choose to turn from the stronghold. This repentance includes commanding the negative thoughts to be still, learning to hate these strongholds, and allowing Jesus to put them to death by His death on the cross.

You must build new ways of thinking that exalt the name of Jesus. These strongholds are overcome by the Bible being read over and over and over. You must not only read the Word, but also grasp the meaning of the Word. As you get strength from the Word of God, self-centeredness will be destroyed.

Corporate strongholds are shared ways of thinking. This is a type of tradition that actually controls masses of people. The Nazi movement is a good example of a corporate stronghold that controlled a large group of people in nearly destroying the Jewish nation. Corporate strongholds rob a person of rationality and the ability to contradict the stronghold. They rob a person of freewill, create tunnel vision, and block the Word of God. Corporate strongholds make the spirit fall asleep.

TODAY'S SCRIPTURE

"I will walk about in freedom, for I have sought out your precepts" (Psa. 119:45).

TODAY'S PRAYER

My heart is in anguish within me; the terrors of death have fallen on me. Fear and trembling have beset me; horror has overwhelmed me. I said, "Oh, that I had the wings of a dove! I would fly away and be at rest. I would flee far away and stay in the desert."

As for me, I call to God, and the LORD saves me. Evening, morning and noon I cry out in distress, and he hears my voice. He rescues me unharmed from the battle waged against me, even though many oppose me. God, who is enthroned from of old, who does not change—he will hear them and humble them.

Cast your cares on the Lord, and he will sustain you; he will never let the righteous be shaken (Psa. 55:4-7, 16-19a, 22).

TODAY'S JOURNAL ENTRY

Write about your freedom in Christ.

DAY SEVEN

REALITY

There are countless examples of people caught up in addiction. Alcohol and prescription drugs present a particular problem because they are considered legal but are deadly.

Audrey's husband first contacted me about her alcohol use. She was married to a pastor and had the world by the tail. The family lived in a house built with her money, since she worked in a highly lucrative industry. He pastored in a well-respected resort town in an old, established church. Financially, they were set. Physically, they were beautiful. Nothing was missing in their world, except peace.

She was "pretty sick," he said. Pretty sick meant that she was no longer able to maintain household chores, and her job was requiring treatment—or else. It was apparent that her husband would like to keep "it" quiet; that is why he brought her to us. The other reason was he didn't have insurance to cover a lengthy stay in a hospital. He wanted her to have spiritual help.

Her smile was infectious. Her personality was troubling. Not that she had a bad personality—that was not the problem. It was that she repeated the stories of her life over and over. I remember talking to her about the alcohol problem, and it was like she didn't—or couldn't—understand what I would say to her.

This type of conversation is not unusual because alcoholics live in denial. But, there was something more. Audrey completed her ninety days, and then she went home. Her husband hoped she would return to work, but that didn't happen. Her short-term memory was totally gone.

A couple of years passed, and her husband called me again. This time she was very, very sick. Her diagnosis was grim. The alcohol had caused senile dementia which, to the untrained eye, appeared to be Early-onset Alzheimer's. She walked with a stumbling gait, and what she could remember, she talked about like it was yesterday. She spoke of being pregnant, which was at least sixteen years prior. She spoke of her once-successful career as though she had worked yesterday. She could not remember that alcohol was bad for you. She had to be kept far away from alcohol of any kind. She was forty-nine years old, but alcohol had taken her life—though she didn't die until she was fifty-four.

I guess the saddest part of this story is the way the other women in addiction treated Audrey. Even though they were told that she was a victim of alcoholism, they believed she could be "saved." These women tried everything to "save" her. They would argue with her and demand she listen to them. Audrey would say that she would change, but the next day, it was all the same. She would ask the same questions over and over, day after day after day. We put signs up to remind her not to rake leaves in the rain. Her mind was prone to compulsive acts, and she had raked her yard as a child. Now, in order for her to think she was helping, she had to rake yards. The weather was terrible one day, and I looked out the window to see Audrey drenched from head to toe, raking leaves.

"Come inside," I said as I led her into the house.

She said, "I need to rake these leaves. I don't know where they come from."

Finally, Audrey began to get hostile, and the women were hostile to her, so she had to leave Bethesda. She was placed in a personal care home, where she died about two years later. I went by to see her from time to time, but she didn't remember me. My heart was broken. She was a real-life example of what excessive alcohol can do to the brain. You might not believe the reports of science or medicine until you live with an Audrey.

Virginia was in her early thirties when she came to Bethesda. Her mother was so grateful that she had someplace to go. This was another case in which the residents did not believe what was happening to this woman. She seemed sober when she arrived. Her mother did say that she had been drinking. I cautioned them both that alcohol can be dangerous to detox from without medical help. They both agreed that she had been "through it" many times, and they signed off on the medical release.

We had planned a baptismal service on the night she arrived. The entire group of women always travel with me, since the ministry is a family-style ministry. Before the baptism started, Virginia started to mumble under her breath. She then got louder and louder. All at once, she began cursing as loud as she could. The group with us and those at the church were stunned. She was slipping into a fantasy world or delirium caused by the alcohol leaving her body. By the grace of God and some good training, I was able to calm her down, but not until she ran out of the church and started down the roadway.

Later that night, she began hallucinating, telling the girls that her daddy was downstairs waiting on her. One of the other women in the program came to me to tell that "she was faking." I explained that Virginia wasn't faking anything. She was in psychosis from drinking too much alcohol. When the alcohol began to leave her brain, she was confused. But the other woman could not believe it. But, you see, I could believe it because I was the one to calm her down. I prayed earnestly that her mind would return to her. I am not sure how sane she was after that because when the "miseries" set in, she convinced herself that she could return home and remain sober. The last I heard, she was drinking again.

It took about three years for one of our clients to return to sanity. She had auditory and visual hallucinations for about a year after she stopped using drugs. She would say, "Do you hear them? The drugs are calling me to come to them." I asked an addiction counselor what was happening to her. She told me it was cocaine psychosis. She told me to pray that she would come back to her senses because, sometimes, they remain like that until they die.

---

*"We teach that there is always another relapse in every person, but there may not be another *recovery*."*

Two things about these particular stories stand out. One is that the other women didn't believe what was happening, and the other is that the women who suffered from the debilitations could not get better. One group could not stand to look in a mirror that reflected what drugs or alcohol can really do to the brain. The other group crossed a line and could not return. We teach that there is always another relapse in every person, but there may not be another recovery.

TODAY'S SCRIPTURE

"You have been set free from sin and have become slaves to righteousness" (Rom. 6:18).

TODAY'S PRAYER

Show me your ways, LORD, teach me your paths. Guide me in your truth and teach me, for you are God my Savior, and my hope is in you all day long. Remember, Lord, your great mercy and love, for they are from of old. Do not remember the sins of my youth and my rebellious ways; according to your love remember me, for you, Lord, are good.

Good and upright is the Lord; therefore he instructs sinners in his ways. He guides the humble in what is right and teaches them his way. All the ways of the Lord are loving and faithful toward those who keep the demands of his covenant (Psa. 25:4-10).

TODAY'S JOURNAL QUESTION

What does transformation look like in your life?

❧ CHAPTER ELEVEN ❧
DUNG GATE: GATEWAY TO RESTORING MY FUTURE

"I had the leaders of Judah go up on top of the wall. I also assigned two large choirs to give thanks. One was to proceed on top of the wall to the right, toward the Dung Gate" (Neh. 12:31).

"Over the Gate of Ephraim, the Jeshanah Gate, the Fish Gate, the Tower of Hananel and the Tower of the Hundred, as far as the Sheep Gate. At the Gate of the Guard they stopped" (Neh. 12:39).

"By night I went out through the Valley Gate toward the Jackal Well and the Dung Gate, examining the walls of Jerusalem, which had been broken down, and its gates, which had been destroyed by fire" (Neh. 2:13).

"The Valley Gate was repaired by Hanun and the residents of Zanoah. They rebuilt it and put its doors with their bolts and bars in place. They also repaired a thousand cubits of the wall as far as the Dung Gate" (Neh. 3:13).

"Your people will rebuild the ancient ruins and will raise up the age-old foundations; you will be called Repairer of Broken Walls, Restorer of Streets with Dwellings" (Isa. 58:12).

DAY ONE

LOST

The lost are all around us. They struggle with their relationships. The lost look like us, but inside, they are lost. They are wandering aimlessly through the mire of broken dreams, wounded hearts, and thoughts of what could have been and what should be.

I was privy to one such struggle recently. I will try to explain in words the best I can as I look from the outside into this struggle. She was brought up in a Southern home, complete with a demanding father and a controlling mother. It seems the parents stayed together in a form of love which required a lot of codependency. He didn't go to church, but she did. Perhaps it was the holiness of the mother that finally brought the father to the Lord. I really can't say. What I know is that the change in the father brought a change in the household—but not really. He was saved clean through, or so she says.

The father and the mother went to church together. He became a deacon, and she continued in her submission. The children, however, were somewhat affected by all of this. Having lived a deeply religious life with their mother, they rejected that lifestyle and pursued, with restraint, a life without God. What I mean by "with restraint" is that they had a sense of morality. They would go so far, and then stop . . . well, they would try to stop. In respect to their mother, they would commit adultery but not prostitution. They could live with a man getting a divorce but never break up a marriage. This is the thinking of the world—sin with restraint, sin in the name of love.

When I met my friend, she had an idea of what God was. I say what God *was* because her concept of our Lord was limited with her upbringing and years of living separated from God, His Word, and His people. She only came in contact with His church when she went home to her mama and daddy. They tried to reintroduce her, but she says their tactics were harsh. The god she knew about could be reduced to a plastic cross hanging on a piece of yarn. She did not know anything about God being a real, loving Father.

When she came to Bethesda, she was polite, but guarded. Anything I said was filtered through her morality. She was here to get her life back, not to change her life. She laid down her bottle, picked up her Bible, and began to pray, with reserve, that she could be sober, with God a little on the edge of her life. In fact, her sister, a very persistent Christian, tried to push her into a commitment to Jesus, but my friend held her ground. As most of us know, guarded Christianity is not Christianity at all. She left our house, not drinking, living with "a little bit of God." But "a little bit of God" is a dangerous thing.

Two years later, she was back at Bethesda. As soon as I spoke to her on the phone, I knew she was down, and she was with me—and God, mostly—alone. And let me tell you, that "me and God" stuff is pretty hard at first.

She had a dream prior to her arrival at the house. It was a spiritual dream about her boat being blown up. In the middle of the explosion, she found herself floating and feeling total peace. Two months later, she had another dream that she had killed a man and that she had to do it. She felt no remorse in the dream, for it was something she had to do to help the man be saved from some terrible torture. I am not a great dream interpreter, but I kind of knew that God was trying to say to her, "Surrender."

Her dream allowed her struggle to come to her conscious mind. Her first dream offered her peace if her boat was blown up. Her life raft, though it was small, would offer her more peace in the time of trouble than her boat. The second dream showed her the internal fight with herself. In order to live, really live, she would have to kill the part of herself that pushed her into hell. That part was unbelief. The best thing for her to do was kill the "man" who was going to be tortured or go to hell. It wasn't long after that, she surrendered at an altar service. These were her words to me: "I can't stand it anymore; the struggle is too much; I give up."

This was just the beginning for her. She has a man in her life. He is lost as well, and he is struggling. She calls him about once a week. I was walking by one day when her conversation became strange. She kept saying, "There is nothing wrong. I've had the best week I've had since I've been here. It must be your phone. I am okay. You can ask Cathy."

He was asking her what was different. He could hear it in her voice. He could hear the change in her voice. The struggle with the world had changed.

She told him her salvation experience on the phone, and now the ball was in his court. What would he do? He would do nothing.

It just isn't that simple to convert another person. This one—though she had something that her loved one would want—found out that he was quite satisfied with his life. It was her life that he wanted changed. He just really wanted her to quit drinking, and that would, by his estimation, solve their problems. Now she knew something different. She knew that she couldn't stay sober without surrender. Surrender to the highest power was her only hope for sobriety. Yet that would mean a lifestyle change. Changes that could end this relationship. Changes that could result in financial difficulty. It is easy to say, but hard to do.

"I give up," she said. But give up what? She says today that she gave up heartache, confusion, desperation, alcohol, family conflict, and sudden death. She gained a life of freedom of choice, joy in the bad times, hope in the worst times. My friend's surrender gave her many years of life to live—sober living with her loved ones.

THE DUNG GATE

The Dung Gate was where all the waste of the city was taken and destroyed and made into a usable product. It is at the Dung Gate that you deal with your past. The past pain you have caused and the past suffering you have felt must be picked up and taken outside of yourself. You must come clean from the past.

KEY TO MY FUTURE

You can rebuild. The future depends on a new foundation. Use this key to remind you that rebuilding the future will be work.

ACTION STEPS

- Make a list of people you have hurt.
- Pray daily for these people.
- Make a list of things you can do to heal their hurt.

- Make a list of the people you have hurt who don't know how you have hurt them. (Example: shoplifting, adultery, lies, etc.)
- Pray for direction as to how to make restitution to the people on both lists.

PRAYER

"I have been placed right in the middle of the Dung Gate. It feels pretty rotten here right now. 'Deal with my past,' they say. But I don't know how. Show me how to deal with my past mistakes and failures; and when this restoration is complete, use my past to help someone else.

"I know I don't always believe that I am salvageable, but, today, I believe Your love makes me worthy. I can be saved from my past and from a future like my past. While I am here, make me able to take the baking and the heat of the 'Gehenna pile.'

"There are others at the Dung Gate today, seemingly thrown out and stinking. I pray that they will know that You are the Master of restoration. You, Lord, have put me in this place to be restored and to bring about restoration—just like the dung piles outside the cities of old where the refuse was taken. There, in the pile of trash, a fire was kindled from on high, and the flames and heat from that which was not completely ready to be used started the work of restoration in the fresh dung. Help me today to bring the fire of revival to others thrown here today. I was once thrown away; help my fire to stay so hot that others will catch the heat. Please, bless other ministries like this one. Bless their coming in and their going out of the community. Grant your favor on them today as I pray for specific ministries. Prepare the hearts of others to help with drug and alcohol restoration. Prepare my heart to help."

TODAY'S SCRIPTURE

"Whoever steals an ox or a sheep and slaughters it or sells it must pay back five head of cattle for the ox and four sheep for the sheep" (Exod. 22:1).

TODAY'S PRAYER

Prayer for Spiritual Restoration

"Forgive me, Father God. I have realized that I have become so engrossed in my own affairs and interests that I have wandered far away from You, and my life seems to be pretty meaningless.

"Thank You, Lord, that, in Your grace, You have sustained me thus far; but I know, Father, that I need to get my life back on a spiritual level. I do thank and praise You that, in Your grace, You have got[sic] my attention and made me realize my need to return back into a right relationship with You.

"Thank You for sustaining me, even when I had wandered far from You. And thank You that Your steadfast love never ceases and that Your tender mercies are new every morning. You are a great and faithful God. Help me, I pray, to get a proper perspective on life, and I ask that You would restore the joy of my salvation and help me to keep my eyes looking to Jesus, my feet firmly planted on the road of righteousness and peace. This, I ask in Jesus' name, Amen."[85]

TODAY'S JOURNAL QUESTIONS

What do you think is fair repayment for things that have been taken from you?

---

85 "Prayer for Spiritual Restoration." In Prayers for Restoration. Knowing-Jesus.com, http://prayer.knowing-jesus.com/Prayers-for-Restoration#sthash.a6z4tFfh.dpuf (accessed August 18 2017).

DAY TWO

RETHINKING THE PAST

Many people get stuck in the past and refuse to leave it. They become bitter and angry over things they cannot change. The past is their present and will become their future, unless it is dealt with.

Warren Wiersbe wrote, "The sanitary disposal of waste materials is essential to the health of a city. This gate did not have a beautiful name, but it did perform an important service! It reminds us that, like the city, each of us individually must get rid of whatever defiles us, or it may destroy us."[86]

The Dung Gate was an important gate for the city. Inside the city walls, everyone could feel safe. Outside of the walls, enemies could attack at will, but inside the gates, residents felt safe. As you can imagine, people had trash. Inside the city, there was a lot of waste material that had to be gathered and taken outside. Refuse from animals and people accumulated inside the city walls, so a dung gate was necessary to take the waste materials outside. What was interesting about the waste pile was that on one side of the pile was the fresh dung, and on the other was dried, hard dung. The fresh dung was useless as it was. It smelled. It carried disease. It was ugly.

At Jerusalem, the Dung Gate led to Gehenna. Gehenna was a place of never-ending fire. Nobody had to start the fire; the fresh dung, piled high, released methane gas, and the heat from the sun sparked a blaze. The fire never went out because fresh dung was the fuel, and the city never ran out of fresh dung.

As the dung deliverer disposed of his or her cargo, he would go around to the other side of the pile and pick up some of the hard, dried dung and take it home. The dried, hard dung, baked in the heat of the pile and the daily sun, was used to fuel household cooking stoves. The waste had become useful. It is very important that we see the working of the Gehenna pile in relationship to the dung. The dung had to be disposed of. The waste had to be carried away. It also had to be fired for some time before it would become useful again.

---

86 Warren Wiersbe. "Nehemiah 3." *The Wiersbe Bible Commentary: Old Testament.* Colorado Springs: David Cook, 2007. 761.

This is the way of recovery. Those in recovery must first be willing to carry the waste products of their lives outside of themselves by confession, repentance, restitution, and making amends. The restitution is where the firing takes place. You see, everybody doesn't desire restitution or amends. But, in order to work the past out of the present, a person may need to make restitution. This is a self-esteem builder, in my opinion. Now, this may go against the grain, but for recovery to be full recovery, people need to make restitution.

At the Dung Gate, you must dig up the past mistakes, admit them, carry them away, and then allow God to bake them in His furnace until they can be used for something good. For example, you hurt your children by failing to take time with them. You miss important events, spend money on yourself while your children are neglected, etc. When you come into recovery, as part of healing, you should ask forgiveness of your children and then, as restitution, begin to spend time and money on them. Now, some wrongs cannot be righted. For example, adultery may or may not be made right. This will depend on the hurt party. But you can still make amends by being faithful in all present and future relationships.

At the Dung Gate, you are taking the ugly things out of your life by making the list of those you have harmed and coming to grips with the fact that you have harmed others. At this time, you are digging up the old to carry it out of your life and learning that you can bury the "dung of your life" outside. Once the "dung" is removed, you can let go and rebuild the waste places of your life.

TODAY'S SCRIPTURE

The Lord said to Moses: "If anyone sins and is unfaithful to the Lord by deceiving a neighbor about something entrusted to them or left in their care or about something stolen, or if they cheat their neighbor, or if they find lost property and lie about it, or if they swear falsely about any such sin that people may commit—when they sin in any of these ways and realize their guilt, they must return what they have stolen or taken by extortion, or what was entrusted to them, or the lost property they found, or whatever it was they swore falsely about. They must make restitution in full, add a fifth of the value to it and give it all

to the owner on the day they present their guilt offering. And as a penalty they must bring to the priest, that is, to the Lord, their guilt offering, a ram from the flock, one without defect and of the proper value. In this way the priest will make atonement for them before the Lord, and they will be forgiven for any of the things they did that made them guilty" (Lev. 6:1-7).

TODAY'S PRAYER

"Just for today, I believe that my past can be forgiven and that I can overcome all the sins I have committed. I trust You, Jesus, to help me to make the list of those I have harmed and to take responsibility for those wrongs. Amen."

TODAY'S JOURNAL QUESTION

What sins in your life do you consider character defects? Which of these character defects have caused the most problems in your relationships?

DAY THREE

SIN/DISEASE CONCEPT: DELIVERANCE

In studying deliverance, let's take a look at the most famous deliverance in all of biblical history. The deliverance of the children of Israel from their bondage in Egypt to their arrival in the Promised Land parallels deliverance from the bondage of negativity. Their initial deliverance, through the parting of the Red Sea, seemed to be complete with safety from the hands of Pharaoh; but, in reality, they were only in the beginning stages of their journey of deliverance.

The plight of the Israelites seemed hopeless. Many became resigned to their fate and continued in their forced labor, not believing that anything would ever change. Others cried out, desperate for relief, yet there was no escape. Perhaps some, in their desperation, attempted to free themselves, but there was no freedom to be found. Every attempt at flight was foiled by the cruel hands of those in power, whether it be the overseer or the master himself.

Today, you may be in a similar situation, for there is nothing new under the sun. Unable to free yourself—even in your desperation—you become resigned to your fate. Believing there is no way out, you will continue in your addiction until death. Some cry out and attempt to escape under their own power but are, inevitably, hunted down and ensnared once again by people or events of the past. Ultimately, it is the past itself which renders you powerless.

In your mind, there must be some external influence powerful enough to deliver. You are unable to deliver yourself because every cell of your body is in bondage. You cannot love yourself enough to come out. Your will was turned over long ago, and you have been beaten into total submission. The small spark of life left in us can only be fanned into flame by the hand of God touching us through the hands of another human being. A physical deliverer must come.

In the days of Moses, the Israelites understood the concept of a deliverer. Today, we would translate it as a friend, a sponsor, a counselor, a family member, a member of the clergy, and, of course, ultimately, Jesus Himself.

The children of Israel sought deliverance, and God sent it in the form of a man, Moses. The hearts of the people were ready for true deliverance, their desperation having kept the sparks alive until they could see and recognize their deliverer. Moses, likewise, had been prepared, for God had told him that deliverance would come but that the Pharaoh would not easily relinquish his hold on the people. He also made it clear to Moses that because of the extreme measures it would take to ensure deliverance, the children of Israel would have no doubt that it was God Himself Who was their ultimate Savior.

A key factor in the deliverance of the Israelites was the occurrence of the plagues used to demonstrate to Pharaoh and the people the ultimate power of God. The plagues began, and while they were difficult to bear, they were understandable under natural law. As the severity of the plagues increased, however, they became more terrible and inexplicable. The plagues also were selective. Those children of Israel, dwelling in the land of Goshen, remained untouched by the destruction around them, and their normal lifestyle, though still one of bondage, remained unchanged.

Ten plagues haunted the Pharaoh, the people, and the "gods" of Egypt. It became obvious that their powers were limited, at best; and no matter what happened, God would deliver His people. What was happening was that prayers, which had reached heaven long before the deliverance began, set the stage for the release from the land of Goshen. Every time the Pharaoh thought he would release the captives, he would reconsider and demand that they stay. Time after time, the Israelites expected to be out of bondage, only to be stopped by the continued power of the Pharaoh.

"Like those bound in slavery in Egypt, we are caught by the hand of Satan in the battle for sanity."

Like those bound in slavery in Egypt, you are caught by the hand of Satan in the battle for sanity. Prayers for those caught in negative lifestyles set the stage for deliverance as the pervasive power of the enemy releases you only momentarily. You are only flirting with the chance for release. Many times, you will continue your day-to-day existence of bondage with only a single glimpse of the deliverance ahead. Sometimes, the power of Satan to hold you becomes stronger during this beginning stage of deliverance. You may increase your tolerance to bad habits, worsened living conditions, and more demanding lifestyle changes. The bondage seems to be getting worse, instead of better.

Trips to detox centers and hospitals for treatment often end in vain attempts to help. This becomes quite frustrating for everyone concerned. The attitude of instantaneous delivery is so prevalent that if the first or second try doesn't result in a complete change, many give up at this point. In truth, like the Israelites, you need to not give up because deliverance will come. This is so like the children of Israel as they waited for the day of exodus. They, too, tired from the long years of waiting, wanting to leave immediately, and grew angry and upset with their deliverer before the release came.

When the day for exodus arrived, the Israelites were instructed to be ready. They could not be wishy-washy or hesitant when the time came to go. When it was time to go, they must be packed with everything they needed for the journey. There would be no turning back.

Often in the field of addiction, you hear a counselor say, "You can't help them if they are not ready." How true this was for the day of exodus so long ago, and how true it is today for the chemically enslaved. You may readily voice the desire to stop and make the steps toward treatment. Then, just as everything seems to be all right, a huge problem has to be overcome. Just like the Red Sea, the Israelite's deliverance would only end in death if they could not believe God for a way out. For you, the Red Sea could be a job loss, loss of children, or the loss of a spouse if you follow the way out. Only until the Red Sea was parted could the children of Israel begin to believe that their deliverance was real.

In a case study for Bethesda Recovery, these exodus examples are easy to identify. A young woman in her mid-thirties was caught in a series of addictions, which started at the age of twelve. She began with alcohol and progressed to cocaine, mixed with alcohol and various prescription drugs. Her lifestyle influences were filled with slavery to addiction issues, since most of her acquaintances were addicts and dealers. This woman, however, was able to maintain a job and to present to the working world a somewhat functioning human being. She was truly caught in bondage and had, on occasion, sought a way out. But, quite frankly, the addiction was so strong, there was little or no hope for true deliverance.

Someone invited the young woman to a Christian revival service; and though she was using cocaine, marijuana, and pills at the time, she decided to attend. Mainly, her purpose for the attendance was to be with people, but what happened was something she had not expected. At the end of the service, an altar call was given; and the young woman, for the first time in a long time, recognized that the Deliverer, Jesus Christ, just might be able to help her. She prayed a prayer herself and allowed the others there to pray for her and with her. This was the beginning. Like the children of Israel, she had sought escape from bondage and cried out to God to deliver. But she did not know that when the process began, things could and would get worse.

The days and weeks that followed proved quite painful for the young woman. After all, the slave owner did not want to give her up. Satan, symbolic in Pharaoh, had a good slave; she was obedient and dependable to him, so he was not about to let her go on the first try.

At first, there were Christian women around her to try to help her, but nothing really happened. One by one, each of them got discouraged by the attempts for freedom and soon left her alone with her Pharaoh. Her drug buddies knew she was trying to stop the addiction, but they continued to call her and leave messages.

One attempt after another to tell the Pharaoh to turn loose was botched by an ever-changing mind. At first, it seemed that Satan would turn her loose, and, momentarily, she would find peace; but then, from nowhere, the addiction would return stronger and more powerful than ever before.

Ten months passed until Satan was ready to turn her loose, and she was ready to escape. There was only a small window of opportunity. Everything had to be done just exactly by design. Nothing could be left undone, or this woman would not cross her Red Sea. What was her Red Sea? Loneliness. One morning, after the bondage had gotten to the point of her attempting suicide, this woman was nearly ready for her escape. But not quite. Drastic measures had to be taken for her deliverers to get her out of immediate danger—like those of God to get the children out of Egypt. Moses had to direct and plan a Passover meal and time of preparation for the people, so when the time came, the Red Sea would be no problem.

It was during this time that the woman in the study was prepared to be taken to a treatment facility against her will. She was asking for help, but the only way to get it was this way. The parallel with the children of Israel was that they had to follow the plan of God and the directions that Moses gave them, or they would never make it.

Getting the young woman to the treatment facility was not her Red Sea experience. It was seven days later, when she was faced with losing the friendships she had developed and the one safe place she had ever found in her life or going back to the familiar problems of her past. She could stay in treatment long enough to get her mind straightened out, or she could go back. What would she decide? She decided to cross the Red Sea.

The decision that young woman made that day was the beginning of her deliverance. She was unable to rejoice in the fact that she had made it this far. Maybe God the Deliverer would be able to help her. Surely, He would carry her through to the promised destination. For that moment in time, everything seemed to be heading in the right direction.

Too often, the Israelites put their trust in the God of Moses, since they had really never seen or known God for themselves. They had never experienced what miracles God could do. After all, they had been exposed to the gods of Pharaoh for so long, that was all they knew. To trust a God you had only met for a moment and then to see things really get worse in life seemed to them just a little too hard to take. These people decided early on that Moses was the one that knew God, so let him talk to God and have faith in Him.

This is what happens so often in our lives. For a time, at least the faith of the deliverer must be strong enough to sustain us. After all, how can we see or know Jesus Christ unless the deliverer can bring the salvation message to us?

After forty years of wandering around in the wilderness, the children of Israel were faced again with the possibility of going into the Promised Land. The Promised Land was still in the same place it had always been, but something had happened to the Israelites. They had died. A whole new "people" were ready to enter the next phase. What had died in the Promised Land? The answer was ten spies and their followers. God only allowed the two men who had given the positive message of a Promised Land to finally obtain that land.

Of course, as the story goes, twelve spies were sent out by Moses to see what the Promised Land looked like. All came back with the same story. They all had seen lush fruits, green pastures, and plenty of resources with which to live the life of abundance. They all said there were people there in the land that had to be overcome. The spies all agreed that the people were giants. One thing was different in the report that Joshua and Caleb gave than the rest of the spies. They saw the Israelites as victorious.

- Where are you now in your recovery?
- Do you understand the meaning of the death of the "old man?"
- What things in your life need to be put to death?

TODAY'S SCRIPTURE

The LORD sent Nathan to David. When he came to him, he said, "There were two men in a certain town, one rich and the other poor. The rich man had a very large number of sheep and cattle, but the poor man had nothing except one little ewe lamb he had bought. He raised it, and it grew up with him and his children. It shared his food, drank from his cup and even slept in his arms. It was like a daughter to him. "Now a traveler came to the rich man, but the rich man refrained from taking one of his own sheep or cattle to prepare a meal for the traveler who had come to him. Instead, he took the ewe lamb that belonged to the poor man and prepared it for the one who had come to him."

David burned with anger against the man and said to Nathan, "As surely as the LORD lives, the man who did this must die! He must pay for that lamb four times over, because he did such a thing and had no pity."

Then Nathan said to David, "You are the man! This is what the LORD, the God of Israel, says: 'I anointed you king over Israel, and I delivered you from the hand of Saul. I gave your master's house to you, and your master's wives into your arms. I gave you all Israel and Judah. And if all this had been too little, I would have given you even more. Why did you despise the word of the Lord by doing what is evil in his eyes? You struck down Uriah the Hittite

with the sword and took his wife to be your own. You killed him with the sword of the Ammonites. Now, therefore, the sword will never depart from your house, because you despised me and took the wife of Uriah the Hittite to be your own.'

"This is what the LORD says: 'Out of your own household I am going to bring calamity on you. Before your very eyes I will take your wives and give them to one who is close to you, and he will sleep with your wives in broad daylight. You did it in secret, but I will do this thing in broad daylight before all Israel.'"

Then David said to Nathan, "I have sinned against the LORD." Nathan replied, "The LORD has taken away your sin. You are not going to die. But because by doing this you have shown utter contempt for the LORD, the son born to you will die" (2 Sam. 12:1-14).

TODAY'S PRAYER

"Take away my fear of looking into the mirror and seeing what I have become. Help me today to face the past and deal with what I have done to others and to myself."

TODAY'S JOURNAL ENTRY

Describe your responsibility to make amends for the wrongs that you have committed.

DAY FOUR

RESTITUTION/AMENDS

"Through love and faithfulness sin is atoned for; through the fear of the LORD evil is avoided. When the LORD takes pleasure in anyone's way, he causes their enemies to make peace with them" (Prov. 16:6-7).

Restitution is a large part of healing for both the injured and the injuring. Making amends is a lost art in the Christian community. So often in the church, a person is told to ask God to forgive him or her, and that is that. This could be why so much of the church is still in pain over the past and also why so many continue to do the same sin over and over again.

Making amends means more than just saying, "I'm sorry." Making amends means apologizing and repaying the person with an act of contrition. For example, if a person stole one hundred dollars, an apology would be, "I am sorry that I stole your money. I was wrong." Amends would include that same apology, along with one hundred dollars or more repaid to the person.

Jesus said if you go to the altar to worship but discover your brother has something against you, you are to go to that brother and make it right with him (Matt. 5:24). Making amends is making it right with your brother.

There are times when making direct amends may be impossible or inappropriate. Impossible times could include the death of the injured party. Inappropriate times could include times when an injured party does not know the full extent of the injury, and to make direct amends would cause more harm. In these cases, indirect amends can be made. An example of indirect amends could be to do volunteer work for the express purpose of paying back a debt to society.

I once heard of a lady who continues to pay back by taking care of stray animals. This is her way of repaying the kindnesses she received while in addiction and also repaying those who were harmed in her addiction she could not remember.

- What are some ideas you have about making amends?
- Who will you need to make amends to?
- Can you find additional Scriptures to help you decide who you need to make amends to?

"Therefore, if you are offering your gift at the altar and there remember that your brother or sister has something against you, leave your gift there in front of the altar. First go and be reconciled to your brother; then come and offer your gift" (Matt. 5:23-24).

TODAY'S SCRIPTURE

"Fools mock at making amends for sin, but goodwill is found among the upright" (Prov. 14:9).

TODAY'S PRAYER

The Serenity Prayer by Reinhold Niebuhr (1937)

GOD, grant me the serenity

to accept the things I cannot change,

Courage to change the things I can, and

Wisdom to know the difference.

Living one day at a time;

Enjoying one moment at a time;

Accepting hardships as the pathway to peace;

Taking, as He did, this sinful world as it is,

Not as I would have it;

Trusting that He will make all things right

If I surrender to His Will;

So that I may be reasonably happy in this life,

And supremely happy with Him forever in the next. Amen.[87]

TODAY'S JOURNAL QUESTIONS

What things in your life must you accept to go on with recovery? What things must you change to go on with recovery?

---

87   Reinhold Niebuhr. "The Serenity Prayer." Hazelden Betty Ford Foundation, http://www.hazelden.org/web/public/serenityprayer.page?printable=true&showlogo=true&callprint=true.

DAY FIVE

DECLARING TRUTH

Making declarations of truth each day can help change the mind and bring about a mental and spiritual transformation. In **Ephesians 6:11-17**, Paul tells the Christians that they must be strong in the Lord. He said they were wrestling **"against the rulers, against the authorities, against the powers of this dark world and against the spiritual forces of evil in the heavenly realms."** As we seek recovery, there is a similar warfare that comes to destroy us. The visible enemies—such as drugs, alcohol, or triggers—are difficult enough to battle; but there are spiritual enemies at work as well. These spiritual enemies are more than figments of our imagination; they are very real enemies.

One such example of a spiritual enemy is the "call of the wild." This "call of the wild" is that "thing" that grabs us at the front door of Wal-Mart and, without a conscious thought, drags us to the beer and wine aisle. It is also that "spirit" of the drug that redirects our vehicle from home to the dope house, instead of work or church.

The addiction itself has a spirit. It has a voice that we can hear in our spirit. It is not in our mind; it is in our spirit. That spiritual force draws and drags us beyond our will. The Word of God is the only weapon that can take down those spiritual foes.

The following is what you need to do each morning to set the tone of your day. It is taken from Ephesians 6:11-17, where Paul spoke of putting on the whole armor of God, and is adapted to your situation.

- The helmet of salvation protects your mind from the fiery darts of the enemy. The enemy will try to convince you that you are not saved. Put on your helmet.
- The breastplate of righteousness must be put on next—but not your righteousness because it is as filthy rags. The enemy cannot penetrate the breastplate of Christ's righteousness.
- Put on the girdle of truth. Truth holds your armor together. It is important to tell the truth, but it is also important to believe the truth about yourself and others.

- When you put on the shoes of the Gospel of peace, you become a peacemaker, and the Word says that peacemakers will see God (Matt. 5:9).
- Take up the shield of faith. It is not your faith, but His faithfulness that shields you.
- Take up the Sword of the Spirit, which is the Word of God. Hide the Word in your heart. That is your most powerful weapon against Satan.
- Put on the garment of praise; be thankful in everything.
- Finally, with every step you make throughout the day, say to yourself, "Left foot, I am dead to the demands of my flesh," and "Right foot, I am alive in Christ." The flesh demands you do what it wants you to do. You must tell it no. You do not have to follow fleshly demands because you are dead to those demands, and you are alive in Christ Jesus.

DECLARATION

"By faith I put on:

The helmet of salvation to protect my mind from the fiery darts of the enemy.

I put on the breastplate of righteousness—not my righteousness but the righteousness of Christ.

I put on the girdle of truth. I will tell the truth, and I will believe the truth.

I put on the shoes of the Gospel of peace, and everywhere my feet take me, I will take the Gospel of peace.

I take up the shield of faith—not my faith, but your faithfulness.

I take up the Sword of the Spirit, which is the Word of God.

Over all that, I put on the garment of praise, and I will be thankful.

Left foot, I am dead to the demands of my flesh.

Right foot, I am alive unto Christ."

NAMES OF GOD

Jehovah Rohi means "the Lord our Shepherd."[88] Taken from Psalm 23:1, the Scripture indicates the character of God to be as trustworthy as a good shepherd. The shepherd is a symbol of a trustworthy caregiver who is both lord and king to his sheep.

Psalm 23, A Psalm of David

> **The LORD is my Shepherd, I lack nothing. He makes me lie down in green pastures; he leads me beside quiet waters; he refreshes my soul. He guides me along the right paths for his name's sake. Even though I walk through the darkest valley, I will fear no evil, for you are with me; your rod and your staff they comfort me. You prepare a table before me in the presence of my enemies. You anoint my head with oil; my cup overflows. Surely your goodness and love will follow me all the days of my life, and I will dwell in the house of the Lord forever.**

NAMES OF GOD PRAYER

> "You are *Jehovah Rohi*, my Shepherd, and I thank You for that. Thank You for providing green pastures for me, for making me to lie down in them. Thank You for keeping me safe today, yesterday, and tomorrow. Thank You for the hook that caught me when I went too far from the path You showed me. Thank You for breaking my leg when I was so disobedient. Thank You for being the Good Shepherd today."

TODAY'S SCRIPTURE

> **"Do to others as you would have them do to you" (Lk. 6:31).**

---

88 Brandon Web. "The Names of God – Jehovah-Rohi." Brandonweb.com. http://www. brandonweb.com/sermons/sermonpages/psalms96.htm (accessed August 21, 2017).

TODAY'S PRAYER

I love the LORD, for he heard my voice; he heard my cry for mercy. Because he turned his ear to me, I will call on him as long as I live. The cords of death entangled me, the anguish of the grave came over me; I was overcome by distress and sorrow. Then I called on the name of the LORD: "LORD, save me!" The Lord is gracious and righteous; our God is full of compassion. The Lord protects the unwary; when I was brought low, he saved me. Return to your rest, my soul, for the LORD has been good to you.

For you, LORD, have delivered me from death, my eyes from tears, my feet from stumbling, that I may walk before the LORD in the land of the living (Psa. 116:1-9).

TODAY'S JOURNAL ENTRY

Describe how you want others to treat you.

DAY SIX

THE SHEPHERD

Unless you live in sheep country, the picture of the shepherd looks romantic. We see photos of shepherds tending sheep in beautiful scenery, experiencing tranquil, peaceful moments. The life of a shepherd, however, is more than beautiful scenery and tranquility. It is a life made to look simple by skill and determination.

The shepherd prepares the pasture before the sheep arrive by removing any dangerous weeds or underbrush. He carefully surveys the terrain for stones, which can injure the sheep. Once the shepherd has led the sheep to the pasture, he then begins his vigilant watch over them. He watches for bears, lions, or wolves, which could devour his flock. He watches the sheep to make sure they do not fall over from their heavy wool coat, especially taking care that they do not fall into the water.

One of my favorite shepherd stories is one of patience. Occasionally, a sheep will step in a hole, fall over on its side, and not be able to get up. The shepherd will go to the sheep and stand him up between his own legs. He will be wobbly for a little while, but the shepherd just patiently holds the sheep steady until he regains his balance. Oh, how a shepherd must love his sheep. To the sheep, the shepherd is protector and provider. He is their leader and king—a good king who knows his subjects by name.

Jail time has a way of breaking you down. It takes pride and puts it in a whole new dimension. Women go into jail with dignity and come out either busted down to dirt or like a mad bull, destroying everything in its path. One woman, in particular, was busted. Like a kitten left on your doorstep, she wanted to come close to get the milk, but she was pretty afraid, so she spit and tried to be bad. And just like a kitten, one scoop, and she was in your hands, lapping up the warm milk and purring to the affectionate petting.

I learned the art of drawing in the hurt and wounded from Janice. Janice is the shepherd of all run-away or abandoned animals. She taught me about the wounded and abandoned through a cat that strayed up to the recovery center.

The cat was beautiful—well, at least on one side. She was white, but on the "other" side, she was blood red. That's because she had blood on her neck and side from a fight with something a little bit "bigger and badder." Shepherd Janice saw the wounded animal and, at once, tried to get the cat to come near. The cat refused. At first, Janice offered the cat water and a little dry cat food. No luck. Then she offered canned tuna or something of the fish sort, and that enticed the wounded cat. Of course, the cat did not eat while the shepherd was close enough for the cat to see her. But Shepherd Janice waited out of sight and, hopefully, out of smell to peek at the cat eating the food.

This went on for days. Then, one morning, I saw her take an old shirt she had worn and put it on a chair on the porch.

"What are you doing?" I asked.

"I am letting her get used to my smell," Janice said.

Little by little, the cat surrendered to the help of the shepherd. Little by little, the shepherd waited with loving patience. Finally, one day, the cat was in Janice's lap, and not many days later, the blood was gone, and the cat was named Izzy.

I saw something pretty wonderful happen with a creature alone, hurt, and abandoned. What the creature needed first was physical care in the form of food. Then, the creature needed safety in the form of a familiar smell. Finally, the cat needed love that could be found in the lap of a loving shepherd.

How could this creature care be incorporated into people care? Here was a woman, hurt from the world's abuse, abandoned by family and friends because of her personal choices, and in desperate need of nurture to heal a wounded spirit. Could I take the steps of Shepherd Janice and become Shepherd Cathy to women?

Let's go back to the woman from jail. She was so hungry. She received no canteen money from family or friends because she had been cut off. The food in jail caused her allergies to flare up, so she hardly ate anything for months because no one would rescue her from her jail cell. She was abandoned. Though she did drugs, she was not familiar with the jail clientele. She had been alone. She needed to be nurtured.

I tempted her with food. Pizza and biscuits and fried chicken and spaghetti and candy all made up for some of the lack in jail. Conversations, hugs, and laughter began the healing of abandonment. Motherly discipline and respect solved the problem of nurture.

It was a long haul. It took many days and many nights, but, slowly, self-esteem returned. Restoration came to her and her family. Her dream of being restored to her daughter was fulfilled. She went to college, got a good job, and found out that her past could be left in the past.

Thanks, Janice, for teaching me a thing or two about being a good shepherd.

TODAY'S SCRIPTURE

When they had finished eating, Jesus said to Simon Peter, "Simon son of John, do you love me more than these?" "Yes, Lord," he said, "You know that I love you." Jesus said, "Feed my lambs." Again Jesus said, "Simon son of John, do you love me?" He answered, "Yes, Lord, you know that I love you." Jesus said, "Take care of my sheep." The third time he said to him, "Simon son of John, do you love me?" Peter was hurt because Jesus asked him the third time, "Do you love me?" He said, "Lord, you know all things; you know that I love you." Jesus said, "Feed my sheep. Very truly I tell you, when you were younger you dressed yourself and went where you wanted; but when you are old you will stretch out your hands, and someone else will dress you and lead you where you do not want to go." Jesus said this to indicate the kind of death by which Peter would glorify God. Then he said to him, "Follow me!" (Jn. 21:15-19).

TODAY'S PRAYER

"Lord, I do not know exactly what I am to do. I know I need to make amends, but I need strength and wisdom. Help me to follow Your leading as You are my Good Shepherd."

TODAY'S JOURNAL ENTRY

Explain what it means to "feed my sheep."

DAY SEVEN

THE SLEEPING SPIRIT

Time and time again, the psalmist uses the term *awaken* to speak to the Israelites. It is obvious they are not physically sleeping, but have fallen asleep in their spirits. John and Paula Sandford did some research in this area of the slumbering spirit. After studying their materials, I have compiled my own research standing on their broad shoulders.

In their book *Healing the Wounded Spirit*, the Sandfords list several areas in which the human spirit must function properly. A fully awakened spirit can worship with others freely, maintain private devotions, heal physically and emotionally, has creativity, is not locked in a moment of time, has good communication skills, has a mature conscience, knows how to hear from God, and understands the marital sexual union as being holy and pure. A fully awakened spirit is open to God and to man, as you can see from the list of how the spirit functions. When the spirit is partially awakened, it is like a foot trying to wake up. The foot tingles and almost hurts as it becomes awake. During the awakening, sometimes the foot tries to go back to sleep, but the full function of the foot will be realized only if it is fully awakened.[89]

A person whose spirit is slumbering may resist attending church because it is uncomfortable or because they "don't get anything out of it." Likewise, that same person will neglect private devotional times because those times will not be significant for him or her. When a person is partially asleep in his or her spirit time, they have a great problem. What may have happened years ago will still, in many ways, control a slumbering spirit.

The conscience of a fully awakened, fully alive spirit works before there is a negative behavior to warn the person. For those who are not fully awakened, they will suffer from a guilty conscience because they did not know ahead of time what the negative consequence would be for the behavior.

Strongholds of religious thinking, manmade traditions, and societal propaganda will cause a person to fall asleep spiritually. This is a rather common occurrence in the world of recovery. In this lesson, we are only exploring

---

89   John and Paula Sandford. *Healing the Wounded Spirit*. Tulsa: Victory House Publishers, 1985.

these ideas. As we study the restoration and recovery process, we will identify specific healing techniques.

TODAY'S SCRIPTURE

"A new command I give you: Love one another. As I have loved you, so you must love one another. By this everyone will know that you are my disciples, if you love one another" (Jn. 13:34-35).

TODAY'S PRAYER

"Lord, help me to love others. I want to love people in a way that brings glory to You. Please help me be Your disciple."

TODAY'S JOURNAL QUESTION

In what ways have you already learned to love others?

CHAPTER TWELVE
FISH GATE: GATEWAY TO RESTORING RELATIONSHIPS

"Afterward he rebuilt the outer wall of the City of David, west of the Gihon spring in the valley, as far as the entrance of the Fish Gate and encircling the hill of Ophel; he also made it much higher. He stationed military commanders in all the fortified cities in Judah" (2 Chron. 33:14).

"The Fish Gate was rebuilt by the sons of Hassenaah. They laid its beams and put its doors and bolts and bars in place" (Neh. 3:3).

"Over the Gate of Ephraim, the Jeshanah Gate, the Fish Gate, the Tower of Hananel and the Tower of the Hundred, as far as the Sheep Gate. At the Gate of the Guard they stopped" (Neh. 12:39).

————

DAY ONE

RESTORING SELF TO OTHERS

Rebuilding relationships is one of the hardest parts of recovery. Up until now, recovery has been about restoring self to God and restoring self to self. In the efforts to restore self to God, we discovered the need to restore reality, authority, and truth in our lives. As we began to restore self to self, we found that accountability, trust, empowerment, and freedom needed rebuilding. In the restoration of self to others, we have already looked at letting go of the past by facing the truths and taking responsibility for the wrongs we did to others.

As we continue to learn about healthy relationships, we must learn to give. Much of the world believes that giving is all about financial and material gifts. That is actually only one small aspect of the giving we will be learning. This giving will include giving of time, talents, intimacy, and material gifts. Most importantly, it will include giving of ourselves.

"Good, strong, positive relationships are built on
a foundation of trust and mutuality."

Good, strong, positive relationships are built on a foundation of trust and mutuality. Each person in the relationship is trustworthy and gives reciprocally in the relationship. In a positive relationship, no one person gives all the time. However, it is never a contest to see who has given the most or who gave the last time either. This mutuality is open and honest. In a mutual relationship, all parties respect and admire each other. There are no jealousy issues, which could lead to competition between the parties. All parties in this type of relationship are happy to see the other party succeed.

Restoring relationships which have been broken must take extra work on the part of both parties. Trust must be rebuilt to make the relationship function properly. The injuring party must work to build trust. The injured party must be willing to accept what the injuring party does to rebuild trust. This will take communication. Those wishing to restore the relationship must have open and honest communication. Sometimes those who have injured the other party must be willing to listen to the complaints of the one who has been injured. The guilty party must be willing to take responsibility for the restoration. The victim of the hurt or pain must be restored.

How is trust rebuilt? First, it takes time. Any broken relationship should proceed with caution after forgiveness is established. This means that both parties should pay attention to being faithful in the smallest of matters. Establishing integrity in the smallest things can lead to more trust in bigger things.

Be prepared to give time to restoration. This time could be spent in waiting. It could be spent in volunteering to help the injured party or someone else. Plan periods of time to be spent in sharing with someone. Most of addiction is centered around the personal needs of the addict. In restoration of self to others, the recovering person must learn to give time generously.

Sharing talents is yet another form of giving. The talents of those in recovery may have been stifled by their drug of choice. Nevertheless, everyone has abilities that are useful. Learn what your talents are, and give them generously.

Sharing yourself is intimacy. This intimacy has nothing to do with sex. It is allowing another human being to know the "real you." Sharing your dreams, your failures, your successes, and your hopes with another communicates your desire to have an open relationship with another human being.

As you go to some of the people you have hurt in the past to make amends, always think of them first. Consider the timing of the conversation, and consider exactly what you need to say, saying no more than necessary to ease the pain of the past. In other words, do not belabor the amends-making process by going on and on about your addiction. Take full responsibility, and consider how they may have felt. If you do not have a specific direct amends to give with the apology, ask the person to give you an idea of how to repay the pain and restore the relationship. If a person does not wish to restore the relationship, then let it go. Give to that person the respect they deserve, and go on with your life.

Remember, in making amends, do not make the victim feel responsible for your negative actions. After the amends are made, allow the person time to gather his or her thoughts, and let them decide if the relationship is to be rebuilt. Not everybody will want to restore the relationship. Some, however, may want a new relationship with new limits and boundaries. Respect that type of relationship.

FISH GATE PRAYER

"I have hurt many people in my life. Most of the time I am thinking that I have been the hurt one, but I am learning that I have hurt others as well. Show me how to have a right relationship and how to heal the relationships that I have broken. I don't even know which relationships need to be restored. Forgive me where I have hurt others and show me which ones I need to make direct amends to.

"Jesus, today there are thousands of foreign missionaries who are getting ready to go fishing for souls in countries all over the world. There are home missionaries who are leaving their families and friends to go fishing for souls in our country today. Multiply Your blessings on them today. Anchor their hearts in Your kingdom so that when the enemy attacks them, their desire to serve You will not change. Plant their feet in soil that You have prepared and make their harvest plentiful. Give them heathen for their inheritance. Protect these missionaries wherever they may be.

"Please send missionaries to the churches of our land to help bring about revival in the churches of America. Today I pray for missionaries to be called out of this place. I pray that there will be those who hear Your voice call and will answer, 'Here am I; send me.' Protect these missionaries from the separatism, which will try to raise its ugly head in the fields they are in. Give them favor with You and favor with the people they serve today.

"I pray for those going into recovery that they will be met with the Spirit of God before they are met with human hands. I pray that Your Holy Spirit will lead those to these missionary recovery houses with the necessary preparation to grow in Your love. Prepare my heart for every new person You send my way today. Help me to remember that I am a missionary, called by Your loving voice to take my light to others."

BUILDING RELATIONSHIPS

"People from Tyre who lived in Jerusalem were bringing in fish and all kinds of merchandise and selling them in Jerusalem on the Sabbath to the people of Judah. I rebuked the nobles of Judah and said to them, 'What is this wicked thing you are doing— desecrating the Sabbath day?'" (Neh. 13:16-17).

The Fish Gate was a gathering place for people of all kinds. Fisherman brought in fish from the Sea of Galilee through this gate to sell in the city. Other merchants brought their wares through this gate as well. With fishermen and merchants selling their merchandise, people from all over gathered together. How many relationships do you know of that began in a public place? How many relationships were destroyed in a public place? At the Fish Gate, relationships can be rebuilt.

At the Fish Gate and the Harvest Gate, the merchants profaned the Sabbath day by buying and selling the fish and other items. They broke relationship with God and caused personal relationships with others to be strained. Nehemiah sought to restore relationships with God and others by pointing out the problem and offering solutions.

Humility is a key to good relationships. Humility means thinking of others more than yourself. C.S. Lewis said in *Mere Christianity*, "Humility is not thinking less of yourself but thinking of yourself less."[90] Restoring relationships which have been broken must take extra work on the part of both parties. Trust must be rebuilt to make the relationship function properly. The injuring party must work to build trust. The injured party must be willing to accept what is done to rebuild trust. This will take communication. Those wishing to restore the relationship must have open and honest communication. Sometimes those who have injured the other party must be willing to listen to the complaints of the one who has been injured. The guilty party must be

---

90   C.S. Lewis. *Mere Christianity*. New York: HarperOne, 1952.

willing to take responsibility for the restoration. The victim of the hurt or pain must be willing to be restored.

How is trust rebuilt? First, it takes time. Any broken relationship should proceed with caution after forgiveness is established. This means that both parties should pay attention to being faithful in the smallest of matters. Establishing integrity in the smallest things can lead to more trust in bigger things.

Remember, in making amends, do not make the victim feel responsible for your negative actions. After the amends are made, allow the person time to gather their thoughts, and let them decide if the relationship is to be rebuilt. Not everybody will want to restore the relationship, but some may want a new relationship with new limits and boundaries. Respect that type of relationship.

KEY TO RESTORING RELATIONSHIPS:

You can forgive. Relationships are about give and take. Sometimes you give; sometimes you take. In the giving and taking, forgiveness is essential. Use this key to build relationships.

ACTION STEPS

- Give away something you own today.
- Plan what you will give back for the things you have received.
- Offer to help a needy person today.

TODAY'S SCRIPTURE

If I speak in the tongues of men or of angels, but do not have love, I am only a resounding gong or a clanging cymbal. If I have the gift of prophecy and can fathom all mysteries and all knowledge, and if I have a faith that can move mountains, but do not have love, I am nothing. If I give all I possess to the poor and give over my body to hardship that I may boast, but do not have love, I gain nothing.

Love is patient, love is kind. It does not envy, it does not boast, it is not proud. It does not dishonor others, it is not self-seeking, it is not easily angered, it keeps no record of wrongs. Love does

not delight in evil but rejoices with the truth. It always protects, always trusts, always hopes, always perseveres.

Love never fails. But where there are prophecies, they will cease; where there are tongues, they will be stilled; where there is knowledge, it will pass away. For we know in part and we prophesy in part, but when completeness comes, what is in part disappears. When I was a child, I talked like a child, I thought like a child, I reasoned like a child. When I became a man, I put the ways of childhood behind me. For now we see only a reflection as in a mirror; then we shall see face to face. Now I know in part; then I shall know fully, even as I am fully known. And now these three remain: faith, hope and love. But the greatest of these is love (1 Cor. 13).

TODAY'S PRAYER

A Prayer to Choose Life

"Lord, I acknowledge that I have not chosen this life. I never would have chosen my circumstances, my family, my personality, or my body. I have not understood nor appreciated how You have formed me, and I surely would never have chosen to come into the pain of this life. I confess I am angry, having consciously believed You could have done better for me. I have judged my family and authorities as lacking in ability, wisdom, and sensitivity; and I judged You, Lord, for creating me as deficient.

"I have come to see how others have wounded me, and I choose to forgive them for hurting me. My sinful responses have created trouble for myself and others. I can see the damage my rebellion has caused, and I ask You to forgive me for running away and never completing what I was supposed to complete. I know I have wounded You by not receiving Your gift of family and life, even though I don't feel life is a gift, nor do I feel gratified by life. I choose, by faith, to accept myself and the life You have given me as a blessing to You and to others.

Jesus, I choose life. Help me to continue choosing You, choosing to be here. Lord, I ask You to open my eyes to see the gift of life. Release me into the abundant life You promised. That joy that comes from knowing I am wonderfully made, a blessing to You and to my family and friends. Help me to know the abundant joy that comes from moving toward the destiny You have planned for me. Lord, lead me into the joy of my birthright, the blessing of my inheritance in You."

TODAY'S JOURNAL QUESTION

How can love help you make amends?

DAY TWO

CODEPENDENCY

Many songs over the years have been written on the subject of love.

The purpose of a man is to love a woman,

And the purpose of a woman is to love a man.

So, come on, baby, let's start today; come on, baby, let's play

The game of love, love, la la la la la love.

It started long ago in the garden of Eden,

When Adam said to Eve, baby, you're for me.

So, come on, baby, let's start today; come on, baby, let's play

The game of love, love, la la la la la love.[91]

"Love hurts, love scars, love wounds, and marks."[92]

I took my troubles down to Madam Ruth.

You know that gypsy with the gold-capped tooth.

She's got a pad down on Thirty-Fourth and Vine.

Sellin' little bottles of Love Potion Number Nine.

I didn't know if it was day or night.

I started kissin' everything in sight.

But when I kissed the cop down on Thirty-Fourth and Vine,

He broke my little bottle of Love Potion Number Nine.[93]

Oh, the games people play now,

Every night and every day now,

---

91   Wayne Fontana and the Mindbenders. Game of Love. Fontana. TF535,267420, 1965. 7," Single.
92   Nazareth. Love Hurts Down. Vertigo. 6078209, 1974. 7," Single.
93   The Searchers. Winners Circle Series. A Kapp Record. KJB-27, 1964. 7."

Never meaning what they say,

Never saying what they mean.[94]

The music industry has given us a definition of what love is. The worldview creates a certain mystique about love, and we get lost in the confusion of what love is supposed to be.

Codependency is a sin/disease which attacks the heart. Codependency is a love disease. Codependency was first determined to be an extension of the disease of addiction, which affected the family members of the addict. The sin/disease of addiction somehow goes viral in the family members, friends, and associates of most addicts. Since we do not understand what love really is, we adjust our feelings to mean love when we are often caught up in codependent relationships, which only perpetuate harmful, addictive behaviors.

The mind tricks of addiction are so contagious. We are certainly in denial and repression, but so are family members. Addiction is never a completely individual thing; it always involves others. Any and all mind tricks are designed to perpetuate the addictive behavior. The only thing that ends addiction is stopping the behavior. Anything that does not support ending or stopping the behavior supports the behavior; thus, codependency is born. Even though all parties concerned want the addiction to end, they find themselves in collusion with the addiction. Collusion is "a secret agreement between two or more parties for a fraudulent, illegal, or deceitful purpose."[95]

Family members, friends, and co-workers will often make excuses for you. Family members will call in for you when you are not sick. They will cover for you. All of these behaviors only serve as addiction support. The term "tough love" is used to describe what the family member should do in order to help you. Family members and friends should never tell lies to protect you. Guilt is a major trigger for codependents, so you will play on the guilt of those who know about your addiction. Codependents do not understand that love is not always saying yes. Sometimes, the most loving thing a person can do for someone who needs recovery is to say no. Codependency is often described as an addiction to people, places, or things. This addiction comes with its own

---

94   Inner Circle. Games People Play. WEA. 4509-96595-2, 1994. compact disc.
95   *Dictionary.com, s.v.* "Collusion," accessed October 26, 2017, http://www.dictionary.com/browse/collusion.

withdrawal. True love is found in God. In 1 Corinthians thirteen, Paul describes what love is in verses four through eight:

> **Love is patient, love is kind. It does not envy, it does not boast, it is not proud. It does not dishonor others, it is not self-seeking, it is not easily angered, it keeps no record of wrongs. Love does not delight in evil but rejoices with the truth. It always protects, always trusts, always hopes, always perseveres. Love never fails. But where there are prophecies, they will cease; where there are tongues, they will be stilled; where there is knowledge, it will pass away.**

That is the true love of God.

TODAY'S SCRIPTURE

> **"Brothers and sisters, do not slander one another. Anyone who speaks against a brother or sister or judges them speaks against the law and judges it. When you judge the law, you are not keeping it, but sitting in judgment on it" (Jas. 4:11).**

TODAY'S PRAYER

"Lord, today I need Your help. I am facing my past. Help me to be brave and to brace myself for any rebuttal I may deserve from those I wish to make amends with. Help my amends be about how they feel and not about how I feel. Amen."

TODAY'S JOURNAL QUESTION

How have you judged others? How have they judged you?

DAY THREE

WORD STUDY

Love

In English, we use one word to describe our feelings toward our friends, family, chocolate, pets, spouses, television programs, and favorite movies. We also use it for anything else that gives us a warm, fuzzy feeling. That word is *love*. It is no wonder people get confused about love. If you love your dog, food, and people all the same way and to the same degree, you can get confused.

Love was never meant to be confusing. God is love, and He wants us to love Him, love others, and love ourselves. God's essence is love; therefore, everything that comes from Him comes through love. This is hard for sinful man to understand. In the Bible, there are several words used to better understand what love means.

God's love is described in Greek as *agape* love, which is selfless love with the other party's best interest at heart.[96] In Greek, there is also *philia*, which is translated as "brotherly love."[97] The Bible speaks of *philargyria*, the love of money.[98] The love of a spouse is *philandros*.[99] All of these are used in the New Testament to better explain the meaning of love.[100]

In the Old Testament, the Hebrews had several definitions of love. *Ahab* was used for love when there was a desire for another."[101] *Chashaq* means "to be joined together or to cleave to another."[102] *Racham* means "tender affection."[103]

---

96   *Wikipedia, s.v.* "agape," accessed August 23, 2017, https://en.wikipedia.org/wiki/Agape.

97   *Wikipedia, s.v.* "philia," accessed August 23, 2017, https://en.wikipedia.org/wiki/Philia.

98   *Latin Dictionary, s.v.* "phylargyria," accessed November 13, 2017, http://www.latin-dictionary.org/Latin-English-Dictionary/philargyria.

99   *Strong's Concordance, s.v.* "philandros," accessed August 30, 2017, http://biblehub.com/greek/5362.htm.

100 *Wikipedia, s.v.* "The Four Loves," accessed November 13, 2017, https://en.wikipedia.org/wiki/The_Four_Loves.

101 *Bible Tools, s.v.* "Ahab," accessed August 30, 2017, http://www.bibletools.org/index.cfm/fuseaction/Lexicon.show/ID/H157/ahab.html.

102 *Blue Letter Bible, s.v.* "chashaq," accessed August 30, 2017, https://www.blueletterbible.org/lang/lexicon/lexicon.cfm?strongs=h2836.

103 *Blue Letter Bible, s.v.* "racham," accessed August 30, 2017, https://www.blueletterbible.org/lang/lexicon/lexicon.cfm?t=kjv&strongs=h7356.

Dodavahu, in Hebrew, was used to describe being beloved.[104] *Ra'yah* is "a female friend or a girlfriend."[105]

Love is never using another person for selfish motives. That is lust—an overwhelming desire or craving. When we crave something, we will go to whatever lengths it takes to get that craving satisfied. A craving indicates selfish motives. What do you crave? How do you know if you are experiencing love or lust?

TODAY'S SCRIPTURE

"Not looking to your own interests but each of you to the interests of the others" (Phil. 2:4).

TODAY'S PRAYER

Husband or Wife

In the space provided on the next page, draw the handprint of your spouse; and as you pray, place your hand over theirs by faith to bless them and ask for their protection.

Five areas to pray for:

- Perseverance
- Protection from temptation
- Growth in their love
- Increased knowledge of Christ
- Strength in their innermost person

---

104 *Bible Hub, s.v.* "dodavah," accessed August 30, 2017, http://biblehub.com/topical/d/dodavah.htm.

105 *Messie2vie, s.v.* "rayah," accessed August 30, 2017, https://www.messie2vie.fr/bible/strongs/strong-hebrew-H7474-rayah.html.

If you are single and wish to be married, begin praying this prayer for your future spouse, speaking life and liberty into them, even before you meet them.

TODAY'S JOURNAL ENTRY

Make a list of the things you are grateful for about your relationships.

DAY FOUR

DELIVERANCE

From the day Moses led the people out of Egypt until the day the spies went to take a look at the Promised Land, much transpired. God parted the Red Sea; Moses received the Ten Commandments; the golden calf was formed; instructions were given for the building of the Tabernacle; and the cloud and the fire appeared. Manna was given; bitter water was made sweet; and quail were given to the people for meat. Over and over, God was doing miraculous signs and wonders before the people.

You might think that with all of those miracles, the spies would be supercharged with faith. Also, with the promise before them, you would think that they would be ready to charge the giants and get on with their new lives. But that is not what happened at all.

Numbers 13:33 gives an indication as to the problem: **"We saw the Nephilim there (the descendants of Anak come from the Nephilim). We seemed like grasshoppers in our own eyes, and we looked the same to them."**

"We seemed like grasshoppers in our own eyes." The spies, at least ten of them, saw themselves as small and crushable. They assumed the people of the land of Canaan saw them as crushable as well. All through the study of deliverance, we have discussed the attributes that cannot go into the Promised Land. This view of self is found in each of the names of the ten spies who could not believe God could change the way others viewed them.

Gaddi, son of Susi, was from the tribe of Manassah; and Ammiel, son of Gemalli, was from the tribe of Dan. They were two of the spies sent to Canaan. *Gaddi* means "fortunate."[106] This can be translated to mean fortunate, as with money. The love of money will not enter into the Promised Land. Gaddi saw himself as one who was more blessed than others. This attitude is often known as one of superiority. People who have superior attitudes or personalities often have low self-esteem. It is easy to see that this man would see himself as a

---

106 *Blue Letter Bible, s.v.* "Gaddi," accessed August 30, 2017, https://www.blueletterbible.org/lang/lexicon/lexicon.cfm?t=kjv&strongs=h1426.

grasshopper if he saw the great wealth of the Promised Land compared to his wealth. He would easily be crushed in his spirit.

Ammiel means "people of God." The original "el" referred to a Canaanite God and was later attributed to Jehovah. Part of Ammiel means "darkness associated with it or to make secret."[107] His name would point us to the darkness of the past or the associates from the past who would convince you that this deliverance won't work. The associates of your old ways must go. Even some of the ones who call themselves Christians may not be able to continue to be associates. All negative attitudes will have to go to get to the destiny of the promise. For those in addiction, the destiny and the promise are restoration and sobriety.

TODAY'S SCRIPTURE

> " . . . Any man or woman who wrongs another in any way and so is unfaithful to the LORD is guilty and must confess the sin they have committed. They must make full restitution for the wrong they have done, add a fifth of the value to it and give it all to the person they have wronged" (Num. 5:6-7).

TODAY'S PRAYER

In the space provided on the next page, draw the handprint of each child, and pray for them in these areas:

- Growth in the knowledge and admonition of the Lord
- Protection from temptation
- Growth in their love for God and others
- Increase in the knowledge of Christ
- Strength in their innermost person

---

107 *Abarim Publications, s.v.* "Ammiel," accessed August 30, 2017, http://www.abarim-publications.com/Meaning/Ammiel.html#.WabR2siGPZY.

Also pray that their spouses are being prepared by God and to keep them chaste until they come together.

If you have no children but wish to have a child, begin by praying for children. Just as Abraham and Sarah waited, so we must wait for God's perfect timing.

TODAY'S JOURNAL QUESTION

How can you make amends to the children in your life?

DAY FIVE

NAMES OF GOD

When Moses was questioning Who he would say had sent him to deliver the Israelites out of Egypt, God told him to say, "I AM has sent me to you" (Exod. 3:14b). The people of Goshen, the land where they lived in Egypt, knew about gods. The Israelites had tried to hold on to the God of Abraham, Isaac, and Jacob; but over time, the Egyptian gods had infiltrated their beliefs. A new religion was embedded in them. Moses would have to present to them the one, true God. He would have to tell them of Jehovah God in a fresh and new way. "I AM"—*Ehyeh Asher-Ehyeh*—speaks to the God of creation, the God Who is, Who was, and Who shall be. This is the name of God revealed in Exodus 3:14.[108] The people of Goshen would understand this God was the true God of all being, bigger than all of the gods of Egypt.

PRAYER

"You are the Great I AM, all that I need. You were the Great I AM when I started this journey. You were the Great I AM when I needed Your help to continue this journey. You are still the Great I AM in my life today, and I thank You for that. O praise Your Name that You are the Great I AM."

TODAY'S SCRIPTURE

"Fools mock at making amends for sin, but goodwill is found among the upright" (Prov. 14:9).

TODAY'S PRAYER

Write the name of the person to whom you will make amends to first in the blanks below and then pray this prayer for that person.

---

108 J.K. Cronin. "The Name of God as Revealed in Exodus 3:14." Exodus-314.com. http://exodus-314.com/part-ii/the-meaning-of-ligehyeh-asher-ehyehlig.html (accessed August 30, 2017).

PAUL'S PRAYERS

"May God give _____ wisdom and revelation to know Jesus better. May the eyes of his (or her) heart be enlightened in order that he may know the hope to which Jesus has called him, the riches of his glorious inheritance in the saints, and Jesus' incomparably great power for us who believe. May that power that raised Jesus from the dead be the power that keeps _____ from temptation and from harm and makes him to be the new creation in Christ he is meant to be. I pray that out of his glorious riches, Jesus may strengthen _____ with power through the Holy Spirit in his inner being, so that Christ may dwell in his heart through faith. I pray that he be rooted and established in love and have power to grasp how wide and long and high and deep is the love of Christ and to know this love that surpasses knowledge that he may be filled to the measure of all the fullness of God.

"Jesus, fill him with the knowledge of Your will through all spiritual wisdom and understanding and that he may live a life worthy of the Lord and may please Him in every way, bearing fruit in every good work, growing in the knowledge of God and strengthened with all power according to His glorious might so that he may have great endurance and patience and may joyfully give thanks to the Father Who has qualified him to share in the inheritance of the saints in the kingdom of light."

TODAY'S JOURNAL QUESTION

What is your plan to maintain your life of recovery?

DAY SIX

BASIC TRUST

Growth and development play an essential part in the way relationships will form throughout one's lifetime. From conception until death, human beings will continue to develop. Each one's maturity level is unique, but in growth and development, basic trust is the key element for restoration and recovery.

Basic trust begins long before a person recognizes or can communicate trust. A baby before birth can sense trustworthiness; and as that baby is born, trust will develop or not develop according to the nurture given to the baby. More than one scientific study has proven that pre-birth infants can hear, recognize voices, and even sense fear or experience trauma.

Once, a family brought a young boy to counseling because he was experiencing great fear. His mother could not leave him. The boy was about nine years old. There was no apparent reason for the fear the child was experiencing. To the inexperienced ear, the story sounded as if the young boy was in trouble at school or that he was experiencing some trauma at home. But, after examination, it was found that the child was not in trouble at school. In fact, his grades were good, and his social skills were acceptable. His parents were not facing anything out of the ordinary, and his home life was secure. The counselor, a child psychologist, and a Spirit-filled minister began asking questions of the family that seemed to me not to be relevant to the problem. After a few minutes, a fact that had been left out of previous counseling was revealed.

During the mother's pregnancy with the baby, a severe tornado had hit the family's home. The mother was in bed when the tornado hit the house. A tree had crashed into the bedroom, and limbs hit her bed, pinning her there. Recently, nine years after the tornado, the family had gone to see a movie about a terrible storm. It was discovered that the boy's pre-birth fear manifested after seeing the movie. After the source of the fear was determined, the treatment became more effective. His basic trust had been broken through the manifestation of a fear that had set in before he was born. The remaining therapy would prove to be restoring basic trust by behavior modification and prayer counseling strategies.

Basic trust, as stated earlier, is formed by nurture. When a baby is born, the baby does not know how to love; he or she only knows basic instincts for survival. The parental nurturing teaches the baby a lot about the world. As a baby is fed in a loving and nurturing environment, he or she learns that his or her needs are met, providing a feeling of security. The more often the baby's needs are met without causing the baby to experience trauma (i.e. having to cry for long periods of time without his or her needs being met), the more satisfied the baby is and the more secure. Basic trust is formed with the caregiving parents; love is established; and the baby grows and matures with limited emotional issues, such as basic trust.

"Basic trust is formed by nurture."

Some studies have indicated that a child who has the interactive love of both mother and father early in life will learn to have a secure, basic trust of humanity. The opposite will happen to a child if parental love is withheld or if caregiving is abusive or neglectful. Of course, there are no hard and fast rules for exactly how much nurture is needed to help a child develop basic trust. The more secure the child feels, the less likely it will be that he or she will develop self-esteem issues or other relationship issues as they mature.

Often, a child can have two loving parents and receive basic trust as an infant, but, for some reason, basic trust will be broken at a later date. Basic trust can be broken by sexual abuse, emotional trauma, physical abuse, or emotional neglect. Rape, incest, violence, or drug abuse can cause basic trust issues. Basic trust issues can show up in anger issues, relationship issues (such as multiple marriages), bonding issues, loneliness, and other ways. When a person doesn't have basic trust, it becomes extremely difficult for them to form solid relationships during their life.

Basic trust issues can be related to bonding issues. Teens with bonding issues sometimes join gangs to replace the need for positive relationships. These teens with basic trust issues rationalize their hostile and negative behaviors as being "okay" because "nobody cares, anyway." Adults with bonding issues move in and out of relationships with little or no guilt for hurting another person.

Spiritually speaking, a person with basic trust issues will have a hard time trusting God. This lack of trust can cause many spiritual problems.

> **"Yet you brought me out of the womb; you made me trust in you, even at my mother's breast" (Psa. 22:9).**

> **"For You have been my hope, Sovereign LORD, my confidence since my youth" (Psa. 71:5).**

> **"It is better to take refuge in the Lord than to trust in humans" (Psa. 118:8).**

According to the *American Heritage Dictionary*, *trust* means "firm belief on the integrity, ability, or character of a person or thing."[109] In order to build basic trust, two things must happen. First, there must be a trustworthy person; and next, there must be exposure to that trustworthy person. Since this basic trust is formed in the early years, children need trustworthy parents. Trustworthy parents are those parents who can meet the physical and emotional requirements of an infant. They must know how to love, respect, and care for others.

(Much of the following information is based on John and Paula Sandford's book *Transformation of the Inner Man*, but includes original material from the author as well.)

Emotional development is sometimes measured in years, but mental years and emotional years are different than calendar years. The mental year is a measurement of the developmental accomplishments and lasts from six months to three calendar years. It has been said that basic trust is formed in the first mental year or the calendar years of birth to age two. If basic trust is not formed during this time, the other developmental stages of a child will be underdeveloped.

The stages of mental and emotional development are as follows:

- Basic trust: first mental year or zero to two years of age;
- Independence: second mental year or two to four years of age;

---

109   *American Heritage Dictionary, s.v.* "Trust," accessed September 5, 2017.

- Initiative: third mental year or three to six years of age;
- Gang Age: fourth mental year or seven to twelve years of age;
- Teenage: fifth mental year or thirteen to twenty years of age.

A baby learns basic trust from the primary experience of appropriate, affectionate touch. This appropriate, affectionate touch should come from both parents, but children who get touching affection from their fathers are the most emotionally mature in their development. Spiritually, the father draws his children to life and teaches them how to meet the world, according to John Sandford.[110]

Discipline defines the limits for the child when he or she reaches the independent stages. As basic trust is established, discipline from a loving, trusted parent establishes more trust in the child. This trust is continued to be established as the parent teaches that the correction equals the mistake and that consequences never outweigh the transgression. The consequences for wrongdoing should never be higher than necessary to teach the lesson.

As a child develops independence formed out of basic trust, initiative is gained, and the child now feels secure to enter and sustain peer relationships. The child can freely experience the give and take of sharing emotions and space with others. He or she, at this stage, finds security within self, not others. This child will have a mind of his or her own and will not comply with or dominate others.

From initiative, the child moves into what is called the "gang age," or better called the "group age." A child who has basic trust and develops independence and initiative now can belong to a group of peers with values that may not be the same as the parents without losing individuality. At this stage, the child will begin to experiment with adult life skills. Without basic trust, which brings independence and initiative, the child who is quickly becoming an adult will begin to comply with the gang and take on the gang's attitude and opinions.

Finally, with basic trust fully developed, a child will enter the teenage years able to have mature and equal relationships. He or she will be able to

---

110 John and Paula Sandford. *Transformation of the Inner Man.* Tulsa: Victory House Publishers, 1982.

make decisions based on a growing sense of right and wrong. This child will say no when appropriate.

When a person without basic trust grows up and hits the teenage calendar years, that person may be acting out at a much younger age mentally and emotionally. If an adult has started using drugs, there is a good chance that this adult never developed basic trust or that trust was destroyed by some traumatic emotional event.

The problem that I see happening so often in recovery is that adults are acting like the "premature" people that they really are. A forty-year-old woman may be acting like a two-year-old, who is screaming and throwing a temper tantrum because life isn't going her way. The person helping this woman must be able to treat the woman with respect while helping her to "make up" the years that she never developed emotionally.

> "Families provide teaching opportunities for their children and others who will spend time in their homes."

A person can lose basic trust, as has been said, by some type of trauma. Divorce, teasing, bullying, and ridicule are all traumatic enough for a person to lose basic trust, especially if these events are ignored by loving and caring parents or other adults.

Families provide teaching opportunities for their children and others who will spend time in their homes. These teaching opportunities do not necessarily have to be labeled by the parent as "I'm going to teach you something" times. Families teach a child how to respond by being who they are. So much of what children are later in life is not taught, but caught. By "caught," I mean that the child is observing the behaviors and just picks up things. In a very abnormal home setting, children catch a lot of negative behaviors and negative reactions. Families are the greatest influence in society and provide children the first information they receive.

In Genesis, God told Adam it was not good for him to be alone. God made Eve as a helpmeet for Adam, and then God told them to produce children and populate the world. That family would eventually grow to be the family of mankind. Families would leave other families and settle the entire world.

Families usually are responsible for the children's development of emotional pain. Therefore, the family unit, called the body of the family of God, is responsible to bring healing and restoration of basic trust. In a family unit, an adult can be healed, and basic trust can be restored. How it happens is simple, yet time consuming. The new family, called "the Church," must pray for the person; give appropriate, affectionate touch; encourage the person with books; and provide a life coach for the wounded person.

The adult who has lost basic trust must learn to pray confessional prayers. They must forgive their parents for the wounding that has happened. Forgiveness of others who have wounded them is important, as is letting go of angry feelings toward God for putting them in the family that He gave them. This prayer should include an admission of the lack of trust; the need for healing; and a plea for new eyes to see, new ears to hear, and a new heart to receive whatever God has in store for that person.

There's a saying in the recovery world that you have to "get sick and tired of getting sick and tired." Old timers (or what AA members call people who have long-time sobriety) will say, "You've got to hit bottom." But how do you know when you have "hit bottom" or gotten "sick and tired of being sick and tired"? The addicted brain is compromised by its confused logic. You may need help long before you hit bottom because your bottom can be death.

One key to getting help is to seek help with recovery and never with drugs. This will take work on the part of the family members and other enablers. Families spend thousands of dollars a year trying to keep addicts out of jail, off the streets, and in a job. All of these things end up costing the family more money and the addict more time in addiction.

Although many people believe addiction is the addict's problem, addiction is a family disease. The drug of choice will often overtake the whole family, although only one person is actually using the drug. By this, I mean that the family will be so preoccupied with keeping one off of drugs that they will lose their normal life. Drug activities can be the focus of a person's life, even if they are not using the drug. Families must make a decision to eliminate drugs from their life. All areas of family life must be restored for an addict to become responsible and sober.[111]

---

111   Ibid.

TODAY'S SCRIPTURE

"Therefore, if you are offering your gift at the altar and there remember that your brother or sister has something against you, leave your gift there in front of the altar. First go and be reconciled to them; then come and offer your gift" (Matt. 5:23-24).

TODAY'S PRAYER

"Lord, help me to remember the ones I have hurt. I am so sorry that I did the things I did to each one. I will, with Your help, make amends to these people. Amen."

TODAY'S JOURNAL QUESTION

How will you make amends?

DAY SEVEN

PERFORMANCE ORIENTATION

The lack of basic trust is closely related to another personality problem found in people with addictions. This problem is performance orientation. Performance orientation is also closely related to people-pleasing, workaholism, perfectionism, and a lot of other "isms." Although those in the throes of addiction don't seem to be performance-oriented, many will begin immediately showing this tendency as soon as they start in recovery.

Take, for example, this one woman I knew. She had lived for years in prostitution, selling her body for crack. For days, this woman would work the streets, unbathed, uncombed hair, and totally disheveled. But within a few days of abstinence and in the earliest recovery, she would come to breakfast with her clothes starched and every hair in place. She was "working" for approval in her recovery. If she could just be perfect on the outside, then the inside might not hurt so much.

You foolish Galatians! Who has bewitched you? Before your very eyes Jesus Christ was clearly portrayed as crucified. I would like to learn just one thing from you: Did you receive the Spirit by the works of the law, or by believing what you heard? Are you so foolish? After beginning by means of the Spirit, are you now trying to finish by means of the flesh (Gal. 3:1-3).

A person coming into recovery must learn to be in Christ and then do good works. Performance orientation is an attitude of accepting a lie about oneself; it is a striving to win acceptance, which in some cases has already been given. It is doing the right things for the wrong reasons.

Some of the signs of performance orientation include needing to succeed, needing compliments (even while not believing them), being unable to receive criticism without becoming compulsively defensive, and taking responsibility for everything and everyone's business.

Those with the "doing" problem tend to blame others for problems; they are tired and angry, and often will serve others but refuse to be served by others. These doers cannot receive gifts without reciprocating and will find it hard to be intimate.

All of this doing will result in countless fears, endless striving, lots of insecurity, a compulsive need for approval, depression, abusiveness, and a loser attitude.

The performer is caught in a cycle of being on top of the world but wondering if "it" is really working. As his doing wanes, he realizes that he can't work enough to earn love, and then he slides into a black hole of depression, thinking, "Maybe if I do something . . . " Then, as he does something, things get better. Then there is more work, and maybe more love—or maybe not. This cycle goes on and on throughout the performer's life.

All of this doing comes from a lack of affection or a lack of feeling affection. Sometimes, the person gets affection, but it is not the affection he has decided is necessary for him. Conditional love helps to make a child a performer—along with unwise discipline, poor family values, and sometimes the position in the lineup of the family.

What will help to heal this is appropriate love and acceptance, recognition of sin, confession of that sin, repentance, and forgiveness. The performer must also learn to hate the structures he has built into self. Also, the performer will need appropriate physical touch and learn to laugh at himself. The performer must learn right motives and build friendships with which he or she can begin to risk failure.

TODAY'S SCRIPTURE

"Settle matters quickly with your adversary who is taking you to court. Do it while you are still together on the way, or your adversary may hand you over to the judge, and the judge may hand you over to the officer, and you may be thrown into prison. Truly I tell you, you will not get out until you have paid the last penny" (Matt. 5:25-26).

TODAY'S PRAYER

"Lord, as I go to those whom I have hurt, help me to express to them the deepest regret and to make amends where possible. Help each one to be healed and not hurt by this. Amen."

TODAY'S JOURNAL ENTRY

Write a practice apology and amends to each of those you will speak to personally.

CHAPTER THIRTEEN
HARVEST GATE: A GATEWAY TO RESTORING A NEW HARVEST

"Do not be deceived: God cannot be mocked. A man reaps what he sows. Whoever sows to please their flesh, from the flesh will reap destruction; whoever sows to please the Spirit, from the Spirit will reap eternal life. Let us not become weary in doing good, for at the proper time we will reap a harvest if we do not give up" (Gal. 6:7-9).

"Jehoash king of Israel captured Amaziah king of Judah, the son of Joash, the son of Ahaziah, at Beth Shemesh. Then Jehoash brought him to Jerusalem and broke down the wall of Jerusalem from the Ephraim Gate to the Corner Gate—a section about four hundred cubits long" (2 Chron. 25:23).

"So the people went out and brought back branches and built themselves temporary shelters on their own roofs, in their courtyards, in the courts of the house of God and in the square by the Water Gate and the one by the Gate of Ephraim" (Neh. 8:16).

<hr>

DAY ONE

HARVEST/ EPHRAIM GATE

NEW HARVEST

Earthy—that is how John F. was. A man of the earth. Sweat, blood, and grime were all symbols of who he was and what he did. They defined him. He was my father. Two things I will always remember about him were his hands and his scars. His hands were big and tough. They were lined with the marks of life. They were always stained with the grime of his work, for he was a fixer. He could fix anything. His scars—oh, his scars—thick and marbled, covered his chest and arms. They had faded over the years but were still quite visible to the eye. When he was bare-chested, which was rare, one would wonder exactly what could cause such deep scars.

John F. had a glass eye, yet another scar of his changes in life. I remember when I was a kid, he would take that glass eye out and show it to me. It didn't scare me because it was Daddy's eye. He would laugh, almost a snicker, and say he had a special eye that he could take out of his head. I would try to take my eye out, but he would laugh again and say, "No, you can't take your eye out."

John F. was named for a preacher. He had no middle name because my grandmother didn't know the preacher's middle name. (That's what I think, anyway.) His name, like his scars, made him stand out. They made him have to answer a lot of questions because people have questions about things that are different. Maybe that is what helped him to change so easily.

Things were quick with my father. Quick temper, quick wit, quick friendships, quick moves, and quick decisions all made him a force to be dealt with around the house. But some things were sure—like his word, his family love, and his commitment to my mother. Well, commitment might be the one word that steadied him. He once told me, "When I lived for the devil, I gave him everything. Now I am living for Jesus, and I will give Him everything." Once the decision was made, John F. stood by it.

He was a drunk. I don't call him an alcoholic because when he was a drunk, he was a real drunk. He fought; he cussed; he cried; he threatened the neighbors with his shotgun; he played his guitar and sang Christian songs; and he beat my mother. But he changed.

When he changed, he went to church every time the doors opened, read his Bible every day, threw out his television, stopped drinking, stopped cussing, stopped threatening his neighbors, and became a preacher. Everything about him changed. John F. was my first real example of a changed life. I saw firsthand what life could do to a person, and that person became better, not bitter. He was forever changed.

A blast of heat, a sudden, shocking pain, flames from the motor—no, flames from him. John F. was on fire. His face, his hands, his arms, his chest, blazing. His head hit the hood of the car as he jerked his body from the flaming automobile, screaming, "Help me." But there was no help; at least, that is what John F. knew. The sandy earth beneath him and the ditch close beside offered the only relief in sight. So, he rolled. And he rolled. And he rolled—until, at last, the blaze had subsided, and he was no longer on fire. Or was he still burning?

Others were there when the carburetor on the auto ignited into flames, but the shock of the sight of John F. on fire paralyzed them. Somebody finally called the ambulance and Cleo, my mother, John F.'s wife. She met them at the hospital. She was pregnant and afraid. She didn't know how bad it was until she saw him. His face was swollen; his ears were just hanging. He was black from the burning and rolling in the dirt. He was still screaming—screaming so loud that everybody in the hospital could hear him. Morphine didn't stop the pain; it only eased it enough to get him to therapy. Therapy, then, was a bath. Cleo thought it was salt water—and maybe it was—because he was screaming again. Every day for days and days, Cleo would take her two children, Norma Jean and John Robert, to the hospital to see John F. The doctors didn't know if he would live or what condition he would be in if he did. The burns were severe. And the rolling did stop the flames, but the sand was ground into his body.

Infection, more pain, more infection, swelling, more screaming. John F. survived. The time of recovery was a blur. John F. finally walked out of the hospital, scarred. But this wasn't the first time he had survived. He remembered losing his eye, being buried alive, losing his son, and being told that his firstborn was handicapped. He remembered leaving school in the third grade to work on the farm for food for his mother and siblings. He remembered. He walked out of Flagler Hospital in St. Augustine, Florida, scarred for life and changed.

The tiny, white block house was conveniently nestled behind the garage/gas station on US 1 South. John F. built it himself. Well, a few of his friends pitched in and helped, too. They bartered the work, mostly. Block mason Junior Left did a little work for John F., and John F. repaired his vehicle. John F. was a master mechanic; though, in his day, there was no such title. He rebuilt engines, changed tires, and replaced batteries. He did everything that was to be done to a car. John F. bought and sold junk cars. He even bought a crane to help mash the junk cars and load them on to a big truck to recycle. Then, in the style of the Clampetts, he would drive his window-"air-conditioned" truck to Jacksonville to get a little pocket change.

But the house was his castle. He ruled the roost, and nobody ever questioned John F. Cleo was a worthy opponent, for she had to stand her ground with her husband most of the time. She picked her battles carefully, though, because those scrimmages could backfire at any time.

Church folks visited John F.—well, "visited" might not be the exact word. They brought their cars to his shop to be repaired, and, as any good church-going folk would do, they invited John F. to church. John F., bent under the hood of some car, heard the invitations time and time again. He even discussed these invitations with Cleo. She would always reply, "You know I don't have anything to wear." She was from a Methodist background, where the ladies always dressed to a "T," and John F. had a religious background where people swung from rafters and rolled on the floor.

It had been twelve years since his roll in the dirt. He had continued to drink every night, but never while he was working. John F. was a family man, and he took care of his family. It must have been his father dying when he was a young boy that made him so dedicated, but who knows? He drank because of the pain. The fire had left scar tissue inside and out, and if he didn't move his skin enough, the scars would tighten up.

The house was filled with his presence one particular Wednesday afternoon. With supper always ready at about 5:30 p.m. or 6:00 p.m., the family sat down to eat. John F. announced, "I am going to church tonight." Nobody said a word, fearful that he would make them go with him. But I wanted to go—mainly because I could be with my daddy and because the boys weren't going. We went.

I was the one who got "saved" that night. But John F. was touched. Cleo asked him what was going to happen now. Was he going to take me back to church again? "We'll see," he said.

Sunday morning rolled around, and all of us—except John Robert—went to church. John F. walked the aisle that day; that means he made a public confession that he was a sinner and wanted Jesus Christ to be the Lord of his life from that day forward. He walked that aisle and walked away from the bottle, the cussing, the bad friendships, and the liquor store (which, by the way, he visited every night that it was open).

John F. started a walk that day that would take him the rest of his life to finish. Some say he finished his journey on the day he died. He died at the kitchen table, preparing to go to a revival service. He was on his way to church—forever changed.

John F.'s version of "I love you" consisted of "I feed you, don't I?" That is what spelled "love" to him. He grew up in a small, rural, southern Georgia community and lived through The Great Depression, so food was a big deal to him. His father was much older than his mother, Jane. George, John F.'s father, was a widower, and Jane worked in the house for George's first wife. When she died, I guess it just followed that Jane would marry the old man and keep him company. It turned out that the old man wasn't dead, and they had four more children. But then George died, leaving another widow and three young children. John F. quit school in the third grade to work in the field to help put food on the table. He really didn't remember his father, and Jane never remarried. John F. knew hard work and not much fun. He knew how to survive, though, and survive he did. When Cleo would cook a meal, John F. wanted a little extra left over, just in case someone came by who was hungry. He said, "I care about you by giving you food." But that was his way—his only way.

John F. wasn't much on affection. After all, working from sunup to sundown left little or no time to be affectionate—especially when you added in the drinking time. After his conversion, he went to church all the time, and it was only when he got much older that he ever showed his children any loving. But, when he did change, he always hugged you when he saw you and when you left.

John F.'s way was always right—no matter what happened. He was right, even if he was wrong. There was no doubt in his mind—or yours either, if you stayed around very long. He never told Cleo that he loved her. It was a given to him. He stayed with her, and she stayed with him, so words were not necessary. You might say that John F. was not a romantic fellow at all. After years of marriage and no words of "I love you," Cleo became a little bitter. Though everybody knew they loved each other, the words weren't uttered. He left her first, and she grieved until she left us. But the words still never came. The years that John F. was cruel to Cleo were eaten up with years of taking care of her. She was the sickly one, but he left first. She needed him to stay, but he left her anyway. When God called, John F. had to go. When he left, the words would have been nice, but his actions, again, spoke of his love for her. He left her a way to take care of herself. He didn't leave her without food or housing or clothes or other things. He said "I love you" with things. Maybe that isn't so bad—just different. After all, it was John F.'s way.

Some folks say that your character is what you do when no one is looking, but John F.'s character was always showing by what he did when everybody was looking. He didn't talk about it, but it was there—that ever-present honesty. Honesty that was almost intimidating. What he was, was what you got. John F. was a kind man, though some would disagree. He was a thoughtful man and deep with introspection. John F. lived with a lot of imperfections. Birth defects were thought of as curses in those days, so he lived with a child whom most people thought of as a punishment from God. But John F. didn't see it that way. He just made a way for Leroy to be taken care of all of his days. John F., himself, took care of him during his later years. He lived with knowing that he couldn't save his one son, George, who was born with no birth defects, yet died of pneumonia. John F. built the pine coffin that his son was buried in. His thirteen-year-old daughter turned up pregnant; and in those days, that was another curse. The world would consider John F. cursed, but, somehow, he considered himself blessed. He just loved the child. She was his first granddaughter.

Lots of imperfections filled John F.'s life—alcoholism, one eye, burns over two-thirds of his body, buried alive, divorced, a handicapped child, a pregnant teenager, a dead son, the loss of businesses, and the list goes on and on. Somehow, John F. kept going. No real signs of depression loomed in his life—no attempted suicides, no giving up, no stopping the world and getting off for John F. He just continued to live.

John F. helped to build a couple of rural churches. He could do anything with his hands, so carpentry was not a challenge for him. At seventy-three, he was awarded his General Educational Diploma, the oldest man in Georgia at the time to get his GED. That was quite a feat for him. But John F. was smart, just uneducated. He was a character. He never gave up. He was forever changed.

HARVEST/EPHRAIM GATE

The harvest of grains and the exchange of goods were the focus of this entrance into the city. Your new harvest will come to your life as you continually plant goodness and kindness into the lives of others. This gateway restoration is intentional, as is the rebuilding of the others. Harvest comes as a new job or career or, perhaps, new friends. The word *Ephraim* in the Hebrew language suggests a double harvest. God says He will give you "double for your trouble" (Zech. 9:12). As you continue in the ways we are learning, double fruitfulness will surround you. You must also sow good seeds here because Ephraim means "doubly fruitful."[112] In the past, your sowings have often been bad seeds, and, if you don't begin to sow good seeds, you will immediately reap a double harvest of the bad.

You also accept the reaping of what was already sown. Some things must be reaped. Of course, change in your life today will often cause the reaping of the negative to be much less than if you had not changed. God is merciful. At this gate, you will begin to accept the things you cannot change and have courage to change the things you can.

---

112 *Blue Letter Bible, s.v.* "Ephraim," accessed September 5, 2017, https://www.blueletterbible. org/lang/Lexicon/Lexicon.cfm?strongs=H669&t=KJV.

KEY TO RESTORING A NEW HARVEST:

You can do the next right thing. During addiction, you may have done some bad things. This sows seeds into your life that bring up ugly consequences. Use this key to remind yourself that you can sow good deeds by doing the next right thing.

ACTION STEPS

- Review the action steps you have taken so far.
- List those you need to improve.
- Do a daily inventory.
- Write a prayer for each day, which will encourage you now and in the future to never give up.

EPHRAIM GATE PRAYER

"Jesus, You are interested in all the areas of my life, so I know You are interested in finance. Teach me to be thrifty and wise in all my financial matters. Forgive me when I have failed to pay my tithes to You or have withheld any talent, which You have given me. Show me how to seek Your kingdom first so that all other things will be added unto me.

"Today, there are those of us in recovery who need jobs. The jobs must be safe and drug-free, and those who work around us must be safe and drug-free, so we who are in recovery can be safe always. Please provide jobs where Your Word is free to work in lives and where Your ministry is possible.

"Provide the personal finances I need and have mercy on me, for I have wasted much in my life. Especially bless the companies where women and men work who have been in addiction today. (List names of employers in the local area.) _____

_____

_____

"Bless and protect these jobs and companies. Lord, please double their harvest for Your glory. Lord, I need a new harvest in my life. Show me how and where to sow seeds of kindness, love, and generosity. I need mercy from You and others. Help me to sow mercy in the lives of those around me. I need grace and forgiveness; help me to sow forgiveness and grace today."

TODAY'S SCRIPTURE

The farmer sows the word. Some people are like seed along the path, where the word is sown. As soon as they hear it, Satan comes and takes away the word that was sown in them. Others, like seed sown on rocky places, hear the word and at once receive it with joy. But since they have no root, they last only a short time. When trouble or persecution comes because of the word, they quickly fall away. Still others, like seed sown among thorns, hear the word; but the worries of this life, the deceitfulness of wealth and the desires for other things come in and choke the word, making it unfruitful. Others, like seed sown on good soil, hear the word, accept it, and produce a crop—some thirty, some sixty, some a hundred times what was sown (Mk. 4:14-20).

TODAY'S PRAYER

"Lord, prepare me as I sow and reap what I am learning and as I learn to deal with things that I reap from what was previously sown. Help me to remember that all things do work together for my good, and eventually, things will work out for the better."

TODAY'S JOURNAL ENTRY

Write about which type of soil you believe you are at this time, according to the types listed in the Scriptures above.

DAY TWO

THE GATE OF EXCHANGE

At the Valley Gate in your life, reality is restored. At the East Gate, authority is restored. At the Old Gate, truth is restored. These three gates restore a relationship with God that has long been broken in your life. Of course, once the gates are put in place, they serve as openings for allowing the right things about God in and allowing the wrong things you have learned in the past out of your life. The gates must open and close for life. They must be maintained to keep your relationship open and honest with God. As you continue on your journey to full recovery and restoration, daily inventory of how the gates are maintained should be taken. Reality, authority, and truth restore your relationship with God. This is foundational in your restoration to yourself, others, and the community.

At the Inspection Gate, the Fountain Gate, and the Horse Gate, self is restored to self. In the course of life, negative situations can force a person to hide from self. The true self, the one God intended you to be, is often buried in a myriad of hurt and disillusionment. Accountability, trust, empowerment, and freedom restore self to self. The process of restoration is sometimes referred to as a journey, a decision, or a lifestyle. But, no matter what restoration is referred to as, you must pursue it. Restoration will not pursue you. Each person must begin his own restoration process with the help of God and others. No one can be restored alone.

> "It is very important to go through healing with self and God before attempting to restore relationships."

Often, in recovery, people will rush to restore relationships. They will not take the time to restore their relationships with God and self before trying to restore marriages or jobs or even relationships with parents and children. What may happen with that is a false start. It will look good; behaviors will appear changed; attitudes will seem to be real; but over a short period of time, they will be overwhelmed at trying to do things for the sake of others when those things are burdens. It is very important to go through healing with self and God before attempting to restore relationships.

At the Harvest Gate in Jerusalem, people brought what they had produced to sell and trade to others. It was where they exchanged their harvest, so to speak. They worked to produce the grain or other fruits and vegetables to share with others. There had been a process of sowing and reaping. This is how it should be in the lives of those who are being restored to others.

> **His divine power has given us everything we need for a godly life through our knowledge of him who called us by his own glory and goodness. Through these he has given us his very great and precious promises, so that through them you may participate in the divine nature, having escaped the corruption in the world caused by evil desires. For this very reason, make every effort to add to your faith goodness; and to goodness, knowledge; and to knowledge, self-control; and to self-control, perseverance; and to perseverance, godliness; and to godliness, mutual affection; and to mutual affection, love. For if you possess these qualities in increasing measure, they will keep you from being ineffective and unproductive in your knowledge of our Lord Jesus Christ. But whoever does not have them is nearsighted and blind, forgetting that they have been cleansed from their past sins. Therefore, my brothers and sisters, make every effort to confirm your calling and election. For if you do these things, you will never stumble, and you will receive a rich welcome into the eternal kingdom of our Lord and Savior Jesus Christ (2 Pet. 1:3-11).**

As a person comes to Christ, the power of the Holy Spirit gives that person everything needed for a godly life. As everything needed for a good life is given, the person is to make every effort to add some things to life.

First, faith is a necessary foundation for restoring a good harvest. **"Now faith is,"** according to **Hebrews 11:1, "confidence in what we hope for and assurance about what we do not see."** Confidence in God begins the new planting season. Add to that goodness. This goodness is in word and deed. We must do the next right thing and say the next right thing to produce or add to our faith. This progression is the essence of change. Add knowledge to faith and goodness. Being teachable is an attribute that must be developed to produce a good harvest. To knowledge, add self-control. In the addiction, self-control is lost, but in recovery, self-control is learned and applied. As self-control is added to knowledge, then comes perseverance, which simply means "don't quit." To perseverance, godliness is added. No amount of desire will produce godliness without following this path of discipline. To godliness, you add love of others in your family and the family of God, and, finally, you add love of others outside your sphere of reference.

Verse eight of Second Peter chapter one says that **"if you possess these qualities in increasing measure,"** you will be effective and productive. Those who do not possess these qualities will be nearsighted and blind or ineffective and nonproductive. To restore a productive harvest, these attributes of faith, goodness, self-control, perseverance, godliness, brotherly love, and love for others will need to be present in your life.

TODAY'S SCRIPTURE

"Where there are no oxen, the manger is empty, but from the strength of an ox come abundant harvests" (Prov. 14:4).

TODAY'S PRAYER

"God of life, there are days when the burdens we carry chafe our shoulders and wear us down; when the road seems dreary and end-less, the skies gray and threatening; when our lives have no music in them, and our hearts are lonely, and our souls have lost their courage. Flood the path with light, we beseech you; turn our eyes to where the skies are full of promise."[113]

TODAY'S JOURNAL QUESTION

How will you get strength to have an abundant harvest?

---

113   Woodeene Koenig-Bricker, ed. *Prayers of the Saints: An Inspired Collection of Holy Wisdom.* San Francisco: Harper Collins, 1996.

DAY THREE

SIN/DISEASE CONCEPT

REJECTION

Feelings of rejection from early childhood are a source of pain, which may cause a person to turn to negativity or some medicating behavior or activity. Rejection is commonplace. No one lives life without feeling rejection, but it is the type of rejection that leads to other extreme feelings which we address here. When rejection becomes an idol, a person becomes subject to rebellion, unforgiveness, and bitterness. These four things can become a root system through which all the fruits in a person's life are formed. Such fruit as self-hate, willfulness, irresponsibility, anxiety, paranoia, shame, malice, anger, attention-seeking, and others become the most often produced in a person's life when the root systems include rejection, rebellion, unforgiveness, and bitterness.

The root system changes as we recognize the need to surrender to the authority of Christ. When a life is fully surrendered to Jesus, the fruit will be gentleness, patience, joy, goodness, self-control, love, peace, kindness, faith, and meekness. Out of the root system of the Holy Spirit will flow life to others, thus a new harvest.

The root of rejection is turned to acceptance. The root of rebellion becomes willingness; bitterness becomes sweetness; and unforgiveness becomes mercy.

TODAY'S SCRIPTURE

"Now he who supplies seed to the sower and bread for food will also supply and increase your store of seed and will enlarge the harvest of your righteousness" (2 Cor. 9:10).

TODAY'S PRAYER

Eternal Father, your Son has promised that whatever we ask in His name will be given to us. In His name I pray: give me a burning faith, a joyful hope, a holy love for Jesus Christ. Give me the grace of perseverance in doing Your will in all things. Do with me what

You will. I repent of having offended You. Grant, O Lord, that I may love You always and never let me be separated from You.[114]

TODAY'S JOURNAL QUESTION

Write about how God supplies your seed. What do you think your seed is?

---

114 "Only One Thing is Necessary: A Prayer of Saint Alphonsus Liguori." In *Prayers. The Apostolate of Hannah's Tears.* http://www.hannahstears.com/2011/08/saint-alphon-sus-de-liguori-only-one/ (accessed September 6, 2017).

DAY FOUR

WORD STUDY

NEW HARVEST

A definition of *harvest* is "the result or consequence of any act, process, or event."[115] Consequences rarely mean anything to a person who is in active addiction. A consequence is something that happens as a result of a particular action or "set of conditions."[116] For example, a family member may wonder why an active addict will continue to risk his or her job to continue using. We would see the addictive behavior in two ways. One way is that the addiction is worth whatever consequences we will have to pay if caught. The other way is that the consequences do not exist for us. Forcing consequences brings reality to the situation, but rarely changes behavior.

A mother who stands to lose her child because of using drugs or alcohol will rarely count the cost. She will certainly have feelings of remorse and, perhaps, even act out when the child is taken away, but will rarely stop using drugs because of this. Going to jail will rarely stop an addict. Jail often serves as a respite.

It is only during early recovery that consequences begin to make a difference. Boundaries placed on those in early recovery can help them question if a relapse is "worth it." It is important to impose consequences on those in addiction. It is also important for them to expect to pay consequences for former behaviors. We all must learn that consequences are the logical outflow of any behavior. One of my friends often tells me, "There are consequences for everything."

TODAY'S SCRIPTURE

"Let us not become weary in doing good, for at the proper time we will reap a harvest if we do not give up" (Gal. 6:9).

---

115   *Dictionary.com, s.v.* "Harvest," accessed October 27, 2017, http://www.dictionary.com/browse/harvest.

116   *Merriam-Webster Dictionary, s.v.* "Consequence," accessed October 27, 2017, www.merriam-webster.com/dictionary/consequence.

TODAY'S PRAYER

"Lord, grant me today that I may continue to give, that I may continue to love regardless of the cost and regardless of how long it takes to receive my harvest."

TODAY'S JOURNAL ENTRY

Write about how you will not get weary in doing good.

DAY FIVE

DELIVERANCE

It took approximately two years before the Israelites were camped at Kadesh Barnea. The Lord God gave Moses the Ten Commandments at Mount Sinai after the worship in the tabernacle was established, and the group had learned to fight against enemies who tried to attack them. In the book of Numbers, the history of the wilderness journey unfolds. Chapter one of Numbers tells of the preparations for departure from Sinai. Each of the tribes was counted, and the arrangement of how the camp was to move and be set up is described. In chapter seven of the book of Numbers, Moses set up the tabernacle, anointed it, and sanctified it. The people celebrated Passover. They experienced the cloud and the fire, which hovered over the tabernacle; the cloud covered it by day and the fire by night. In chapter ten, Israel moved the tabernacle and marched for the first time to Kadesh Barnea.

In chapter thirteen, the Lord told Moses to send out the twelve spies. The spies were gone from the camp forty days. As I have stated before, the names of the spies indicate the character defects and flaws, which were not allowed to go into the Promised Land of Canaan. The character defects reflected in each name will need to be put to death by those in recovery in order for recovery to become a successful lifestyle, filled with joy and peace.

Sethur, son of Michael, was from the tribe of Asher. *Sethur* means "hiding self."[117] The hidden self is the problem caused by addiction. Until the hidden self is revealed to you and to others, the Promised Land cannot be reached. Keep in mind that all these people died before anyone could enter the Promised Land.

Hiding is such a part of active addiction. Hiding self, drugs, and behaviors all have a negative part in the addiction process.

NAMES OF GOD

Abram was ninety when *El Shaddai* appeared to him and made a covenant with him to make him the father of many nations. At ninety, Abram was

---

117   *Bible Study Tools,* s.v. "Sethur," accessed October 27, 2017, https://www.biblestudytools. com/dictionary/sethur.

beyond his prime to father a nation. But, regardless of what the natural claimed, God is almighty and could pour His power into Abram—not only to father a child, but also to father a nation. El Shaddai established His covenant with him and changed his name to Abraham.

PRAYER

"You are El Shaddai, 'all-sufficient.'[118] Thank You that You are all-sufficient for those in my life as well as for me. Thank You that You have known what to do when things looked really bad in my life. Thank You that You are more than enough, more than I ever hoped or imagined."

TODAY'S SCRIPTURE

"They sowed fields and planted vineyards that yielded a fruitful harvest" (Psa. 107:37).

TODAY'S PRAYER

"Lord, forgive me for sewing negative words into the lives of others. Forgive me for sewing negative seed into the lives of those I have loved. Give me opportunities to sew positive words and positive deeds today. And when those negative opportunities arise, nudge me by Your Holy Spirit to ignore those opportunities."

TODAY'S JOURNAL QUESTION

There are fruitful crops for a negative harvest. How will you stop reaping the negativity that you have sown in your life?

---

118   *Blue Letter Bible*, s.v. "El Shaddai," accessed October 27, 2017, https://www.blueletter-bible.org/study/misc/name_god.cfm.

DAY SIX

HOW TO SOW SEED FOR THE NEW HARVEST

So often, we speak in metaphors as we work a program for change. Metaphors can be a little confusing, so let's look at practical ways to sow seeds for a new harvest.

Consider any reaping you may be doing at this moment in terms of consequences. All negative consequences are a result of some negative action you were a part of. If you examine the consequences of your life with complete honesty, you will discover the actions it took to reap these consequences. It would seem obvious to eliminate those actions to prevent future reaping of similar consequences. But so many times, it doesn't occur to us to stop the negative behaviors to stop negative consequences. However, this is the first step toward a new harvest.

The next step in the new sowing is to choose positive, life-giving actions. These actions may include offering help to others, volunteering for a positive organization, being an encourager, and, most of all, not breaking any law—whether natural or spiritual. It is only as you stop the negative behaviors and replace them with positive that your new harvest will begin. Remember, all of this takes time.

TODAY'S SCRIPTURE

"The Lord will indeed give what is good, and our land will yield its harvest" (Psa. 85:12).

TODAY'S PRAYER

"Jesus, You are good, and You give me good things. I pray that the seed of the Word will multiply in my life, and it will yield a bountiful harvest in me—so much so, that there will be an outflowing of the harvest to others."

TODAY'S JOURNAL ENTRY

Write about what you are doing now to produce a good harvest.

DAY SEVEN

TREES TO EAT FROM

Adam and Eve were given instruction concerning the tree of the knowledge of good and evil, but not the tree of life. Had they been as interested in life as they were curious about being like God, they would be alive now. We might all be living in the Garden of Eden. However, they chose to eat, or take in, knowledge, instead of life. Mankind still thinks knowledge brings life, but that is the oldest trick in the book. It is life which brings knowledge and wisdom.

How do we eat from these trees? Knowledge does not necessarily make us want to change; life is a change agent. As we gain more and more knowledge without life, we end in despair. We need to learn to recognize only life-giving pursuits. If the choice ends in destruction, make another choice.

TODAY'S SCRIPTURE

"Then he said to his disciples, 'The harvest is plentiful, but the workers are few. Ask the Lord of the harvest, therefore, to send out workers into his harvest field'" (Matt. 9:37-38).

TODAY'S PRAYER

"Lord Jesus, please send laborers into the world to harvest souls. Please send me."

TODAY'S JOURNAL ENTRY

Write about what a harvest looks like in your life.

CHAPTER FOURTEEN

SHEEP GATE: GATEWAY TO RESTORING BELONGING

"My sheep listen to my voice; I know them, and they follow me" (Jn. 10:27).

"Eliashib the high priest and his fellow priests went to work and rebuilt the Sheep Gate. They dedicated it and set its doors in place, building as far as the Tower of the Hundred, which they dedicated, and as far as the Tower of Hananel. The men of Jericho built the adjoining section, and Zakkur son of Imri built next to them" (Neh. 3:1-2).

"Over the Gate of Ephraim, the Jeshanah Gate, the Fish Gate, the Tower of Hananel and the Tower of the Hundred, as far as the Sheep Gate. At the Gate of the Guard they stopped" (Neh. 12:39).

"Now there is in Jerusalem near the Sheep Gate a pool, which in Aramaic is called Bethesda and which is surrounded by five covered colonnades" (Jn. 5:2).

DAY ONE

SHEEP GATE

Everything that pertained to sheep happened at the Sheep Gate. Sheep were very important to the people of Jerusalem. They were a means to God, so to speak. The sheep were the sacrifice that paid for their sins and brought them into right standing with God. Sheep are helpless and social animals. They gather in flocks and tend to wander off and fall into crevices or get caught in thorny bushes. Sheep know the shepherd, and he knows each sheep by name.

As sheep ourselves, we will sometimes wander off and get stuck in some thoughts that are not of God; but if we continue sacrificing to build the discipline of prayer, we will one day see the results. Prayer and meditation take a lot of sacrifice on our part. We must be willing to spend time—lots of time—in prayer to get the knowledge of His will and the power to carry His will out.

A VIRTUOUS WOMAN

A lifestyle of cocaine and prostitution usually lends itself to a few days in jail every couple of months. The routine is "in the front door, out the back door," with a call to a family member and then to the bail bondsman. But this time, it was different. Nobody was answering. She couldn't believe it; she cursed them at first. The nonstop calling finally netted an answer, but it wasn't what she wanted to hear. No help? What did they mean? They were supposed to get themselves right up to that jail and get her out. Now. This time, no amount of calling changed their minds. No amount of threats or cries or curses—nothing changed their minds. She was in jail, and she wasn't getting out. The food was killing her, and the stale air was killing her. Her soul was being rendered.

One morning—was it Sunday? Yes, it was Sunday, and some church ladies came to the jail. Oh, they had been coming to the jail all along, but today was her first time going to the room to hear what they had to say. They talked about Jesus. They talked about a life without drugs. They talked about virtue. They talked about a virtuous woman. *That was a joke*, she thought. She was no virtuous woman—not now or ever.

Sunday after Sunday, they came. Sunday after Sunday, she went. She listened to the church ladies. Day after day, she waited. She called her family for a while after she met the church ladies, but then she just stopped. It wasn't going to change things anyway. They weren't coming to get her.

One day, a lawyer showed up. He told her she could try to get into a rehab for drugs, and, maybe, the judge would let her spend the rest of her time there instead of in jail. Once again, she called her family. This time, there was no begging, just asking if they could find her a place where she could get some help for her drug addiction. She was ready, she told them. She needed to call the rehab herself. The rehab accepted her call. Week after week, she pleaded with them, "Please save my bed."

It took some time for the judge to hear her case again. She forgot that she had charges in another county. She would never get help. Meanwhile, she kept listening to the church ladies. Every week, they told her of the possibility of becoming a virtuous woman. "Proverbs thirty-one," they would say. She could be a Proverbs thirty-one woman.

After months, she landed in front of the judge, complete with a rehab address and a hope for a new life. The judge agreed that if she could get a ride to rehab, she could go. It was a Saturday afternoon when she arrived at the beginning of her new life. Standing at the end of the stairwell, she asked the director, "Can I become a virtuous woman? Those church ladies said that somebody like me can change. Do you think I can leave here a virtuous woman?" Tears streamed down her face as she spoke the words.

"Yes," I said. "You can."

Family members still refused her calls. She was still isolated. She wrote letters to them—letters asking for forgiveness, letters that said she was to blame for her addiction and her problems. Then, slowly, ever so slowly, one-by-one, they picked up the phone.

It was months later, and she was riding in the rehab van with a group of children. One of the children said to the woman, "What do you church ladies do?" The woman was caught off-guard. She was speechless. Nobody had ever called her a "church lady" before. I guess you can become a virtuous woman, after all. A life of total depravation can be restored. Even though she didn't quite see herself as a "church lady," the innocent child could see her for what she had become.

About eighteen months after leaving jail, she returned home, a virtuous woman, restored to family and community. She had found where she truly belonged.

ABOUT SHEEP

Israel was a nation of shepherds. Sheep were the livelihood of Israel. Sheep offered as sacrifice freed them from sin. Sheep provided food and clothing and were a source of fellowship as the shepherds gathered together at night with their flocks. Sheep taught many life lessons to the Israelites.

From the earliest settlements to the time of Jesus, sheep were important to the lifestyle of the Israelites. Abraham and Lot separated because there was not enough pasture land for their flocks. Abraham let Lot choose where he would take his flocks. Lot chose the plains around Sodom and Gomorrah, while Abraham stayed in Canaan. Moses left Egypt and became a shepherd. He learned how to lead the people out of Egypt by tending the flocks of his father-in-law.

The Sheep Gate was essential to the lifestyle of Jerusalem. At the Sheep Gate, the priest selected the best sheep for sacrifice. At the Sheep Gate, the flocks were corralled for protection and shearing. Jesus said in **John 10:27, "My sheep listen to my voice; I know them, and they follow me."** He also said in **Matthew 7:14, "But small is the gate and narrow the road that leads to life, and only a few find it."** He might have been talking about the Sheep Gate. The shepherd would stand at the gate and call for his sheep. He knew them each by name and called them one by one. Only his sheep responded, leaving the sheepfold behind to follow the shepherd.

Sheep have a great sense of identity. They follow the shepherd and know they belong to him. They are satisfied with belonging to the shepherd. Sometimes, a sheep will stray away from the pathway or place appointed for him, and the shepherd will leave the flock to go and find him. If the sheep continues to stray, the shepherd takes his staff and strikes the sheep on the leg. Often, the leg is broken, so the shepherd will pick the sheep up and carry it on his shoulders until the leg heals. This close, healing relationship will convince the sheep never to stray again. The shepherd has loved the sheep into life.

The Sheep Gate is where you find your identity and restore yourself to community. It is only as a true identity is created that you are able to go out into the world and find a job and keep it. You can join a church or other group and participate in them as you discover that you belong to the Shepherd.

KEY TO RESTORING BELONGING

You can serve. While it seems unusual to think that serving can help you restore a sense of belonging, it really works. Serving out of your heart puts belonging into your core. You will feel more a part of community as you serve others. Use this key to remind you that belonging comes out of service.

ACTION STEPS

- Improve your sense of belonging by volunteering at a food bank, your church, or another community group.
- Ask a friend to come to dinner at your home.
- Offer to help a neighbor this week with a project.

SHEEP GATE PRAYER

"Your sheep hear Your voice and know it. Help Your sheep today, O Lord, for Your sheep are dumb. I am Your sheep, and I listen; but, sometimes, I can't hear Your voice clearly. Please help Your voice come clearly to me for direction.

"I need to know which way to turn today, what to do about tomorrow, and how to live my life according to Your plan. I need help with direction for all areas of my life—relationships, marriage, children, school, work, etc.

"Some of Your sheep are straying from their path today; gather them to You, Jesus. Some of Your sheep are wounded and hurting today; give them strength, and heal their wounds. Some of Your sheep have wandered from You; send a Shepherd to them today. Some of the little ones need to be trained in Your ways; teach them, Jesus.

"Bless these sheep today. (List loved ones, children, Christian friends, church friends.)_____

_____

_____

_____

"I am Your sheep, and I need Your shepherding hand today. Help me to remember that You are the Good Shepherd, and I am Your sheep, not the other way around."

TODAY'S SCRIPTURE

"And you also are among those Gentiles who are called to belong to Jesus Christ" (Rom. 1:6).

TODAY'S PRAYER

"Lord, I desire to belong to those who are called to belong to Jesus Christ. Help me to know my worth in You and to realize who I am in You."

TODAY'S JOURNAL QUESTION

How do you remind yourself that you belong to Jesus Christ?

DAY TWO

RESTORING A SENSE OF BELONGING

All of the work in restoration hinges on the power of prayer and the intimate knowledge of Jesus Christ. From the first day of restoration until now, you have been given a set of tools to help you rebuild the boundaries of your life. At this point in the restoration process, you should be feeling more and more like a human being. Sin steals the sense of humanness from you. Finding Jesus and finding yourself leads to being a more humane person. Being humane is often linked to animals (i.e. the humane society), but I have found that being humane includes becoming a real human being. Jesus reflects what a human being should look like. He offers us a pattern for knowing God, knowing ourselves, and knowing others. He also shows us where and how we are to belong.

I am the true vine, and my Father is the gardener. He cuts off every branch in me that bears no fruit, while every branch that does bear fruit he prunes so that it will be even more fruitful. You are already clean because of the word I have spoken to you. Remain in me, as I also remain in you. No branch can bear fruit by itself; it must remain in the vine. Neither can you bear fruit unless you remain in me. I am the vine; you are the branches. If you remain in me and I in you, you will bear much fruit; apart from me you can do nothing. If you do not remain in me, you are like a branch that is thrown away and withers; such branches are picked up, thrown into the fire and burned. If you remain in me and my words remain in you, ask whatever you wish, and it will be done for you. This is to my Father's glory, that you bear much fruit, showing yourselves to be my disciples. As the Father has loved me, so have I loved you. Now remain in my love. If you keep my commands, you will remain in my love, just as I have kept my Father's commands and remain in his love. I have told you this so that my joy may be in you and that your joy may be complete. My command is this: Love each other as I have loved you. Greater love has no one than this: to lay down one's life for one's friends.

You are my friends if you do what I command. I no longer call you servants, because a servant does not know his master's business. Instead, I have called you friends, for everything that I learned from my Father I have made known to you. You did not choose me, but I chose you and appointed you so that you might go and bear fruit—fruit that will last—and so that whatever you ask in my name the Father will give you. This is my command: Love each other (Jn. 15:1-17).

In John 15:1-4, Jesus describes how we are disciplined in love by the Father through a picture of a vine and a gardener. In this picture, Jesus shares His heart with the disciples, telling them that they are to remain in Him. You will bear much fruit if you remain in Jesus, or the Vine. In John 15:5, Jesus again tells us to remain in Him. As we remain in Jesus, we find our sense of significance and success. Without this "remaining," we can do nothing, according to the Scriptures.

Our belonging comes from abiding in Jesus. Our significance comes from abiding in Jesus. Our success comes from abiding in Jesus. Jesus calls us friends. He speaks to us as One who sincerely knows us. He desires for us to sincerely know Him and His Father.

The longer we are in the Vine, the more we become like Him. The more we become like Him, the more we know that we belong. That feeling of insecurity diminishes with each day of knowing and abiding. We grow stronger in doing the next right thing.

The gatekeeper opens the gate for him, and the sheep listen to his voice. He calls his own sheep by name and leads them out. When he has brought out all his own, he goes on ahead of them, and his sheep follow him because they know his voice. But they will never follow a stranger; in fact, they will run away from him because they do not recognize a stranger's voice (Jn. 10:3-5).

According to those who know about sheep, the shepherds of the East gave names to each sheep in the flock. The individual sheep learned the name quickly and would respond to the shepherd as he called them by name. The idea that the shepherd would stand at the door of the sheepfold and call to his sheep reminds us that as His followers, each individual believer must spend time with Jesus to know His voice as He leads us through life.

Sheep cannot be driven anywhere. It is said that when sheep are attempted to be driven, they huddle together and refuse to move. Sheep must be led. Jesus leads us gently by calling us by name. What a sense of belonging is felt by the sheep as the shepherd calls each by name and gently leads them from place to place.

- What does it mean to you to "remain in Jesus?"
- How do you describe belonging?
- Where do you feel you belong?

TODAY'S SCRIPTURE

"This is how we know that we belong to the truth and how we set our hearts at rest in his presence" (1 Jn. 3:19).

TODAY'S PRAYER

"Lord, forgive me for the actions that do not show that I belong to You. Help me to do the next right thing, so I will be confident when I stand before You. Amen."

TODAY'S JOURNAL ENTRY

List the actions you take that make you know you belong to God.

DAY THREE

WORD STUDY

The word *sober* occurs twelve times in the King James version of the Bible. The first time it is used in the Scriptures is **2 Corinthians 5:13: "For whether we be beside ourselves, it is to God: or whether we be sober, it is for your cause."** In this sense, it means to have a sane or sound mind.

In **1 Thessalonians 5:6, "Therefore let us not sleep, as do others; but let us watch and be sober."** The word refers here to sobriety or calmness of spirit.

In **1 Timothy 3:2, "A bishop then must be blameless, the husband of one wife, vigilant, sober, of good behaviour, given to hospitality, apt to teach."** The word *sober* refers to self-control.

In **1 Timothy 3:11, "Even so must their wives be grave, not slanderers, sober, faithful in all things."** The word *sober* refers to not drinking wine.

In **Titus 2:4, "That they may teach the young women to be sober, to love their husbands, to love their children."** *Sober* refers to being restored to one's senses.

Sober is "abstaining from or habitually abstemious in the use of alcoholic drink or other intoxicants; not intoxicated or affected by the use of alcohol or drugs."[119] For our use, sobriety means the return to a sound mind and thinking, along with the abstaining from intoxicating chemicals or behaviors. A person in recovery may abstain from the use of chemicals or habitual behaviors but not be sober. Sobriety is a process of restoring the mind to rational, responsible thinking and subsequent actions.

We need a picture of sobriety. While doing a group with recovering addicts, I asked what sobriety looks like. One young man said, "I don't know what sobriety looks like." He had never experienced sobriety in his adult life, so he had no reference for what a picture of his life would look like. How sad that is. Without a picture, a guide, or a roadmap, how can you get there?

Let me propose what sobriety may look like—waking up in the morning, knowing that life is more than chasing a drug; waking up, wanting to build a

---

119   *The Free Dictionary, s.v.* "Sober," accessed October 27, 2017, https://www.thefreedictionary.com/sober.

life of good things; knowing where you are headed, having goals, working a job, having a place to lay your head, and having ownership of your life. That is what sobriety looks like, and so much more. It is having respect for one's self, fewer regrets, and more hope. It is living life one day at a time with a commitment to life. It is joy in the middle of a mess; it is hope in the middle of chaos and love for the unlovable. It is forgiveness and mercy.

TODAY'S SCRIPTURE

"You, dear children, are from God and have overcome them, because the one who is in you is greater than the one who is in the world" (1 Jn. 4:4).

TODAY'S PRAYER

"Lord, You have, by Your own action, given me everything that is necessary for living righteously here and now, by allowing me to know and have Jesus, Who has called me through His own glorious goodness. It is through Christ Jesus that these great and precious promises have become available to me, making it possible to escape the inevitable corruption that lust produces in the world and for me to share in Your essential and permanent nature. For this very reason, Lord, I must do the utmost from my side and see that my faith results in real moral excellence—real goodness of life. My goodness must be accompanied by knowledge; my knowledge, then, by self-control; my self-control by the ability to endure. My endurance, too, must always be fueled by complete devotion to You, which, in turn, will result in my showing the quality of brotherly kindness, and my brotherly kindness must lead on to supernatural Christian love. Lord, if I have these qualities manifesting and growing within me, then it means that I really do know Jesus as Lord, and I can be sure that the power of Christ in me will keep my life from becoming either complacent or unproductive. If I fail to exhibit these qualities, it means I am blind or short-sighted, that I can't remember how great Your salvation is from my former sins. I want to set my mind, then, on endorsing, by my conduct, the fact that You, God, have really called and chosen me. If I grow in these qualities, there is no reason why I should ever stumble. As long as I am living a more Christlike life, then I can be completely sure that the Father will grant me a rich welcome into the eternal kingdom of our Lord and Savior Jesus Christ" (based on 2 Pet. 1:3-11).

TODAY'S JOURNAL QUESTION

What have you won the victory over in your life?

DAY FOUR

DELIVERANCE

How often in the field of addiction do you hear a counselor say, "You can't help them if they are not ready?" How true this was for the day of exodus so long ago, and how true it is today for the chemically enslaved. At first, you readily voice the desire to stop, and steps are made toward treatment. Then, just as everything seems to be all right, a huge problem has to be overcome. At the Red Sea, the Israelites' deliverance would only end in death if they could not believe God for a way out. For an addict, the "Red Sea" could be a job loss, loss of children, or the loss of a spouse if you follow the way out. Ahead is the destruction of life as you know it. Only until the Red Sea was parted could the children of Israel begin to believe that their deliverance was real. Only as you walk through detox and the first ninety days of abstinence can you believe that deliverance is possible.

Maturity could almost be substituted for the word *deliverance* as it is known in recovery. How many levels of deliverance are there? The Israelites were delivered from the hand of Pharaoh as the death angel passed over the country of Egypt. They were delivered through the Red Sea, as Pharaoh's army chased them. The same Israelites were delivered from sure death as manna came down from heaven; and then, Moses got water from the rock when they needed water. They were also delivered from the Canaanites and received the promise of the land of milk and honey. We can see the different levels of deliverance from evil and problems throughout the history of Israel. Deliverance is not a onetime, once-and-for-all event, which never needs repeating. Deliverance is a complete reliance upon God, now and throughout the course of a lifetime.

I see this so often in the life of the women we help at Bethesda. Families almost demand that treatment "work this time." But the way I see it, every time a woman is saved from death and has another chance to sober up, it is a type of deliverance. The disease of addiction is so insidious, that it can almost never be routed with one "trip" to rehab. It is a lifetime problem, as was the lifestyle of the Israelites. Over and over, God reached down to deliver His people. When God said to Moses, "I have heard the cries of My people and have come down to deliver them,"[120] it was not a onetime, once-and-for-all event. God saved and delivered the same people on countless occasions, and He can and will deliver us countless times. Do you suffer loss? Yes. Does your family suffer loss? Yes. But no matter what the loss, God has still made a way for you and your family to have a period of rest and peace. If you can mature as you are delivered, you have a better chance of being completely changed. If, however, you act as the Israelites did and continue to get in trouble, then it may take much deliverance to bring about full maturity. It may be the reason that many of those who master the disease say a person must be "sick and tired of being sick and tired."

As we have seen, personal responsibility and accountability play important roles in the deliverance from addiction. Even when the hope and promise of a much better life faces you, you may not get sober. It is much like the story of the twelve spies.

According to Scripture, twelve spies were sent out by Moses to see what the Promised Land looked like. All came back with the same story. They all had seen lush fruits, green pastures, and plenty of resources to live the life of abundance. They all said there were a people there in the land that had to be overcome. The spies all agreed that the people were giants. But one thing was different in the report that Joshua and Caleb gave from the rest of the spies. That one thing was that the giants could be defeated. The ten spies thought the giants were too big and too many for the Israelites. The Israelites saw themselves as grasshoppers compared to the giants.

The names of the twelve spies have great importance to our study, since each name represents a person that could not go into the Promised Land. As we study the names of these spies, we see the things that will not be profitable in our new life of recovery.

One of the spies from the tribe of Gad was named *Geuel*, which means "the majesty of God."[121] The majesty of God is the maturity and completeness of all that is powerful and holy. It is a type of fullness in which nothing else is needed. Geuel, by the very nature of his name, had the ability to be majestic or, perhaps, to grow to his fullness in God. However, fear gripped him, and he

---

120 Paraphrased from Exodus 3:7-8.
121 *Bible Study Tools*, s.v. "Geuel," accessed October 27, 2017, http://www.biblestudytools. com/dictionary/geuel.

was stunted. Geuel had only to take his place as the mature man he should have been, and he (and his family) would have seen the Promised Land. Because he sided with those who did not trust God to deliver them again, he died in the wilderness. Only those willing to grow in the fullness of God will enter the Promised Land. This old man, at the thought that all of the childhood dreams must be fulfilled, had to be put to death before the next phase could happen.

Fame, judgment, performance, running away, idols of self, idols of money, associates, the hidden self, ties with the occult, and the fear of growing up all have to be put to death in everyone wishing to cross the Jordan River into Canaan. The Jordan River represents the final deliverance into the new life. The day and the hour that the need for fame, the desire to pass judgment, performance orientation, running away, idols of self, idols of money, associates, the hidden self, ties with the occult, and lack of maturity have been exposed and dealt with in your life, the new life will be cemented in you, and you will no longer fear the past.

NAMES OF GOD

The name *Adon Adonai* is translated "the Lord of lords."[122] It is used in Scripture in Exodus 6:1 and is translated "Lord." Almost anytime you see the word "Lord" with a capital letter, it is translated from *Adonai.*

Elohim is used in **Genesis 1:1. "In the beginning God created the heavens and the earth."** *Elohim* refers to the Creator God, to the Father God. He is the greatest of all. His name proclaims His greatness.[123]

PRAYER

You are *Adon Adonai,* the Master of the universe. You set the stars in place; You make the sun to shine; You cause the rain to come and go; You tell the moon when to change; You make the grass to grow. You call the birds to sing. You formed the world; You made gravity, and You made the laws of the universe to work. You hold me on earth by Your bidding. Thank You for all that,

122   *Hebrew for Christians, s.v.* "Adonai," accessed October 27, 2017, http://www.hebrew-4christians.com/Names_of_G-d/Adonai/adonai.html.
123   *Hebrew for Christians, s.v.* "Elohim," accessed October 27, 2017, http://www.hebrew-4christians.com/Names_of_G-d/Elohim/elohim.html.

and so much more. Thank You for making a speck like me and allowing me to know You by name.

"You are *Elohim*, the Three-in-One, and I thank You for that. You are Father to me when my father has failed to teach a daughter to be a daughter. You are the Son to me to pay my pardon and ransom me from sin. You are the Holy Spirit to fill me with love when there was no love in me. You are wonderful, marvelous, Counselor, Friend. You are everything I need. Thank You for that."

TODAY'S SCRIPTURE

"You are judging by appearances. If anyone is confident that they belong to Christ, they should consider again that we belong to Christ just as much as they do" (2 Cor. 10:7).

"If you belong to Christ, then you are Abraham's seed, and heirs according to the promise" (Gal. 3:29).

TODAY'S PRAYER

"Hear my prayer, O Lord, and let my cry come unto thee. Hide not thy face from me in the day when I am in trouble; incline thine ear unto me: in the day when I call answer me speedily. For my days are consumed like smoke, and my bones are burned as an hearth. My heart is smitten, and withered like grass; so that I forget to eat my bread" (Psa. 102:1-4 KJV).

"I will sing of mercy and judgment: unto thee, O Lord, will I sing. I will behave myself wisely in a perfect way. O when wilt thou come unto me? I will walk within my house with a perfect heart" (Psa. 101:1-2 KJV).

"Have mercy upon me, O God, according to thy lovingkindness: according unto the multitude of thy tender mercies blot out my transgressions. Wash me thoroughly from mine iniquity, and cleanse me from my sin. For I acknowledge my transgressions: and my sin is ever before me" (Psa. 51:1-2 KJV).

"Create in me a clean heart, O God; and renew a right spirit within me. Cast me not away from thy presence; and take not thy holy spirit from me. Restore unto me the joy of my salvation" (Psa. 51:10-12a KJV).

"Surely [You will] deliver [me] from the snare of the fowler ... " and I "shalt not be afraid for the terror by night; nor for the arrow that flieth by day ... for [You shall] give [your] angels charge over [me] to keep [me] in all [my] ways" (Psa. 91:3a, 5, 11 KJV).

"Some trust in chariots, and some in horses: but [I] will remember the name of the Lord [my] God" (Psa. 20:7 KJV).

"Many a time have they afflicted me from my youth: yet they have not prevailed against me" (Psa. 129:2 KJV).

"Behold, how good and how pleasant it is for brethren to dwell together in unity" (Psa. 133:1 KJV).

TODAY'S JOURNAL QUESTIONS

How do you recognize that you belong to Jesus Christ? Are you satisfied with belonging to Jesus? Explain.

DAY FIVE

A SENSE OF BELONGING IS SCRIPTURAL

"But you are a chosen people, a royal priesthood, a holy nation, God's special possession, that you may declare the praises of him who called you out of darkness into his wonderful light" (1 Pet. 2:9).

Peter, who was a disciple of Jesus from day one, so to speak, developed his sense of belonging in Christ. He was a hot-headed fisherman, who knew who he was as a fisherman, but not as a disciple. He had to develop that through his relationship with the risen Christ. Peter struggled with becoming a new person just as we do. He spent time with Jesus but refused to create his new identity until after Jesus spoke to him concerning Peter's love for Jesus.

We are not unlike Peter. We know Jesus to a point. We call ourselves Christians, but our identities are still mingled with our past lives. It may take a personal encounter with Jesus to strike a chord in our souls to be new and have a sense of true belonging. But Peter got it, and so can we.

We know the changes he made through his writings. In the Scripture above, Peter is declaring to us that we are a chosen people. Peter knew what it was like to be chosen because Jesus sent for him after he had denied ever knowing Christ.

Peter also tells us that we are a royal priesthood. He now understands his own role in the kingdom. He understands for himself that he can speak to God through the shed blood of Jesus Christ. That fact alone gives him significance. Remember, prior to Jesus, Peter was only a fisherman, not a priest.

Peter calls us "a holy nation." Peter is the Jew who was sent to Cornelius to share the Gospel. He is the one who was told by God to not call what God had called clean, dirty. This was after a vision of unclean animals was offered to him to eat. Peter calls all of us "a holy nation"—a people set apart to God.

Peter says we are "a people for His own possession." We are bought with the price of Jesus' blood. We belong to God—not in the sense of a slave, but in the sense of a precious jewel. We belong to God as His love, His child, not as a possession which is tossed away when it is no longer of use. We belong to God forever. He will never throw us away. There is empowerment in knowing that.

TODAY'S SCRIPTURE

"Those who belong to Christ Jesus have crucified the flesh with its passions and desires" (Gal. 5:24).

TODAY'S PRAYER

"I pray for myself 'that the message of the Lord may spread rapidly and be honored' in me and that I 'may be delivered from wicked and evil people'" (2 Thess. 3:1-2).

TODAY'S JOURNAL QUESTION

Who are the "wicked and evil men," or perhaps the people who are unreasonable in your life, that you must be delivered from?

DAY SIX

INHERITANCE BECAUSE OF BELONGING

As people who belong to God, we are eligible for an inheritance. **"So that, having been justified by his grace, we might become heirs having the hope of eternal life" (Titus 3:7). "And giving joyful thanks to the Father, who has qualified you to share in the inheritance of his holy people in the kingdom of light" (Col. 1:12).** So, what do we inherit? We inherit eternal life in Jesus Christ. When does this inheritance begin? Today. We are sharing in eternal life today, not when we die. We are receiving the privileges of the worship of our great God today.

We inherit the earth. **"Blessed are the meek, for they will inherit the earth" (Matt. 5:5).** We have the privilege of enjoying all the earth has for us.

We inherit the kingdom of God. In a brief sentence, we inherit the privilege of living a life as a King's kid in the kingdom of God. We don't live totally under the rules of natural law, but under the laws of God and how things work in His kingdom.

We inherit a blessing. **"Do not repay evil with evil or insult with insult. On the contrary, repay evil with blessing, because to this you were called so that you may inherit a blessing" (1 Pet. 3:9).**

We inherit a position with God. **"Blessed and holy are those who share in the first resurrection. The second death has no power over them, but they will be priests of God and of Christ and will reign with him for a thousand years" (Rev. 20:6).**

We inherit salvation. The word *salvation* comes from the Greek *sozo*, which translates as wholeness or completeness.[124] We therefore inherit wholeness— wholeness in the spirit and also wholeness in the natural. This wholeness is eternal, as we are complete in Christ. Our inheritance includes joy and peace now and forever. It includes right standing with God and the ability to give and receive reconciliation. As sons and daughters, we are eligible for blessing due to our right standing with God and man. We must understand that our

---

124   *Bible Hub*, s.v. "Sovo," accessed October 27, 2017, http://biblehub.com/greek/4982.htm.

belonging to God empowers us to live as heirs. We know God is our Father and has bequeathed us blessings that are ours just because He says they are. We do not have to work hard to be heirs; we only have to believe. **"Therefore, there is now no condemnation for those who are in Christ Jesus" (Rom. 8:1).**

TODAY'S SCRIPTURE

> **"This mystery is that through the gospel the Gentiles are heirs together with Israel, members together of one body, and sharers together in the promise in Christ Jesus" (Eph. 3:6).**

TODAY'S PRAYER

> **"May the Lord make [my] love increase and overflow for...everyone else . . . so that [I] will be blameless and holy in the presence of [my] God and Father when our Lord Jesus comes with all his holy ones" (1 Thess. 3:12-13).**

TODAY'S JOURNAL QUESTION

How do you know that you are sober?

DAY SEVEN

WORSHIP

Worship as Celebration

Each Sunday, as we enter the sanctuary, we should count this time as a celebration. The reason we come together as Christians is because the early believers met each week, on the first day of the week, to celebrate the resurrection of Jesus. The early believers were mostly Jews, so their day to worship at the synagogue was Saturday. The Sabbath was the holy day set aside from the Garden of Eden. Until Jesus rose from the grave, there was no day of celebration set aside weekly. Of course, the Jews celebrated at their feasts, but now, because of Jesus, we celebrate each week.

In the worship service, there are many ways to celebrate. We are emotional creatures, so we show celebration through our emotions and by our bodies. We may weep for joy as we remember our sins are forgiven. We may leap for joy as we think of the healing power of Jesus. We may raise our hands in celebration, or clap, or dance.

Normally, when we think about celebrating, we think about having a party. A party is where friends come together to enjoy an event. Celebrating the risen Christ can be similar to that with reverence and truth. We can come together and enjoy the fact that Jesus is risen, and, because of that, our lives are changed.

TODAY'S SCRIPTURE

"Rejoice in the Lord always. I will say it again: Rejoice!" (Phil. 4:4).

TODAY'S PRAYER

"Jesus, I am so happy You rose from the grave. I am so happy that You called my name and that I was able to believe, so that I can belong to Your family and inherit salvation and eternal life. Please show me how to celebrate You all day, every day. Amen."

TODAY'S JOURNAL QUESTION

What can you celebrate because of Jesus?

CHAPTER FIFTEEN

WATER GATE: GATEWAY TO RESTORING JOY

"Nehemiah said, 'Go and enjoy choice food and sweet drinks, and send some to those who have nothing prepared. This day is holy to our Lord. Do not grieve, for the joy of the Lord is your strength'" (Neh. 8:10).

"And the temple servants living on the hill of Ophel made repairs up to a point opposite the Water Gate toward the east and the projecting tower" (Neh. 3:26).

"All the people came together as one in the square before the Water Gate. They told Ezra the teacher of the Law to bring out the Book of the Law of Moses, which the LORD had commanded for Israel" (Neh. 8:1).

"Beyond him, Nehemiah son of Azbuk, ruler of a half-district of Beth Zur, made repairs up to a point opposite the tombs of David, as far as the artificial pool and the House of the Heroes" (Neh. 3:16).

DAY ONE

LET'S CELEBRATE

Who knows what life will bring. I have heard it asked, "What will you do when life shows up at your door?"

Real life is filled with all the messy stuff. Take, for example, the birth of a baby into a family. The couple is excited and thrilled, but the life brings smelly diapers; wounded feet from toys on the floor; loud, unexpected noises; and so much more. The once-quiet space of the couple is interrupted with "life."

Well, real life has shown up many times at my friend's door, but she continues to celebrate her newfound, overcoming power in Christ. Her "new life" is filled with unexpected stuff. "Life showing up" means heartache, but Christ encourages us to not lose heart in **John 16:33b**: **"In this world you will have trouble. But take heart! I have overcome the world."** My friend hasn't lost heart and has started her "new life" in Georgia.

I didn't know what she looked like; I only knew I was to meet her there. It was a little funny if you think about it—how did I know which woman it would be? So, what would make her stand out? Was it that lost look on her face? Or was it an internal knowing sent by God to her and to me? No matter what it was, it always worked. I would show up at the bus station, and she would arrive on the bus. I'd say, "I'm Cathy," and then she would say her name.

And so it was this afternoon, except she wasn't the usual quiet one. She was busy talking and talking and talking. In the van, I finally said, "You have to slow down; I can't hear that fast." But, you know, she never really did slow down. She hit the ground running, both with her feet and with her tongue.

It's like that with so many of the women who come to Bethesda for recovery. They are glad be here in the hope of change. It takes a change of mind, a change in body, and a change in soul to reach the point of celebrating their stay at Bethesda. We have a sign up in the house that says, "Home is where your story begins." And for many women, their old story ends at our front door, and their new story begins.

I think of many women who are celebrating their new lives today. There's the one who had lost her child to "the System," due to alcoholism, but, now, she is celebrating being with her every day. There's the one whose family refused to have any contact with her, and now she is very involved with her grandchild. Then there's the lady whose husband left her; and now she is remarried to a great guy, and they are making a life together. Over and over, when a negative lifestyle is changed to a positive, Christ-centered life, celebration erupts.

She was sure exactly why God had sent her to our house. She knew everything. It was quite amazing. (I say that with a little bit of sarcasm.) She found a book about the Holy Spirit and decided that was her answer. She wrote notes during class, and that would be her answer. She was "something else" (as we say in the South).

She decided when her time was up and what she would do next, and you had better get out of her way because nothing could stop her now. With 120 days of no cocaine or cigarettes, she was sure that she would make it. And she did, kind of. She went home, changed from what she was, but not to what she would be. She went home, got into a good church, and started her life over. There were no drugs, but there *were* a lot of problems to face.

Heartache showed up at her door; she fought through that. Disappointment showed up at her door; she fought through that. Overwhelming circumstances showed up at her door; but she fought through that, too. Every day was not full of fun, but she learned to celebrate the victories. When she found herself pregnant before marriage, she quickly repented and gave herself over to raising her child. She readily admitted that she got ahead of the plan God had for her life, but she rejoices in the fact that He is a merciful God of grace.

Her health is not the best, but she keeps her head held high, even though she is plagued with unwanted pain. Life has continued to show up at her doorstep with all its surprises, but she keeps moving onward. She battles her sorrow with a smile and by knowing the joy of the Lord is her strength.

Certainly, life's issues may cause us to take a detour from time to time, but we can learn the lesson of strength from this woman and so many others—to get up quickly. We may fall, but we can get up with celebration, not with shame and guilt. We get up and move forward because there is another chance to rebuild the broken places of our lives.

She decided what sobriety would look like and began the journey to get to her picture. She is celebrating a life filled with joy these days. Oh, life still shows up, but she has fought through enough battles that she keeps smiling because she knows that the joy of the Lord is her strength. From that day at the bus station until now, she has followed the path that was laid before her. She has made mistakes and taken a couple of detours, but she has quickly gotten back on the path that God has laid out for her. I have watched her, and, now, I celebrate with her. One day, "her children [will] arise and call her blessed (Prov. 31:28). Now, she has a testimony as a witness of what Christ can do for a person who surrenders their life to Him.

KEY TO CELEBRATION:

You can speak. Celebration gives you a voice. Your voice to speak is a freedom that brings joy and lasting fulfilment. Use this key to remind you that you celebrate with your new voice.

ACTION STEPS

- Plan a celebration.
- Make a list of those you wish to celebrate with you.
- Make the plan as big or as small as you need to express the celebration of your life's victories.
- Make a list of the victories in your life.
- Keep making a list of the victories, and celebrate each one.

PRAYER

"Lord, many of my loved ones are lost and need Your water to drink from today. They are in a dry and barren place in their lives and need the living water You offer to us to live. Help me be able to offer that water to them, flowing from my belly as living water.[125] Help my words offer life to others as I pray for them who are lost today.

---

125   John 7:38 KJV.

"I pray that You will send Christians to witness to them and help me not to hinder Your ways of salvation in the lives of my loved ones.

"Lord, I want to stop here and drink of Your Living Water myself. I need refreshing each day. I forget that You are in control of my life; forgive me. I want You to take control today. Show me Your ways and help me to be more like You, Lord.

"Your Word says that if I confess my sins, You are faithful and just to forgive me and 'cleanse me of all unrighteousness.'[126] I claim this for my life today and ask You to wash me thoroughly and cleanse me from my sin."

TODAY'S SCRIPTURE

"While the morning stars sang together and all the angels shouted for joy" (Job 38:7).

TODAY'S PRAYER

"Now, Lord, consider their threats and enable your servants to speak your word with great boldness. Stretch out your hand to heal and perform signs and wonders through the name of your holy servant Jesus" (Acts 4:29-30).

TODAY'S JOURNAL QUESTION

What do you have to shout for joy about?

---

126   1 John 1:9.

DAY TWO

RESTORING SELF-COMMUNITY THROUGH JOY

Of all the water on the earth, humans can use only about three-tenths of a percent of this water. Such usable water is found in groundwater aquifers, rivers, and freshwater lakes. Water dissolves more substances than any other liquid. Wherever it travels, water carries chemicals, minerals, and nutrients with it.[127]

There is the same amount of water on earth as there was when the earth was formed. The water that came from your faucet could contain molecules from the time of Adam. Water regulates the earth's temperature. Next to air, water is the most important life-giving agent. Water is not only important to man, but to every living creature. Without water, there would not be life as we know it. This fact has never changed and will never change.[128]

The Bible has much to say about water. Water is used 396 times in the King James version of the Bible.[129] Jesus said in **John 7:37-38, "In the last day, that great day of the feast, Jesus stood and cried, saying, If any man thirst, let him come unto me, and drink. He that believeth on me, as the scripture hath said, out of his belly shall flow rivers of living water."**

When Jesus performed His first miracle in John 2:11, He used water. Baptism, using water, relates to the new life in Jesus. Jesus spoke to the woman at the well about living water.

> "Refusing to bring death to others and ourselves brings life instead as we live out godly principles and tell others about how Jesus has changed our lives."

At the Water Gate, Ezra read the Law to the people, and a great revival started. It was a great celebration. Water brings life and keeps life. At this gate, you are living your faith and bringing life to others. Sharing your faith

127   AllAboutWater.org. "20 Interesting and Useful Water Facts." AllAboutWater.org. http://www.allaboutwater.org/water-facts.html (accessed October 27, 2017).

128   Matter Under Mind. "Life Without Water. Is it Possible?" Matterundermind.com. http://matterundermind.com/life-without-water-is-it-possible/ (accessed October 27, 2017).

129   *Letter Bible, s.v.* "water," accessed October 27, 2017, https://www.blueletterbible.org/search/search.cfm?Criteria=water&t=KJV#s=s_primary_0_1.

is a life-giving lifestyle. Refusing to bring death to others and yourself brings life instead as you live out godly principles and tell others about how Jesus has changed your life. It is through salvation that God has a plan for your life. It is cemented in the love of Jesus for you. God is love. God's plan for you is determined by His great and powerful love for you. Part of that plan is for you to share with others the very things that have helped you the most. Salvation through grace is the most precious gift God gives us. It is through the reconciliation of God to man and man to God that joy, celebration, and, of course, sobriety are born.

As you are changed into the person you were meant to be, God uses you to share the good news of deliverance to others who are lost in the darkness of addiction. Jesus told His disciples to go and make disciples of others (Matt. 28:19). It is your job now to share that good news of how you were once bound by addiction and the sin/disease. You have learned that the body, soul, and spirit must be set free from addiction. You can hate how the body is bound by the disease. You can share how the soul is bound by personality defects of character and how they must be changed. You can share how the spirit is set free through faith in Jesus Christ. You can now open your spirit to be filled with the Holy Spirit, and, by faith, you can ask the Holy Spirit to fill you with His love and to continue filling you as you share the good news of sobriety and Jesus Christ wherever you go.

Wholeness is received at the Water Gate as it is restored to your life. Community involvement, with belonging and acceptance, is complete as you learn to share the celebration revival. You once were dead, but now you live. You are alive and filled with joy and gratitude at being able to share this new life with others.

TODAY'S SCRIPTURE

"Strength resides in its neck; dismay goes before it" (Job 41:22).

TODAY'S PRAYER

"May the God of hope fill [me] with all joy and peace [in believing], that [I] may overflow with hope by the power of the Holy Spirit" (Rom. 15:13).

TODAY'S JOURNAL QUESTION

What sorrow in your life has God turned to joy?

DAY THREE

COMMUNITY INVOLVEMENT

Before sobriety, life is devoid of community involvement. Who thinks of getting involved with social events or maintaining commitments when drugs are the only things that matter? You can't attend school events or functions for your children because, well, you know why. The obsession of the lifestyle of addiction permeates every area of community, family, and personal lifestyle. A celebration only means more alcohol and more drugs. By the time addiction has become the basis for all of your life, a party—as sober people define party—is no longer an option.

You may feel uncomfortable at celebrations at first. People may seem too nice or too boring. Celebrations as a sober participant can trigger feelings for you, or it can make you feel sick because you don't know how to act or what to say. In fact, any social or community involvement may be uncomfortable for you.

Ladies in recovery who used to experience these feelings at celebrations have told me that they now know the only time they have really celebrated is when they are sober. They said to "party" was only an excuse to use in the early days of their addiction; but after the addiction took over, there would be no party or celebration—only maintenance.

When I asked them about community involvement, one of them said, "Are you kidding? I didn't think about that at all. I had no energy for volunteering."

Another woman said that now that she is sober, she enjoys being around people—especially at family gatherings. Prior to being sober, she avoided family gatherings because she didn't like people "that much" when she was using.

Getting involved in community becomes a new joy in sobriety. Women at Bethesda take part in community events, such as feeding shut-ins at Thanksgiving or giving out food at the food bank. They all express excitement and tell their stories of cooking the food or helping another human being over and over. The restoration to community stretches over to the work world as well. Women tell how they can understand instructions, take feedback, and actually enjoy working as sober employees.

You can expect community to become a safe place as your sobriety gets stronger and stronger. At first, it will take some adjustment, but over time, you will find acceptance in a community of people who were waiting on you to join in.

JOB SKILLS

You may get a job, now that you are sober. Your work ethic should be different as you approach your first job sober. Presenting yourself as a mature individual will be appropriate for getting hired. You will need to review how to dress for an interview, as a drug addict's attire is sometimes too trendy for the workplace. You will also need to review etiquette for jobs, such as cell phone availability, cursing, and respect. The workplace will require social skills and boundaries, which you may need to build.

Tardiness is not acceptable for jobs. This is just one boundary you will have to build for successful employment. Absenteeism should not be a problem because sobriety has eliminated the need to lie about drug use.

Bank accounts may be impossible for you to have because of past issues, so be prepared to be flexible about how you will be able to save and distribute your finances.

CHURCH ATTENDANCE

Finding a church to attend is important for your community restoration. You will need to remain open about visiting churches until you find the one that fits you best. Churches have their own personality, so you can find one that feels right; just don't give up.

Look for a pastor who knows about recovery. He or she can be a valuable resource for your recovery. Look for people with realistic attitudes about life. And if you have children, look for a youth or children's pastor who understands families in addiction. Church is not a good place to hide your recovery needs. It should be a safe place to release your feelings.

SCHOOL FUNCTIONS

Attending PTA or other school functions for and with your children can be a challenge at first. You may have feelings of insecurity at first, but do not let these feelings prevent you from attending. People may remember your past at first; but if you continue with your sober lifestyle, the past will soon become a blur to you and to others.

Your child is the most important person in your life, and how he or she feels when you attend these school functions should be your top priority. It causes your child to feel importance when you attend their functions.

SCRIPTURE TELLS OF GOD'S PLAN OF DELIVERANCE

For since the creation of the world God's invisible qualities—his eternal power and divine nature—have been clearly seen, being understood from what has been made, so that people are without excuse. For although they knew God, they neither glorified him as God nor gave thanks to him, but their thinking became futile and their foolish hearts were darkened (Rom. 1:20-21).

"But God demonstrates his own love for us in this: While we were still sinners, Christ died for us" (Rom. 5:8).

"For all have sinned and fall short of the glory of God" (Rom. 3:23).

"For the wages of sin is death, but the gift of God is eternal life in Christ Jesus our Lord" (Rom. 6:23).

"If you declare with your mouth, 'Jesus is Lord,' and believe in your heart that God raised him from the dead, you will be saved. For it is with your heart that you believe and are justified, and it is with your mouth that you profess your faith and are saved" (Rom. 10:9-10).

"For 'Everyone who calls on the name of the Lord will be saved'" (Rom. 10:13).

"Yet to all who did receive him, to those who believed in his name, he gave the right to become children of God" (Jn. 1:12).

"Here I am! I stand at the door and knock. If anyone hears my voice and opens the door, I will come in and eat with that person, and they with me" (Rev. 3:20).

"And this is the testimony: God has given us eternal life, and this life is in his Son. Whoever has the Son has life; whoever does not have the Son of God does not have life" (1 Jn. 5:11-13).

"If we confess our sins, he is faithful and just and will forgive us our sins and purify us from all unrighteousness" (1 Jn. 1:9).

"For it is by grace you have been saved, through faith—and this is not from yourselves, it is the gift of God—not by works, so that no one can boast" (Eph. 2:8-9).

"Therefore, if anyone is in Christ, the new creation has come: The old has gone, the new is here" (2 Cor. 5:17).

"For God so loved the world that he gave his one and only Son, that whoever believes in him shall not perish but have eternal life" (Jn. 3:16).

"For God did not send his Son into the world to condemn the world, but to save the world through him" (Jn. 3:17).

"Now this is eternal life: that they know you, the only true God, and Jesus Christ, whom you have sent" (Jn. 17:3).

"We all, like sheep, have gone astray, each of us has turned to our own way; and the LORD has laid on him the iniquity of us all" (Isa. 53:6).

"Just as people are destined to die once, and after that to face judgment" (Heb. 9:27).

TODAY'S SCRIPTURE

"But let all who take refuge in you be glad; let them ever sing for joy. Spread your protection over them, that those who love your name may rejoice in you" (Psa. 5:11).

TODAY'S PRAYER

"And this is my prayer: that your love may abound more and more in knowledge and depth of insight, so that you may be able to discern what is best and may be pure and blameless for the day of Christ, filled with the fruit of righteousness that comes through Jesus Christ—to the glory and praise of God" (Phil. 1:9-11).

TODAY'S JOURNAL QUESTION

How will you share your joy?

DAY FOUR

SIN/DISEASE CONCEPT REVIEW

The sin/disease concept is an idea or theory of how addiction works in the body, soul, and spirit of mankind. Addiction is identified as any habitual action which cannot be simply stopped by willpower in the life of an individual. In other words, when addiction begins, willpower alone ends. The will is overrun by the power of addiction. Addiction is a chemical reaction in the brain. This chemical reaction can be caused by chemicals introduced into the body or by chemicals in the body which are stimulated by a certain type of pleasure-seeking behavior. A person can be addicted to marijuana or to pornography. A person can be addicted to people or to anger. A person can be addicted to church or to cocaine. Addiction crosses every boundary and destroys all known personal and ethical boundaries.

Sin is any action or thought that violates a moral code—either God's moral code of the Bible or man's moral code of personal ethics. Sin is also missing the mark of a planned end or future. No man or woman ever makes a life plan to be an addict, but addiction easily takes a person off the mark of the plan of their life. Addiction causes a person to miss the mark or goal of life which was and is planned by God.

The sin/disease concept recognizes addiction to be a disease, using the oldest definition of disease and the newest definition of disease. The oldest is "not at ease." The newest definition is "a determined illness with definable symptoms and treatment plans."[130] The concept recognizes that the whole person is affected and, therefore, must be treated for the illness to come into remission. The sin/disease concept accepts remission as a goal, realizing that the addiction is resident in the flesh and that mankind will always be dealing with flesh until heaven is obtained. For the addict, remission is true healing. Remission, in this case, simply refers to remission like that in the disease of cancer, where there is no current cancer residing in the body. Once a person

---

130 *Google, s.v.* "disease," accessed October 27, 2017, https://www.google.com/search?ei=QB_zWeHmCem-jwS1r7S4DQ&q=disease+meaning&oq=disease+meaning&gs_l=psy-ab.3..0i67k1j0l9.4625.9728.0.11915.15.15.0.0.0.0.143.1811.1j14.15.001.1.64.psy-ab..0.15.1808...35i39k1j0i131k1j0i20i264k1j0i20i263i264k1.0.DWyPzLRQHSU.

has cancer, it is always possible for that person to get cancer again. Complete remission refers to the situation where the disease disappears completely with the treatment. Partial remission refers to the situation where the disease shrinks but does not disappear completely. Cure means complete freedom from the cancer. To render someone cured of cancer, one has to wait and see if the cancer will ever come back, so time is the crucial factor. If a patient remains in remission for a few years, the cancer might be cured. Certain cancers can reoccur after many years of remission. This is the way of addiction.

Addiction affects every organ of the body, but it is said to be the disease of the brain. For treatment to be effective, it must cover the physical—body, mind, and soul—and the spirit of a person. The treatment of addiction takes time and dedication by the addict. It is good to admit the disease is present, but always remember that remission is the goal.

DAY FIVE

WORD STUDY

Celebration, in reference to the Bible, means to hold a feast, hold a festival, make a pilgrimage, keep a pilgrim-feast, celebrate, dance, or stagger. The *American Heritage Dictionary* says *celebrate* means "to observe (a day or event) with ceremonies of respect, festivity, or rejoicing."[131]

A party for an addict is about as much celebrating as one does in addiction. Friday night is the night of the big "party" for most people whose lives are wrapped up in addictive behaviors. Of course, if the addiction has gone far enough, any day of the week could be a "party." Those parties usually end up with too much to drink, too many drugs, or a blackout. This type of party is not the type of celebrating we are talking about here. Can recovery have its moments of celebration without the addictive substance or behavior?

Sobriety and the life of recovery does not mean there will be no excitement, no happiness, and no fun. When a person first enters recovery, it is hard for him or her to imagine a lifetime without the drug or lifestyle of choice. Recovery looks pretty boring to those whose lives are filled with drama, but the life of recovery is very exciting.

Once, I was talking to some teenagers about living the Christian life. I asked them how they would describe it. They responded, "Boring." All they saw any Christian do was sit at home and watch television. But the sinners, they told me, were having a "ball."

From the outside, recovery may seem—to a person in active addiction—as "boring." The recovering person must learn the "celebration" techniques of a life of sobriety. The world of recovery has parties without drugs or alcohol. People in recovery laugh, tell jokes, and have fun at amusement parks. They find pleasure in simple things. They enjoy creation, the arts, and sports. Celebration happens in the life of recovery over birthdays, anniversaries, job advancement, a new home, or the birth of a child. Sometimes, celebration erupts on a rough day when they haven't returned to addiction. Celebration is joy unlimited. It is

---

131   *The American Heritage Dictionary, s.v.* "Celebrate," accessed October 27, 2017, www.ahdictionary.com/word/search.html?q=celebrate&submit.x=50&submit.y=20.

pleasure without the heartache of addiction. Life without addiction snapping at your heels is a huge celebration of joy.

TODAY'S SCRIPTURE

> **"You make known to me the path of life; you will fill me with joy in your presence, with eternal pleasures at your right hand" (Psa. 16:11).**

TODAY'S PRAYER

> **"I pray that I 'may stand firm in all the will of God, mature and fully assured'" (Col. 4:12).**

TODAY'S JOURNAL QUESTION

How do you plan to share your story with others?

DAY SIX

Deliverance comes by realizing the blessings of God. Deliverance is achieved by choosing life and obeying the voice of God. When the Israelites were in the wilderness, they were given specific instructions on how to be blessed by God. He also told them what would happen if they did not obey the commandments. The Ten Commandments are found in the Bible's Old Testament in Exodus, chapter twenty. They were given directly by God to the people of Israel at Mount Sinai after He had delivered them from slavery in Egypt. Moses gave the Israelites the Ten Commandments. These commandments, recorded in Exodus, are as follows:

"You shall have no other gods before me" (v. 3).

"You shall not make for yourself an image in the form of anything in heaven above or on the earth beneath or in the waters below" (v. 4).

"You shall not misuse the name of the Lord your God" (v. 7a).

"Remember the Sabbath day by keeping it holy" (v. 8).

"Honor your father and your mother" (v. 12a).

"You shall not murder" (v. 13).

"You shall not commit adultery" (v. 14).

"You shall not steal" (15).

"You shall not give false testimony against your neighbor" (v. 16).

"You shall not covet your neighbor's house. You shall not covet your neighbor's wife, or his male or female servant, his ox or donkey, or anything that belongs to your neighbor" (v. 17).

Jesus summed up the commandments in two—**"love the Lord your God with all your heart and with all your soul and with all your strength and with all your mind"** and **"love your neighbor as yourself" (Lk. 10:27).** In Deuteronomy 28:1-14, the Lord gave the blessings for following the commandments. The blessings include an increase for your children, your properties, your animals, and whatever you do. The Lord promises to conquer your enemies and to establish you in your nation. He promises to give you prosperity in the work that you do by sending abundance. He also blesses you with respect from others, and you will be the head, and not the tail, in life.

THE NAMES OF GOD

El-Olam means "the everlasting God."[132] I love it that in the verse below, Isaiah says, "Do you not know, have you not heard?" It is as if he is saying to us, "Listen, people, God has never changed." He is the everlasting God. He does not get tired. He never grows weary. He never tires of us, even though we are tiresome. God never ends, and He never begins. He also was and always ever will be. The everlasting God stands throughout the ages as the eternal, all-knowing, all-powerful God, Who set the world in order and Who knows our every detail. You can count on the everlasting God.

> **Do you not know? Have you not heard? The Lord is the everlasting God, the Creator of the ends of the earth. He will not grow tired or weary, and his understanding no one can fathom. He gives strength to the weary and increases the power of the weak. Even youths grow tired and weary, and young men stumble and fall; but those who hope in the Lord will renew their strength. They will soar on wings like eagles; they will run and not grow weary, they will walk and not be faint (Isa. 40:28-31).**

As you continue your journey of recovery, it will be important to know that God is the everlasting God. The everlasting, El-Olam, will strengthen you when you are weary. He will make you to soar on the wings of eagles; you will "run and not be weary"; and you will "walk and not faint." You can count on El-Olam.

Prayer

"The everlasting God, El Olam, thank You for giving strength to my limbs, to my mind, and to my heart. You are the God that cannot fail. You have given me a future; You have given me hope. You are

---

132 *Blue Letter Bible, s.v.* "El-Olam," accessed October 27, 2017, https://www.blueletterbible.org/study/misc/name_god.cfm.

the mighty Creator. From the beginning to the end, You never grow weary or weak. Thank You for holding me up and helping me when I stumble and fall. Thank You for increasing my power. Amen."

TODAY'S SCRIPTURE

"For his anger lasts only a moment, but his favor lasts a lifetime; weeping may stay for the night, but rejoicing comes in the morning" (Psa. 30:5).

TODAY'S PRAYER

"Lord, teach me to always find joy in life. Help me not to dwell on the negatives of my past. Help me to seek Your peace in every decision I make. Help me to declare Your Word over my life every day."

TODAY'S JOURNAL QUESTION

What are the things you have learned so far in your journey to joy?

DAY SEVEN

WHY SUFFERING IS IMPORTANT

The very fact that Jesus was willing to suffer must speak to the power of suffering for others. We are lost in a sea that we have created for ourselves if we say that all suffering is wrong. There are times that suffering pays a debt, saves a life, increases stamina, or is necessary for healing. As the human race becomes more and more subjected to the fast pace of technology, we have less and less patience for suffering—even to the point of having to wait more than ten seconds for the computer mouse to catch up.

Mankind has stepped into the lie that utopia is completely without pain. Well, heaven is without sorrow and suffering, but here on earth, there will be pain. How then can we be reconditioned to accept life as pain and pleasure, weeping and laughter?

We can look at the suffering Savior for the example. When I think about the magnitude of His suffering, my suffering seems to be minimized. For example, we hate having to give up things for the sake of others, yet He gave up eternal glory for a trip to the world of pain and sorrow. He left his position to accept a lower position on earth. He had to wait for His body to catch up with earth time to begin His ministry to people who did not want Him. His emotional suffering must have been great, yet He refused depression; He refused anger; and He refused malice.

Jesus suffered rejection on a regular basis, heard ridicule from the very people He created, wore sandals on His kingly feet, and built cabinets with His godly hands. For my sake and yours, He chose to stay in a world that spit on Him. His trip to the cruel cross was His bodily suffering. He went through the agony of emotional turmoil, and He lived through torture. He also suffered spiritually. We know this because of His words on the cross: **"My God, why have You forsaken Me" (Matt. 27:46).** Jesus thought it was important to bear the sins of humanity and to suffer great losses, yet He never despised His suffering. We can and should take a lesson from Jesus about the importance of learning how to suffer.

TODAY'S SCRIPTURE

"Let me hear joy and gladness; let the bones you have crushed rejoice" (Psa. 51:8).

TODAY'S PRAYER

"Lord, when life shows up on my door, make me to hear joy. Make me to feel Your presence, even when my bones are being broken, and life is overwhelmingly hard."

TODAY'S JOURNAL QUESTION

How will you continue in joy when life gets hard again?

❧ CONCLUSION ❧

IF YOU HAVE MADE IT through the many pages of this material, you have had an opportunity to grow in your relationship with God, to examine yourself, to be restored to others, and to find a sense of belonging in the community where you live. So, what is next?

You must go and live. Choose life. Choose the finer things, the best things, and living things. Refuse to choose death. As a reminder of what gives life, let's look at a few Scriptures.[133]

"The fear of the LORD is a fountain of life, turning a person from the snares of death" (Prov. 14:27).

The fear of the Lord refers to the reverential respect due to our Creator. Although we often equate the fear of the Lord with the fear of man, it is not the same. The fear of the Lord carries no undue or unjust punishment, as does the fear of man. Reverential respect for Him reminds us that God is the ultimate Authority, and He is due ultimate respect. It is not the intimidating fear that an abusive controller requires. Our choices need to include the reverential respect for God, since He is the Life-giver.

TODAY'S SCRIPTURE

"The LORD your God is with you, the Mighty Warrior who saves. He will take great delight in you; in his love he will no longer rebuke you, but will rejoice over you with singing" (Zeph. 3:17).

---

133 Pamela Rose Williams. "20 Popular Bible Verses About Life." WhatChristiansWanttoKnow.com. http://www.whatchristianswanttoknow.com/20-popular-bible-verses-about-life/ (accessed October 27, 2017).

TODAY'S PRAYER

I heard and my heart pounded, my lips quivered at the sound; decay crept into my bones, and my legs trembled. Yet I will wait patiently for the day of calamity to come on the nation invading us. Though the fig tree does not bud and there are no grapes on the vines, though the olive crop fails and the fields produce no food, though there are no sheep in the pen and no cattle in the stalls, yet I will rejoice in the LORD, I will be joyful in God my Savior (Hab. 3:16-18).

TODAY'S JOURNAL QUESTION

How will you live from this day forward? What will your creed be?

❧ APPENDIX ❧

So many people who use drugs or alcohol do not know the short-term and long-term effects the drugs will have on their bodies. They are so high most of the time that they really don't know much about the drugs or the side effects. This section is dedicated as a resource for the recovery community to be aware of these facts. Early recovery persons may not be aware of the signs and patterns of different drugs. They will remember the most important symptoms to them but may not know what another drug does. It is important to explore facts so as not to be blindsided by a new drug.

Information concerning drugs which block receptors will help you to be aware of potential help for those not ready for the abstinence-based programs of recovery like the Twelve Gates. Rituals of use will be discussed in this section, along with how to develop new rituals.

SIGNS AND PATTERNS

Denial is a major problem in all early recovery programs. Those attempting recovery for the first—or the fiftieth—time all use this as a great protection device. They deny their use of drugs and, often, the current drug use of others. The mind attempts to protect the "normality" of drug-use, thus keeping the person picking up their drug of choice.

Look out for signs of denial in the people, places, and things you hang around. It is so easy to pretend that old friends won't make a difference in your sobriety, but one visit can be the last visit for you. The first day you want to lay out of work, take a quick inventory. It could be a warning you are getting tired of the new norm of sobriety. Drug paraphernalia, empty bottles, prescription bottles with no name, and unusual-looking cigarettes are all signs of drug use. These items can easily trigger a relapse.

Post-acute withdrawal (PAWS) can show up with physical symptoms, including poor coordination, red and watery eyes, puffiness, changes in facial color, shaking, and frequent illness. PAWS can hit a person in recovery early or late. It can come and go intermittently, be consistent for a period of time, or disappear over time. Be sure you know about PAWS, and pay attention to your body as you may experience these symptoms at any time.

Personality changes are often a giveaway. Sudden, unexplainable outbursts of anger, delusions of grandeur, paranoia, moodiness, secretive behavior, and oversensitivity may be attributed to PAWS.

Cocaine use is often accompanied by a constantly runny nose. An onset of psychosis, grinding teeth, sudden changes in body temperature, weight loss, and shortness of breath are symptoms of cocaine use.

Marijuana users have reddish eyes and dilated pupils. Their face becomes pale and puffy. Their hands tend to shake, and their palms become clammy. They have a dry mouth and fast heartbeats. They usually develop a hacking cough and can have severely stained teeth. Marijuana causes multiple side effects, such as loss of ambition, emotional immaturity, and memory loss. The following side effects last long after use has stopped:

- Short-term memory problems
- Severe anxiety
- Fear that one is being watched or followed (paranoia)
- Very strange behavior
- Seeing, hearing, or smelling things that aren't there
- Not being able to tell imagination from reality (psychosis)
- Panic
- Hallucinations
- Loss of a sense of personal identity
- Lowered reaction time
- Increased heart rate (risk of heart attack)
- Increased risk of stroke

- Problems with coordination (impairing safe driving or playing sports)
- Sexual problems (for males) or sexually transmitted infections (up to seven times more likely than non-users for females).[134]

"A pill user will often have symptoms similar to allergies and can look as if they have a cold."

Pain pills, especially Oxycontin®, show first in the attitude. The withdrawal symptoms are so severe that the addicted person will do things out of character. He or she may become argumentative because of the nausea, chills, and fatigue. His or her mood may change from happy to sad in a matter of minutes. The stronger the addiction, the more pain the addict will feel, forcing him or her to do more of the drug.

Bags under the eyes often are a side effect of opioid use. They may rub their arms or scratch their faces; they may twitch and sweat. Pill abuse will often have symptoms similar to allergies or the common cold. "Doctor shopping" is a common activity in opioid abuse.

PHARMACOLOGY

The following information on the most abused drugs in America comes from the National Institute on Drug Abuse website.[135]

Marijuana

Marijuana (cannabis) is the most commonly used illicit substance. This drug impairs short-term memory and learning, the ability to focus, and coordination. It also increases heart rate, can harm the lungs, and may increase the risk of psychosis in vulnerable people. Research suggests that when regular marijuana use begins in the teen years, addiction is more likely—one in six users, compared to one in nine among adults. In addition, recent research suggests that heavy cannabis use that starts in the teen years is associated with

---

134 Foundation for a Drug-Free World. "Short and Long-Term Effects." Drugfreeworld.org. http://www.drugfreeworld.org/drugfacts/marijuana/short-and-long-term-effects.html (accessed November 11, 2017).
135 National Institute on Drug Abuse. "Addiction Science." DrugAbuse.gov. http://www.drugabuse.gov/related-topics/addiction-science (accessed October 27, 2017).

declines in IQ scores in adulthood. (More information on marijuana can be found at www.drugabuse.gov/marijuana.)

K2/Spice

"K2" or "Spice" refers to a wide variety of herbal mixtures that produce experiences similar to marijuana. Of the illicit drugs most used by high school seniors, Spice is second only to marijuana. It is sometimes called "synthetic" marijuana, but this is a misperception. Labels on Spice products often claim that they contain "natural" psychoactive material taken from a variety of plants; however, chemical analyses show that their active ingredients are synthetic (or designer) cannabinoid compounds.

Poison Control Centers report a variety of K2/Spice symptoms, including rapid heart rate, vomiting, agitation, confusion, hallucinations, raised blood pressure, reduced blood supply to the heart, and, in a few cases, heart attacks. Because the chemicals used in Spice have a high addictive potential and no medical benefit, the Drug Enforcement Administration (DEA) has made it illegal to sell, buy, or possess the main chemicals in these drugs. (More information can be found at www.drugabuse.gov/drugs-abuse/k2spice-synthetic-marijuana.)

Prescription/Over-the-Counter Drug Abuse

Prescription medications and some over-the-counter medications are increasingly being abused (used in ways other than intended or without a prescription). This practice can lead to addiction and, in some cases, overdose. Among the most disturbing aspects of this emerging trend is its prevalence among teenagers and young adults. It is also a common misperception that because these are used medically or prescribed by physicians, they are safe, even when not used as intended. Commonly abused classes of prescription drugs include opioid painkillers, stimulants, and depressants.

Opioids are usually prescribed for pain relief. Commonly prescribed opioids include hydrocodone (e.g., Vicodin®), oxycodone (e.g., OxyContin®), morphine, fentanyl, and codeine. In the United States, more people now die from opioid painkiller overdoses than from heroin and cocaine combined.

Methylphenidate (Ritalin®, Concerta®, Focalin®, and Metadate®) and amphetamines (Adderall®, Dexedrine®) are stimulants commonly prescribed for attention-deficit hyperactivity disorder (ADHD).

Depressants are usually prescribed to promote sleep or to reduce anxiety. As measured by national surveys, depressants are often categorized as sedatives or tranquilizers. Sedatives primarily include barbiturates (e.g., phenobarbitol) but also include sleep medications such as Ambien® and Lunesta®.

Tranquilizers primarily include benzodiazepines, such as Valium® and Xanax®, but also include muscle relaxants and other anti-anxiety medications.

"Syrup," "Purple Drank," "Sizzurp," or "Lean" describe soda mixed with prescription-strength cough syrup containing codeine and promethazine. These cough syrups are available by prescription only. Users may also flavor the mixture with hard candies. Drinking this combination has become increasingly popular among some celebrities and youth in several areas of the country. Codeine is an opioid that can produce relaxation and euphoria when consumed in sufficient quantities. Promethazine is an antihistamine that also acts as a sedative. (More information can be found at www.drugabuse.gov/drugs-abuse/emerging-trends.)

Commonly abused over-the-counter drugs include cold medicines containing dextromethorphan, (DMX), a cough suppressant. Products containing DMX can be sold as cough syrups, gel capsules, and pills that can look like candies. They are frequently abused by young people, who refer to the practice as "robo-tripping" or "skittling." Pseudoephedrine, a decongestant found in many over-the-counter cold medicines, is another over-the-counter medication that is used illicitly. Although not typically abused in itself, it is one ingredient used to produce methamphetamine. (For more information about prescription drug abuse and related health consequences, go to www.drugabuse.gov/drugs-abuse/prescription-drugs-cold-medicines.)

Alcohol

Alcohol consumption can damage the brain and most body organs—including the heart, liver, and pancreas. It also increases the risk of some cancers, weakens the immune system, puts fetal development at risk, and causes deadly vehicle accidents. Areas of the brain that are especially vulnerable to alcohol-related damage are the cerebral cortex (largely responsible for our higher brain functions, including problem-solving and decision making), the hippocampus (important for memory and learning), and the cerebellum (important for movement coordination).[136] (More information can be found on the website of the National Institute on Alcohol Abuse and Alcoholism at www.niaaa.nih.gov.)

Amphetamines/Methamphetamine

Amphetamines, including methamphetamine, are powerful stimulants that can produce feelings of euphoria and alertness. Methamphetamine is a white, odorless, bitter-tasting crystalline powder that easily dissolves in water or alcohol and is taken orally, intranasally (snorting the powder), or intravenously (needle injection).

Methamphetamine's effects are particularly long-lasting and harmful to the brain. Amphetamines can cause high body temperature and can lead to serious heart problems and seizures.

Regular methamphetamine use significantly changes how the brain functions. Noninvasive human brain imaging studies have shown alterations in the activity of the dopamine system that are associated with reduced motor skills and impaired verbal learning, which may account for many of the emotional and cognitive problems observed in regular methamphetamine users. (More information on methamphetamine can be found at www.drugabuse.gov/publications/drugfacts/methamphetamine.)

Anabolic Steroids

Anabolic steroids refer to synthetic variants of the male sex hormone testosterone. The proper term for these compounds is anabolic-androgenic steroids (abbreviated AAS—"anabolic," referring to muscle building, and "androgenic," referring to increased male sexual characteristics.) Steroids can be prescribed for certain medical conditions; however, they are often abused to increase muscle mass and to improve athletic performance or physical appearance. Anabolic steroids are usually either taken orally or injected into the

---

136 ScienceNetLinks. "Alcohol and Your Brain." http://sciencenetlinks.com/student-teacher-sheets/alcohol-and-your-brain (accessed October 27, 2017).

muscles, although some are applied to the skin as a cream or gel. Doses taken by abusers may be ten to one hundred times higher than doses prescribed to treat medical conditions.

Anabolic steroids work very differently from other addictive drugs, and they do not have the same acute effects on the brain. However, long-term steroid use can affect some of the same brain pathways and chemicals—including dopamine, serotonin, and opioid systems—that are affected by other drugs. They, thereby, may have a significant impact on mood and behavior.

Other serious consequences of steroid abuse can include heart disease, liver problems, stroke, infectious diseases, depression, and suicide. Less serious side effects include severe acne and changes in sex characteristics, like shrinking of the testicles in men and growth of facial hair in women. (More information on steroids can be found at www.drugabuse.gov/drugs-abuse/steroids-anabolic.)

Bath Salts

The term "bath salts" refers to an emerging family of drugs containing one or more synthetic chemicals related to cathinone, an amphetamine-like stimulant found naturally in the khat plant. Reports of severe intoxication and dangerous health effects associated with the use of bath salts have made these drugs a serious and growing public health and safety issue. Some users experience paranoia, agitation, hallucinatory delirium, and psychotic and violent behavior. Deaths have also been reported. Flakka is a particularly dangerous form of bath salts.

These synthetic cathinone products—marketed as "bath salts" to evade detection by authorities—should not be confused with products such as Epsom salts for bathing. Bath salts typically take the form of a white or brown crystalline powder and are sold in small plastic or foil packages labeled "not for human consumption." (More information can be found at www.drugabuse.gov/drugs-abuse/bath-salts-synthetic-cathinones.)

Cocaine

Cocaine is a short-acting stimulant, which can lead users to "binge" (take the drug many times in a single session). Cocaine use can lead to severe medical consequences related to the heart and the respiratory, nervous, and digestive systems. Cocaine users can also experience severe paranoia, in which they lose touch with reality.

The powdered form of cocaine is either inhaled through the nose, where it is absorbed through the nasal tissue, or dissolved in water and injected into the bloodstream. Crack is a form of cocaine that has been processed to make a rock crystal (also called "freebase cocaine") that can be smoked. The crystal is heated to produce vapors that are absorbed into the bloodstream through the lungs. The term "crack" refers to the crackling sound produced by the rock as it is heated. (More information can be found at www.drugabuse.gov/cocaine.)

Hallucinogens

The effects of hallucinogens—perception-altering drugs—are highly variable and unreliable, producing different effects in different people at different times. This is mainly due to differences in the amounts and chemistries of active compounds within the drugs. Because of their unpredictable nature, the use of hallucinogens can be particularly dangerous. Examples of hallucinogens include:

- MDMA (Ecstasy, "Molly") (3,4-methylenedioxymethamphetamine) produces both stimulant and mind-altering effects. It can increase body temperature, heart rate, blood pressure, and heart-wall stress. Ecstasy may also be toxic to nerve cells. It is taken orally, usually as a capsule or tablet. Its effects last approximately three to six hours, although it is not uncommon for users to take a second dose of the drug as the effects of the first dose begin to fade. Ecstasy is commonly taken in combination with alcohol and other drugs.

- Molly—slang for "molecular"—refers to the pure crystalline powder form of ecstasy. Users may seek out Molly to avoid the adulterants or substitutes known to be commonly found in Ecstasy, but those who purchase what they think is pure Ecstasy may actually be exposing themselves to the same risks, since Molly often contains toxic additives. In fact, Molly is often nothing more than repackaged Ecstasy. (More information can be found at www.drugabuse.gov/publications/drugfacts/mdma-ecstasy.)

- LSD is one of the most potent hallucinogenic drugs. Its effects are unpredictable, and users may see vivid colors and images, hear sounds, and feel sensations that seem real but do not exist. Users also may have traumatic experiences and emotions that can last for many hours. Some short-term effects can include increased body temperature, heart rate, and blood pressure; sweating; loss of appetite; sleeplessness; dry mouth; and tremors.
- PCP (phencyclidine) was developed in the 1950s as an intravenous anesthetic. Its legitimate use has since been discontinued due to serious adverse effects.
- Psilocybin is obtained from certain types of mushrooms that are found in tropical and subtropical regions of South America, Mexico, and the United States. These mushrooms typically contain less than 0.5 percent psilocybin plus trace amounts of psilocin, another hallucinogenic substance. (More information can be found at www. drugabuse.gov/publications/drugfacts/hallucinogens.)

Heroin

Heroin is a powerful opioid drug that produces euphoria and feelings of relaxation. It slows respiration and can increase the risk of serious infectious diseases, especially when taken intravenously. Regular heroin use changes the functioning of the brain, causing tolerance and dependence. Other opioid drugs include morphine, OxyContin®, Vicodin®, and Percodan®, which have legitimate medical uses; however, using them in ways other than prescribed (or using them without a prescription) can result in the same harmful consequences as heroin use. (More information about heroin can be found at www. drugabuse.gov/drugs-abuse/heroin.)

Inhalants

Inhalants are volatile substances found in many household products (such as oven cleaners, gasoline, spray paints, and other aerosols) that induce mind-altering effects. Inhalants are extremely toxic and can damage the heart, kidneys, lungs, and brain. Even a healthy person can suffer heart failure and death within minutes of a single session of the prolonged sniffing of an inhalant.

People tend to abuse different inhalant products at different ages. New, younger users, ages twelve to fifteen, most commonly abuse glue, shoe polish, spray paints, gasoline, and lighter fluid. First-time older users, ages sixteen to seventeen, most commonly abuse nitrous oxide, or "whippets." Adults most commonly abuse a class of inhalants known as nitrites such as amyl nitrites, or "poppers." (More information on inhalants can be found at www.drugabuse.gov/drugs-abuse/inhalants.)

Ketamine, Rohypnol, and GHB

Ketamine, Rohypnol®, and GHB have come to be known as "date rape" drugs because they can cause someone to lose their memory of an assault. Rohypnol® and GHB can easily be added to beverages and ingested unknowingly. Any of these drugs can also cause someone to lose consciousness. Ketamine and GHB are predominantly central nervous system (CNS) depressants, whereas Rohypnol® is a benzodiazepine. (More information can be found at www.drugabuse.gov/drugs-abuse/club-drugs.)

Nicotine

Nicotine is an addictive stimulant found in cigarettes and other forms of tobacco. Tobacco smoke increases a user's risk of cancer, emphysema, bronchial disorders, and cardiovascular disease. Smoking rates have decreased in the United States in recent years, yet the mortality rate associated with tobacco addiction is still staggering, with more than 480,000 premature deaths in the United States each year—about one in every five deaths. Tobacco use killed approximately one hundred million people during the twentieth century and, if current smoking trends continue, the cumulative death toll for this century is projected to reach one billion. (More information can be found at www.drugabuse.gov/drugs-abuse/tobacco-addiction-nicotine.)

ETHICS IN RECOVERY

Ethics is a moral code or philosophy by which we conduct ourselves to do right. In recovery, forming a safe place for others to recover will be greatly influenced by the code of ethics. At Bethesda Recovery, a high standard of morals and ethics is expected from each volunteer and each staff member.

"Do the next right thing if it kills you" is the code of ethics taught at Bethesda Recovery. It is easy to slip into a wrong thing. Everybody does from time to time. However, if your life rule is to do the next right thing, you can start getting your life back on track little by little by simply doing the next right thing. Simple, little, right things can lead you out of the wrong things. The next right thing is the next thing you see to do which is positive and helps, not hurts, the situation.

Attitude

A person working in recovery must first have a sober attitude. This sober attitude includes thinking clearly about one's self. Good self-esteem is necessary to help others recover. A positive attitude about life, other people, and God is a must for helping others to recover. Attitude is placed first in the code of ethics because almost everything else will hinge on that. If a person's attitude is good, then mistakes can be handled with ease. If a person's attitude is poor, then mistakes will become more than they need to be.

Attitude is also considered a lifestyle. People in recovery can usually see through a fake person. Those working with people in early recovery should be honest in all their dealings, including being honest with their emotions.

There will always be times when people who need recovery will refuse it. Continue a positive attitude even when the person is negative. Learn to let things roll off like "water off a duck's back."

Confidentiality

What happens in recovery, stays in recovery. Meetings are confidential places where those in recovery share private information. Do not tell what is said in a meeting to anyone other than your superior or to your counselor. Learn to keep your mouth tightly closed about what is happening in recovery. Many church members break confidentiality by asking for prayer and going into detail. Learn to pray for the people in recovery at the meetings you attend with them. Don't put them on the prayer list at other church meetings. When someone in recovery asks for prayer, do not give details of what you may know about that person. Trust is built on confidentiality. If you want people to trust you, don't talk about their business.

When a person in recovery begins to tell you deep secrets, learn to respond with compassion. What they tell you may be deplorable to you personally, but they do not need to feel judged. Your job is to lead them to Jesus for repentance and forgiveness, not to send them to hell.

Boundaries

Recovery programs and churches must have strong boundaries. Do not share personal things with those you may be helping in recovery. Learn to discern. Be welcoming, yet protective, of certain areas of your life. Do not disclose private marriage information with those in recovery. There is such a thing as spiritual abuse. Do not cross the line with those in recovery who see you as an authority. Make sure you do not counsel or coach those of the opposite sex unless your spouse is with you. Married men and women must protect the sanctity of the marriage to help provide a safe, nurturing place for recovery.

"Do not date those in recovery."

Do not date those in recovery. Do not text personal messages to those in recovery. Talk only about those things that pertain to recovery. Know your place in Christ and make sure you keep that place. Do not hang out alone with those in recovery. Go places as a group. This keeps vulnerable men and women from thinking that you have a more personal issue with them than you should.

When holding telephone conversations with those you are helping, keep the conversations to the point and make them as brief as possible. Do not receive calls from clients after regular business hours unless you are a sponsor. You should be able to set limits on times for calls and receive only emergency calls from clients after regular hours. Your hours may vary, so set those hours early in the recovery process. For example, some people in early recovery are very needy. If there are no boundaries set, the needy person may become too dependent on you. This is very serious. It could be swapping one addiction for another. You could be setting yourself up for a codependent relationship, which could begin to take over your life.

Meet those in recovery in public places, such as coffee shops and at church. If you volunteer to give rides, make sure you have someone else along with you, at least at first. This sets the personal boundaries that may be needed later.

"Avoid male/female relationships with those you choose to counsel. A dual relationship exists where two or more roles are mixed in a manner that can harm the counseling relationship. This includes sexual or romantic relationships."[137] Dual relationships with church members are potentially troublesome and best avoided. However, when those relationships occur, helpers will take responsible precautions to limit adverse impact in any dual relationship.

Professional Conduct

The clause "Do no harm" is essential for the code of ethics for Christians who help with recovery. To "do no harm" implies that every action will be life-giving. As Christians, we can turn to the Bible to learn the life-giving techniques of Jesus.

Jesus is the Way, and, therefore, He showed the Way to those who were lost. Our job is to know the way out of addiction and then to show that way to others. Jesus is the Truth, and so, truth is the theme of our ministry. Truth is necessary to help others, so all communication must be truthful. Jesus was Light to those in darkness. We must always be light for those we help.

Ending Relationships

When relationships are not life-giving, you must be willing to end that relationship for the sake of the one you are trying to help and for your own sake. This is very difficult, since you want to help everybody. A good code of ethics requires that you examine every relationship and determine if the relationship is continuing to move forward.

Personal and Professional Development

Continuing education is a must. The recovery coach must remain teachable and open to new information or, simply, new ways to present old information. Nobody knows everything. Learning never stops in the life of a minister.

---

137   Tim Clinton. *Caring for People God's Way*. Nashville: Thomas Nelson, 2005. 109.

Respect

Every human being deserves respect as a human being, no matter who the individual is.

Competence

Always operate in your area of expertise. If a question arises which you do not know the answer to, refer the person to someone who can help.

Avoid Areas of Conflict of Interest

A minister working with recovery will use his or her position to promote the best interests of the clients and will avoid personal, commercial, or other conflict of interests.

A minister working with recovery will maintain appropriate professional boundaries and not misuse any client relationship.

A minister working with recovery offers educative service to clients and will work with all people without discrimination.

A minister working with recovery will minister with honesty and integrity, being respectful of both clients and colleagues while protecting their dignity and welfare.

A minister working with recovery will work within the limits of his or her professional training and experience.

A minister working with recovery will not attempt to assess, counsel, or advise on problems outside the scope of their professional training or role as an educator and coach.

A minister working with recovery will, as far as possible, ensure the confidentiality of clients, whether in individual sessions or groups settings. All information disclosed will be treated as confidential, unless the client otherwise gives permission.

A minister working with recovery will respect people's personal boundaries and also their right to choose the level at which they will participate in activities.[138]

---

138 The Baptist Churches of South Australia Inc. *Code of Ethics Applicable to Pastors/Ministers of the Baptist Churches of South Australia*. Unley: Baptist Churches of South Australia Inc., 2012. Accessed October 27, 2017. http://sabaptist.asn.au/wp-content/uploads/2013/12/BCSA-Code-of-Ethics-201210.pdf.

NUTS AND BOLTS

It is suggested that the pastor of the church select a director for the residential recovery program.

Minimum Suggested Requirements for the Director

Deacon or deaconess

Training in addiction/recovery

Preferred Requirements

Licensed minister called to the field of Christian recovery

Counseling training/certificate minimum

Recovery certificate minimum

Member of local church in good standing

Minimum Suggested Requirements for a Recovery Church

Availability of recovery life coach

One weekly, dedicated meeting to the issues of recovery

Preferred Requirements

Five to seven groups each week geared to recovery issues

Anger management

Co-dependency meetings

Overcomers groups

Bible study

Self-esteem

Life coaches for recovering addicts

Christian counseling for deeper problems

Small group leaders

Any church can start a meeting with a dedicated group leader and one recovering person. Once the meetings begin, it is important to be faithful to them. The leader should be dedicated to show up and be prepared, no matter how many others show up. Remember, one person's life is important.

HOW SMALL GROUPS WORK

Small groups are designed for accountability. Each small group should have a meeting to define the level of accountability it will have.

HOW RELIABILITY ENHANCES RESTORATION

The Twelve Gates of Recovery and Restoration are built on the foundations of family and community. It is in relationships that we are wounded and hurt. It is in communities that trust is often destroyed and relationships relinquished to loneliness and disillusionment. Logic may suggest that healing comes in isolation, but healing comes in restored families and solid communities. As you may have noticed, Nehemiah used family groups to rebuild each section of the walls and gates, and the whole community came together to build the whole wall. In the end, the family groups were connected to a solid community of support, and the walls and gates were restored.

This is the premise of restoring lives with the twelve gates. As a small group of wounded people begin the process of restoration together, it is imperative that someone in the group be reliable and trustworthy. The group will learn faithfulness through faithfulness. The group becomes a surrogate family, almost an incubator, for the new life that must be formed. As the one in recovery becomes more mature, he or she becomes reliable and can move more freely in community.

❧ BIBLIOGRAPHY ❧

Abarim Publications, s.v. "Ammiel," accessed August 30, 2017, http://www.abarim-publications.com/Meaning/Ammiel.html#.WabR2siGPZY.

Abarim Publications, s.v. "Shaphat," accessed October 25, 2017, www.abarim-publications.com/Meaning/Shaphat.html.

Abounding Love Bible Ministry. "Seven Hebrew Words for Praise." Albministry. org. http://www.albministry.org/pdf/HebrewandGreekWordsforPraise.pdf (accessed August 18, 2017).

AllAboutWater.org. "20 Interesting and Useful Water Facts." AllAboutWater. org. http://www.allaboutwater.org/water-facts.html (accessed October 27, 2017).

American Heritage Dictionary, s.v. "celebrate," accessed October 27, 2017, www. ahdictionary.com/word/search.html?q=celebrate&submit.x=50&submit.y=20.

American Heritage Dictionary, s.v. "trust," accessed September 5, 2017, https:// ahdictionary.com/word/search.html?q=trust.

American Psychiatric Association. 1994. *The Diagnostic and Statistical Manual of Mental Disorders: DSM-IV-TR.* New York: American Psychiatric Association.

American Society of Addiction Medicine. "Definition of Addiction." ASAM. org. http://www.asam.org/for-the-public/definition-of-addiction (accessed November 13, 2017).

"Anima Christi, The." *Catholic.org.* http://www.catholic.org/prayers/prayer. php?p=1140 (accessed July 25, 2017).

"Another Serenity Prayer." In *Acts International,* by Billy Joe Vaughn, http://www. actsweb.org/articles/article.php?i=322&d=2&c=4 (accessed July 26, 2017).

Baptist Churches of South Australia Inc, The. *Code of Ethics Applicable to Pastors/ Ministers of the Baptist Churches of South Australia.* Unley: Baptist Churches of South Australia Inc., 2012. Accessed October 27, 2017. http://sabaptist.asn.au/ wp-content/uploads/2013/12/BCSA-Code-of-Ethics-201210.pdf.

Bible Hub, s.v. "dodavah," accessed August 30, 2017, http://biblehub.com/topical/d/ dodavah.htm.

Bible Hub, s.v. "hagiazo," accessed August 18, 2017, http://biblehub.com/ greek/37.htm.

Bible Hub, s.v. "Joshua," accessed October 24, 2017, http://biblehub.com/he-brew/3091.htm.

Bible Hub, s.v. "Palti," accessed August 18, 2017, http://biblehub.com/topical/p/ palti.htm.

Bible Hub, s.v. "selfish ambition," accessed August 15, 2017, http://biblehub.com/ greek/2052.htm.

Bible Hub, s.v. "Sovo," accessed October 27,2017, http://biblehub.com/ greek/4982.htm.

Bible Hub. s.v. "worship," accessed August 18, 2017, https://www.blueletterbible. org/search/search.cfm?Criteria=worship&t=KJV#s=s_primary_0_1.

Bible Hub, s.v. "Yhvh Nissi," accessed October 24, 2017, http://biblehub.com/ hebrew/3071.htm.

Bible Study Tools, s.v. "Geuel," accessed October 27, 2017, http://www.biblestudy-tools.com/dictionary/geuel.

Bible Study Tools, s.v. "Hanun," accessed November 13, 2017 http://www.biblestudytools.com/dictionary/hanun.

Bible Study Tools, s.v. "heresy," accessed August 15, 2017, http://www.biblestudy-tools.com/dictionary/heresy.

Bible Study Tools, s.v. "pisteuo," accessed October 24, 2017, http://www.biblestudytools.com/lexicons/greek/nas/pisteuo.html.

Bible Study Tools, s.v. "Sethur," accessed October 27, 2017, https://www.biblestudytools.com/dictionary/sethur.

Bible Tools, s.v. "Ahab," accessed August 30, 2017, http://www.bibletools.org/index.cfm/fuseaction/Lexicon.show/ID/H157/ahab.html.

Bible.org, s.v. "Jehovah-Jireh-Rapha-Nissia," accessed August 23, 2017, https://bible.org/seriespage/60-compound-names-jehovah-jireh-rapha-nissi.

Blue Letter Bible, s.v. "chashaq," accessed August 30, 2017, https://www.blueletterbible.org/lang/lexicon/lexicon.cfm?strongs=h2836:

Blue Letter Bible, s.v. "El Shaddai," accessed October 27, 2017, https://www.blueletterbible.org/study/misc/name_god.cfm.

Blue Letter Bible, s.v. "El-Olam," accessed October 27, 2017, https://www.blueletterbible.org/study/misc/name_god.cfm.

Blue Letter Bible, s.v. "Ephraim," accessed September 5, 2017, https://www.blueletterbible.org/lang/Lexicon/Lexicon.cfm?strongs=H669&t=KJV.

Blue Letter Bible, s.v. "exousia," accessed October 24, 2017, https://www.blueletterbible.org/lang/lexicon/lexicon.cfm?t=kjv&strongs=g1849.

Blue Letter Bible, s.v. "Gaddi," accessed August 30, 2017, https://www.blueletterbible.org/lang/lexicon/lexicon.cfm?t=kjv&strongs=h1426.

Blue Letter Bible, s.v. "Halal," accessed August 18, 2017, https://www.blueletterbible.org/lang/lexicon/lexicon.cfm?t=kjv&strongs=h1984.

Blue Letter Bible, s.v. "Jehovah Mekoddishkem," accessed October 25, 2017, https://www.blueletterbible.org/study/misc/name_god.cfm.

Blue Letter Bible, s.v., "pharmekia," accessed November 8, 2017, https://www.blueletterbible.org/lang/lexicon/lexicon.cfm?t=kjv&strongs=g5331.

Blue Letter Bible, s.v. "phylargyria," https://www.blueletterbible.org/lang/lexicon/lexicon.cfm?t=kjv&strongs=g5365 accessed August 30, 2017.

Blue Letter Bible, s.v. "racham," accessed August 30, 2017, https://www.blueletterbible.org/lang/lexicon/lexicon.cfm?t=kjv&strongs=h7356.

Boggs, Ricky. *Alcohol and Addiction: How It Affects the Brain.* Youtube video, 54:39. Posted [January, 2012]. https://www.youtube.com/watch?v=e9F5wpvq2ho.

Brandon Web. "The Names of God – Jehovah-Rohi. Brandonweb.com. http://www.brandonweb.com/sermons/sermonpages/psalms96.htm (accessed August 21, 2017).

Clinton, Tim. *Caring for People God's Way.* Nashville: Thomas Nelson, 2005.

CLMNWA Family Church. "7 Hebrew Words for Praise: "Shabach." Christlikeministriesnwa.com. https://christlikeministriesnwa.com/2013/02/21/7-hebrew-words-for-praise-shabach/ (accessed August 18, 2017).

Cronin, J.K. "The Name of God as Revealed in Exodus 3:14." Exodus-314.com. http://exodus-314.com/part-ii/the-meaning-of-ligehyeh-asher-ehyehlig.html (accessed August 30, 2017).

Dictionary.com, s.v. "collusion," accessed October 26, 2017, http://www.dictionary.com/browse/collusion.

Dictionary.com, s.v. "harvest," accessed October 27, 2017, http://www.dictionary.com/browse/harvest.

Dictionary.com, s.v. "jealousy," accessed August 15, 2017, http://www.dictionary.com/browse/jealousy.

Drug/Alcohol Abuse Rehab Centers. "The Effects of Alcohol Use." Drugabuse.com. http://drugabuse.com/library/the-effects-of-alcohol-use/ (accessed August 15, 2017).

Easton's Bible Dictionary, s.v. "Jehovah-Nissi," accessed August 18, 2017, http://www.biblestudytools.com/dictionary/jehovah-nissi.

Easton's Bible Dictionary, s.v. "Jehovah-Shalom," accessed August 16, 2017, http://www.biblestudytools.com/dictionary/jehovah-shalom.

Epstein, Murray. "Alcohol's Impact on Kidney Function." NIH.gov. http://pubs.niaaa.nih.gov/publications/arh21-1/84.pdf (accessed August 15, 2017).

Foster, Richard. *Celebration of Discipline: The Path to Spiritual Growth.* New York City: Harper Collins, 1988.

Foundation for a Drug-Free World. "Short and Long-Term Effects." Drugfreeworld.org. http://www.drugfreeworld.org/drugfacts/marijuana/short-and-long-term-effects.html (accessed November 11, 2017).

Fountaingate Loaves and Fishes. "Destiny of the Church: The Gates of the City (Part II)." Churchlink.com. http://www.churchlink.com.au/churchlink/bible_studies/dotc/dotc6.html (accessed October 25, 2017).

Free Dictionary, The, s.v. "sober," accessed October 27, 2017, www.thefreedictionary.com/sober.

Free Dictionary, The, s.v. "sorcery," accessed August 15, 2017, www.thefreediction-ary.com/sorcery.

Global World Ministry. "Praise-Yadah and Towdah." Globalworldministry. org. https://www.globalwordministry.org/worship/praise-yadah-and-todah (accessed August 18, 2017).

Google, s.v. "disease," accessed October 27, 2017, https://www.google.com/ search?ei=QB_zWeHmCem-jwS1r7S4DQ&q=disease+meaning&oq=disea se+meaning&gs_l=psy-ab.3..0i67k1j0l9.4625.9728.0.11915.15.15.0.0.0.0.143.1811 .1j14.15.001.1.64.psy-ab.0.15.1808...35i39k1j0i131k1j0i20i264k1j0i20i263i264k1.0.D WyPzLRQHSU.

Grimm, Carl Ludwig Wilibald, Joseph Henry Thayer, Christian Gottlob Wilke, Christian Gottlob. *A Greek-English Lexicon of the New Testament, Being Grimm's Wilke's Clavis Novi Testamenti, tr., rev. and enl. by Joseph Henry Thayer.* New York: New York American Book Company, 1889. https://archive.org/details/ greekenglishlexi00grimuoft.

Headcoverings by Devorah. "Names of Men in Torah." Headcoverings-by-Devorah.com. https://headcoverings-by-devorah.com/NamesMenTorah.htm (accessed November 11, 2017).

Hebrew for Christians, s.v. "Adonai," accessed October 27, 2017, http://www.he-brew4christians.com/Names_of_G-d/Adonai/adonai.html.

Hebrew for Christians, s.v. "Elohim," accessed October 27, 2017, http://www.he-brew4christians.com/Names_of_G-d/Elohim/elohim.html.

Hitchcock's Bible Names Dictionary, s.v. "Palti," accessed October 25, 2017, https:// www.biblestudytools.com/dictionary/palti.

Hitchcock's Bible Names Dictionary, s.v. "Sodi," accessed August 18, 2017, http:// www.biblestudytools.com/dictionary/sodi/.

Hitchcock's Dictionary of Bible Names, s.v. "Jehovah Tsidkenu," accessed October 25, 2017, https://www.biblestudytools.com/dictionary/jehovah-tsidkenu.

Hurnard, Hannah. *Hinds Feet on High Places.* Carol Stream: Tyndale House, 1979.

King James Bible Page, The, s.v. "idolatry," accessed August 15, 2017, http://av1611. com/kjbp/kjv-dictionary/idolatry.html.

Latin Dictionary, s.v. "phylargyria," accessed November 13, 2017, http://www. latin-dictionary.org/Latin-English-Dictionary/philargyria.

Leshner, Dr. Alan I., "Addressing the Medical Consequences of Drug Abuse," *NIDA Notes,* 15 (2000): 1, accessed November 10, 2017, http://www.nida.nih.gov/ NIDA_notes/NNVol15N1/DirRepVol15N1.html.

Letter Bible, s.v. "water," accessed October 27, 2017, https://www.blueletterbible. org/search/search.cfm?Criteria=water&t=KJV#s=s_primary_0_1.

Lewis, C.S. *Mere Christianity.* New York: HarperOne, 1952.

Matter Under Mind. "Life Without Water. Is it Possible?" Matterundermind. com. http://matterundermind.com/life-without-water-is-it-possible/ (accessed October 27, 2017).

May, Dr. Gerald. *Addiction and Grace.* New York: HarperCollins, 2009.

Merriam Webster Unabridged, s.v. "contention," accessed August 15, 2017, https:// www.merriam-webster.com/dictionary/contention.

Merriam-Webster Dictionary, s.v. "consequence," accessed October 27, 2017, www. merriam-webster.com/dictionary/consequence.

Merriam-Webster Dictionary, s.v. "overcome," accessed August 18, 2017, www. merriam-webster.com/dictionary/overcome.

Merriam-Webster Dictionary, s.v. "transformed," accessed August 23, 2017, www. merriam-webster.com/dictionary/transformed.

Merriam-Webster Dictionary, s.v. "victory," accessed August 18, 2017, http://www. merriamwebster.com/dictionary/victory.

Messie2vie, s.v. "rayah," accessed August 30, 2017, https://www.messie2vie.fr/ bible/strongs/strong-hebrew-H7474-rayah.html.

National Institute on Alcohol Abuse and Alcoholism. "Alcohol Facts and Statistics." NIH.gov. https://www.niaaa.nih.gov/alcohol-facts-and-statistics (accessed August 15, 2017).

National Institute on Drug Abuse. "Addiction Science." DrugAbuse.gov. http:// www.drugabuse.gov/related-topics/addiction-science (accessed October 27, 2017).

National Institute on Drug Abuse. "The Neurology of Drug Abuse: 7: Summary: Addictive Drugs Activate the Reward System Via Increasing Dopamine Neurotransmission." DrugAbuse.gov. https://www.drugabuse.gov/publications/ teaching-packets/neurobiology-drug-addiction/section-iv-action-cocaine/7- summary-addictive-drugs-activate-reward (accessed November 8, 2017).

Niebuhr, Reinhold. "The Serenity Prayer." *Hazelden Betty Ford Foundation,* http:// www.hazelden.org/web/public/serenityprayer.page?printable=true&showlogo =true&callprint=true.

Norton, Merrill. "Clinical and Administrative Pharmacy," *University of Georgia College of Pharmacy.* UGA.edu. http://cap.rx.uga.edu/index.php/people/faculty/ norton/chemicalhealthassociates.press (accessed November 10, 2013).

Norton, Merrill. "Hijacking the Teenage Brain." Seminar, Georgia Council on Substance Abuse, Waycross, accessed February 7, 2008.

"Only One Thing is Necessary: A Prayer of Saint Alphonsus Liguori." In *Prayers. The Apostolate of Hannah's Tears.* http://www.hannahstears.com/2011/08/saint- alphonsus-de-liguori-only-one/ (accessed September 6, 2017).

Parsons, John J. "Hebrew Names of God." Hebrew4Christians.net. http://www.
hebrew4christians.com/Names_of_G-d/Redeemer/redeemer.html (accessed
October 24, 2017).

"Peace Prayer of St. Francis of Assisi." In *Catholic News Agency*, http://www.
catholicnewsagency.com/resources/saints/saints/peace-prayer-of-st-francis-
of-assisi (accessed July 23, 2017).

"Prayer for Spiritual Restoration." In *Prayers for Restoration. Knowing-Jesus.com*,
http://prayer.knowing-jesus.com/Prayers-for-Restoration#sthash.a6z4tFfh.
dpuf (accessed August 18, 2017).

Russell, Bertrand. "Envy." *The Conquest of Happiness*. New York: Liveright, 1996.

"Saint Francis's Prayer in Praise of God, Given to Brother Leo." In *National Shrine
of Saint Francis of Assisi*, Shrinesf.org, http://www.shrinesf.org/franciscan-prayer.
html (accessed July 26, 2017).

Sandford, John and Paula. *Healing the Wounded Spirit*. Tulsa: Victory House
Publishers, 1985.

Sandford, John and Paula. *Transformation of the Inner Man*. Tulsa: Victory House
Publishers, 1982.

ScienceNetLinks. "Alcohol and Your Brain." http://sciencenetlinks.com/student-
teacher-sheets/alcohol-and-your-brain (accessed October 27, 2017).

SensAgent, s.v. "vulnerability," accessed November 12, 2017, http://dictionary.
sensagent.com/Vulnerability/en-en/.

Simple English Wikipedia, s.v. "hatred," accessed October 25, 2017, https://simple.
wikipedia.org/wiki/Hatred https://en.m.wikipedia.org/wiki/hatred.

"St. Francis' Prayer Before the Crucifix." In *National Shrine of Saint Francis of
Assisi*, Shrinesf.org, http://www.shrinesf.org/franciscan-prayer.html (accessed
July 25, 2017).

Stein, Michael Alan. "The Religion of the Israelites in Egypt." JBQ.JewishBible. org. http://jbq.jewishbible.org/assets/Uploads/393/jbq_393_religioninegypt. pdf (accessed August 18, 2017).

Strong's Concordance, s.v. "barak," accessed August 18, 2017, http://biblehub.com/ hebrew/1288.htm.

Strong's Concordance, s.v. "chayah," accessed October 9, 2017, http://lexiconcor-dance.com/hebrew/2421.html.

Strong's Concordance, s.v. "Hamartia," accessed October 9, 2017, http://biblehub. com/greek/266.htm.

Strong's Concordance, s.v. "Igal," accessed October 25, 2017, http://biblehub.com/ hebrew/3008.htm.

Strong's Concordance, s.v. "michyah," accessed October 9, 2017, http://lexiconcor-dance.som/hebrew/4241.html.

Strong's Concordance, s.v. "natsal," accessed October 9, 2017, http://www.eliyah. com/cgi-bin/strongs.cgi?file=hebrewlexicon&isindex=natsal.

Strong's Concordance, s.v. "philandros," accessed August 30, 2017, http://biblehub. com/greek/5362.htm.

Strong's Concordance, s.v. "shabach," accessed August 18, 2017, https://www.bluelet-terbible.org/lang/lexicon/lexicon.cfm?t=kjv&strongs=h7623.

Strong's Concordance, s.v. "shuwb," accessed October 9, 2017, http://lexiconcor-dance.som/hebrew/7225.html.

Strong's Concordance, s.v., "tehillah," accessed August 18, 2017, http://biblehub. com/hebrew/8416.htm.

Strong's Concordance, s.v. "yadah," accessed August 18, 2017, http://biblehub.com/ hebrew/3034.htm.

Strong's Concordance, s.v. "zemar," accessed August 18, 2017, http://biblehub.com/hebrew/2171.htm.

Strong's Exhaustive Concordance, s.v. "Shammua," accessed October 9, 2017, http://biblehub.com/hebrew/8051.htm.

"Suscipe Prayer of St. Ignatius of Loyola." *Loyola Press,* http://www.loyolapress.com/our-catholic-faith/prayer/traditional-catholic-prayers/saints-prayers/suscipe-prayer-saint-ignatius-of-loyola (accessed July 25, 2017).

Vines, William Edwy, M.F. Unger, and W. White. *Vine's Complete Expository Dictionary of Old and New Testament Words.* Nashville: Thomas Nelson, 1984.

Wiersbe, Warren. "Nehemiah 3." In *The Wiersbe Bible Commentary: Old Testament.* Colorado Springs: David Cook, 2007.

Wikipedia, s.v. "agape," accessed August 23, 2017, https://en.wikipedia.org/wiki/Agape.

Wikipedia, s.v. "alcohol intoxication," accessed August 15, 2017, https://en.wikipedia.org/wiki/Alcohol_intoxication.

Wikipedia, s.v., "Four Loves, The" accessed November 13, 2017, https://en.wikipedia.org/wiki/The_Four_Loves.

Wikipedia, s.v. "hatred," accessed November 10, 2017, https://en.wikipedia.org/wiki/Hatred.

Wikipedia, s.v. "Jehovah-jireh," accessed October 24, 2017, https://en.wikipedia.org/wiki/Jehovah-jireh.

Wikipedia, s.v. "murder," accessed November 12, 2017, https://en.wikipedia.org/wiki/Murder.

Wikipedia, s.v. "philia," accessed August 23, 2017, https://en.wikipedia.org/wiki/Philia.

Williams, Pamela Rose. "20 Popular Bible Verses About Life." WhatChristiansWanttoKnow.com. http://www.whatchristianswanttoknow. com/20-popular-bible-verses-about-life (accessed October 27, 2017).

Woodeene Koenig-Bricker, ed. *Prayers of the Saints: An Inspired Collection of Holy Wisdom.* San Francisco: Harper Collins, 1996.

✦ DISCOGRAPHY ✦

Fontana, Wayne and the Mindbenders. Game of Love. Fontana. TF535,267420, 1965. 7," Single.

Inner Circle. Games People Play. WEA. 4509-96595-2, 1994. compact disc.

Nazareth. Love Hurts Down. Vertigo. 6078209, 1974. 7," Single.

Searchers, The. Winners Circle Series. A Kapp Record. KJB-27, 1964. 7."